SCARLET WOMEN

ALSO BY IAN GRAHAM

The Ultimate Book of Impostors

SCARLET
WOMEN

THE SCANDALOUS LIVES OF COURTESANS, CONCUBINES, AND ROYAL MISTRESSES

IAN GRAHAM

THOMAS DUNNE BOOKS

ST. MARTIN'S PRESS ❧ NEW YORK

THOMAS DUNNE BOOKS.
An imprint of St. Martin's Press.

SCARLET WOMEN. Copyright © 2016 by Ian Graham. All rights reserved.
Printed in the United States of America. For information, address
St. Martin's Press, 175 Fifth Avenue, New York, N.Y. 10010.

www.thomasdunnebooks.com
www.stmartins.com

The Library of Congress Cataloging-in-Publication Data is available upon request.

ISBN 978-1-250-06263-5 (hardcover)
ISBN 978-1-4668-6817-5 (e-book)

Our books may be purchased in bulk for promotional, educational,
or business use. Please contact your local bookseller or the Macmillan Corporate
and Premium Sales Department at (800) 221-7945, extension 5442, or by
e-mail at MacmillanSpecialMarkets@macmillan.com.

First Edition: January 2016

10 9 8 7 6 5 4 3 2 1

To Annadale Grammar School, Belfast

CONTENTS

INTRODUCTION

Well-behaved women seldom make history.
—LAUREL THATCHER ULRICH

In 1965, an impoverished elderly woman was found dead in a hotel room in Nice, France. Her death marked the end of an era. She was the last of the great European courtesans. Known as La Belle Otero, she was a volcanic Spanish beauty whose patrons included Kaiser Wilhelm II, the Prince of Wales (later King Edward VII), and Grand Duke Peter Nikolaevich of Russia. She is also sometimes credited as the world's first movie star. She accumulated an enormous fortune, but gambled it all away. Upon her death, a rare species slipped into extinction, quietly and unnoticed.

·

The secret of a great partnership is that each partner contributes something of value to the other. It was said of Fred Astaire and Ginger Rogers that he gave her class and she gave him sex appeal. Together, they were unbeatable. Courtesans and kings danced a similar game. Each benefited from the other's contribution . . . although courtesans didn't face quite so challenging a task as Ginger Rogers in one respect—she had to do everything her incandescently talented partner did, but she had to do it backwards and in high heels!

Marriages in European aristocratic and royal circles in past centuries were almost invariably *not* great partnerships. On the contrary, they could be a lonely business. And "business" is the appropriate description. Marriage in the upper echelons of society was seen as a way of forming alliances between important families, protecting inheritances, and producing heirs. Love was not a consideration. A couple sometimes met for the first time on their wedding day. When the British king, King George III, married Princess Charlotte of Mecklenburg-Strelitz in 1761, the king and his queen had not met before the moment they saw each other at the altar.

Upper-class women were schooled in social etiquette but little else. Their thoughts and limited conversation were rarely of any interest to their husbands. The queen's job was to produce an heir, but, having had a very sheltered upbringing, most queens knew little about how to please their husbands, either in bed or out of it. Husbands looked elsewhere for companionship, conversation, and sexual pleasure, so it was common for the nobility and royalty to take mistresses, providing a fertile hunting ground for ambitious and avaricious courtesans.

Like Astaire and Rogers, ambitious courtesans understood the symbiotic nature of their trade. They contributed companionship, conversation, fun, and sex in return for their patrons' contributions of money, property, status, and maybe even an aristocratic title. The best courtesans underwent years of training for the job. They often spoke several languages. They were well read, up to date with current affairs, and, unlike highborn women, they were also skilled in the arts of seduction and sexual pleasure. There were rich rewards for the most accomplished practitioners. They were provided with money, accommodation, clothing, jewelry, and other possessions befitting the social status of the men they serviced. The most successful courtesans could become spectacularly wealthy or famous in their own right. And they sometimes wielded great political power by virtue of their influence over kings and emperors. King Henry II of France trusted his mistress, Diane de Poitiers, to write and sign royal documents and letters on his behalf. Louis XV's mistress, Madame de Pompadour, was deeply involved in French politics at the highest level.

Initially, a courtesan (*courtisane* in French, *cortigiana* in Italian) was simply a female courtier, a woman who was part of the king's circle of attendants, advisers, informants, and companions. Given the dysfunctional nature of royal marriages, attractive female courtiers often caught the king's eye, and nature took its course. In time, "courtesan" took on a slightly different meaning—a woman who set out to capture the attention of a king or nobleman in return for money, title, or property, preferably all three. Courtesans could come from any part of society. Some started out as common prostitutes who were lucky enough to attract clients from the nobility. Others were highborn women who had fallen on hard times, or whose families couldn't afford the huge dowries they were expected to pay on marriage. They were distinguished from mistresses by the number of clients or partners they had. While a mistress generally had one partner or lover at a time, courtesans frequently had several clients on the go at the same time. Courtesans and mistresses accepted money and property in return for their services, but they didn't see themselves as prostitutes. In prostitution, there is a direct relationship between money and sex, but for courtesans and mistresses, there was no such direct quid pro quo, no payment per sex act.

In addition to mistresses and courtesans, in some countries there were concubines. A concubine is a secondary or alternate wife, a partner taken on by a man who is unable to marry her because he is already married or because of her lower social status. Concubines were common in Ancient Greece and Rome, and in Imperial China. Unlike the offspring of mistresses and courtesans, who weren't usually recognized or legitimized by their fathers, the offspring of concubines were often recognized and could inherit titles. The son of a concubine in Imperial China could become emperor, and several did.

There are no hard-and-fast dividing lines between the definitions of courtesan, concubine, and mistress. They overlap. Courtesans could be described as professional mistresses. Women who set out to be noticed by kings or emperors intentionally in order to become their mistresses, like Madame de Montespan at the court of the Sun King, were courtesans in all but name. The multiple mistresses of kings could also be described as concubines. A few mistresses actually went through a form of marriage with their royal patrons, or claimed they did.

Courtesans and royal mistresses enjoyed a charmed life of freedom and independence that most women of their time could barely dream of, but they paid a price for it. While some women were encouraged by their families to work as courtesans or mistresses, others were disowned and disinherited. They were also often ostracized by polite society. The value and desirability of courtesans rose with each notable lover, whereas the value of "respectable" women fell in the same circumstances.

Because of their relationships with royal, political, and military figures, courtesans and mistresses risked accusations of spying or acting as agents of a foreign power, especially during wartime. And sometimes it was true. An ancient Ionian hetaera (courtesan), Thargelia, was said to have acted for

Cyrus the Great of Persia in the sixth century B.C. by spreading pro-Persian propaganda among her influential Greek lovers during a time of conflict between Persia and Greece. Persia went on to conquer Ionia in 547 B.C. In the seventeenth century, a courtesan called Louise de Kérouaille was sent to England from France to seduce King Charles II and spy on his court. But the most famous name among courtesans associated with spying is, of course, Mata Hari. France and Germany both asked her to spy for them during World War I, and she paid for it with her life.

In earlier centuries, courtesans also risked being accused of witchcraft because of the power they appeared to exercise over men. The infamous Venetian courtesan Veronica Franco successfully defended herself in court against a charge of witchcraft by the Inquisition in 1577. In the early 1600s, the English traveler and writer Thomas Coryat warned men that Venetian courtesans were so skilled that they could cause temporary insanity in men who had any dealings with them. Add to these risks the more mundane hazards of sexually transmitted diseases and unwanted pregnancies at a time when both were potential killers.

THE HARLOT'S PROGRESS

The fortunes of a courtesan, concubine, or royal mistress could decline as fast as they rose. Associating with capricious men who thought they had unlimited power, and often did, was rather like keeping a pet tiger, always fearing that it might turn on its mistress with frightening force. While a courtesan or royal mistress held the attention of a lover, there were rich rewards to be had, but there was no tenure of office—she could be dropped in the blink of an eye and consigned to poverty.

A series of pictures by William Hogarth in the 1730s, called *A Harlot's Progress,* tells the story of a girl called Moll Hackabout. She was named after Daniel Defoe's fictional gold digger, Moll Flanders, and a real prostitute of the time called Kate Hackabout. Moll comes to London to look for work, but she is spotted by a procuress called Elizabeth Needham. In the second picture, Moll has become the mistress of a wealthy merchant and has other lovers. However, by the third picture, she has lost her wealthy benefactor and has become a common prostitute who is about to be arrested. In the fourth picture, she is in prison. In the next, she is dying of syphilis, and most of her clothes and possessions have been stolen. Finally, she dies at the age of only twenty-three. Moll Hackabout's story was fictional, but some real courtesans actually did die at such a tragically young age as this. Others who lasted longer eventually lost their youthful allure and were discarded by their patrons to die in poverty unless they had managed to secure an annuity from their paramour. A few tried to fund their old age by blackmailing former clients, even kings. The most unfortunate were executed because of their association with powerful men who fell from grace or turned on them.

There is no name for the male equivalent of a courtesan, apart perhaps from the "gigolo," but there have always been men who have been attracted to powerful women, and powerful women who have had their favorite men. Robert Devereaux, 2nd Earl of Essex, was a favorite of Queen Elizabeth I . . . at least until he failed to show her the respect a queen of England demanded. He lost his head over her, literally! His foolishly unruly behavior continued until he was put on trial for treason, found guilty, and executed. Catherine the Great of Russia had a string of male lovers. The most famous were Stanislaw Poniatowski, who became king of Poland; Grigory Orlov, who helped to end the reign of Catherine's husband, Peter III, which resulted in Catherine becoming empress; and Grigory Potemkin, a Russian military leader. Her lovers benefited from their affairs with her, because she rewarded them with senior military positions or noble titles. And when she tired of them, she pensioned them off handsomely.

The most famous (or notorious) women whose prey and partners were the wealthiest and most powerful men of their time include:

- Thaïs, a famous courtesan of Ancient Greece, who was responsible for the burning of Persepolis;
- Marie Duplessis, who made such an impact in her short life (she died at only twenty-three) that she inspired characters in Dumas's *La dame aux camélias* and Verdi's *La traviata*;
- Cora Pearl, who is reputed to have served herself naked on a silver platter to dinner guests at one of her legendary parties;
- Harriette Wilson, a British courtesan who tried to blackmail her aristocratic and royal clients;

- Clara Ward, a rare American courtesan who hunted for a European aristocrat to give her the royal title she craved but, having married a Belgian prince, ran away with a gypsy violinist;
- Klondike Kate, the queen of the Yukon during the Klondike Gold Rush;
- La Belle Otero, one of the most beautiful courtesans, whose breasts are said to have inspired the shape of the cupolas on the Hotel Carlton in Cannes;
- Veronica Franco, the most famous Venetian courtesan, who had a brief liaison with King Henry III of France and survived an accusation of witchcraft by the Inquisition;
- Ninon de l'Enclos, who was offered fifty thousand crowns by Cardinal Richelieu for one night in her company—money left in her will bought books for a nine-year-old boy called François-Marie Arouet, better known as Voltaire;
- Mesdames de Pompadour and du Barry, two of the many mistresses of Louis XV;
- Liane de Pougy, who ran away to Paris to become a courtesan after her husband shot her;
- La Païva, whose husband couldn't bear to be parted from her body—so he kept it in the attic, where it was discovered by his next wife;
- Nell Gwyn, the saucy orange-seller and actress who captured the heart of King Charles II;
- Marie Walewska, the reluctant courtesan who was Napoléon Bonaparte's "little Polish wife";
- Jane Digby, the admiral's daughter who married a bedouin sheikh;
- Lola Montez, a fake Spanish dancer who caused a revolution;
- Lillie Langtry, the actress who was one of King Edward VII's many mistresses;
- Cixi, a concubine who rose from obscurity to rule China for nearly half a century.

⚜ 1 ⚜

LES DEMIMONDAINES

The woman who died in a Nice hotel room in 1965, La Belle Otero, was the last of a group of fiercely ambitious and competitive women known as *les demimondaines*. They inhabited a shadow world, particularly in France, where it was known as the demimonde (literally, "half world")—hence demimondaines. In view of their profession, these extraordinary women were also known as *les grandes horizontales*.

In the nineteenth century, France was enjoying the golden age of the Belle Époque following the Second Empire. During this prosperous and peaceful time, science, music, theater, and art flourished before Europe was overwhelmed by the horror of World War I. The most famous, or infamous, courtesans of this period were not shrinking violets. They made no attempt to hide their lifestyle from disapproving eyes. On the contrary, they courted publicity. They were as famous in their time as movie stars or sports stars are today. And, to make the biggest impression, they constantly tried to outdo each other in terms of their flamboyance, fashion, extravagant spending, grand homes, and outrageous scandals. Some of them amassed jewelry collections and palatial homes worth a king's ransom.

Unlike the courtesans of earlier centuries, we can see exactly what *les demimondaines* looked like—not approximate likenesses fashioned by flattering artists, but images of real life frozen in time by some of the first celebrity photographers. The photographs show women who, to twenty-first-century eyes, are often not striking beauties. They appear to be confident women, comfortable to be on show and under the gaze of observers. They often stare straight into the camera lens, courting it as they might flirt with a prospective client. But photographs taken using the slow film of the day, requiring long exposure times, can't convey the demimondaines' most valuable properties—their animation, the way they moved, the way they danced, the swish of their dress, the sparkle of their jewelry, their heady scent, and the sound of their voice. For those qualities, we have to rely on descriptions written by the men and women who knew them and observed them at work and play.

THE ANDALUSIAN VOLCANO— LA BELLE OTERO

One of the most famous, wealthiest, and most sought-after courtesans in Europe arrived in Paris in 1889, the year the city was host to the World's Fair. Known as La Belle Otero, she spent most of her life on the run—from her mother, from her school, and from ex-lovers. She would be feted by kings, but despite amassing a great fortune, she would die in poverty, the last of the great courtesans of the demimonde.

Agustina Otero Iglesias was born in 1868 near the port of Cádiz, Spain. Her mother, Carmencita Otero, had met her father, a Greek army officer called Carasson, there. They set up home outside the town, where Carmencita gave birth to four children, including Agustina. The family called her Nina. Carasson then moved his growing family to Valga in Galicia. When he discovered that Carmencita had taken a lover, he challenged the man to a duel. The challenge was accepted. As a military officer, Carasson expected to win, but the next time Nina saw her father was when his lifeless body was carried home after the duel.

The man who had killed her father moved in with the family and married Otero's mother. One by one, the children left home or were sent away to live with relatives. Nina was sent to boarding school, but her mother refused to pay her school fees, so Nina had to do cleaning work to pay her way. She was desperately unhappy, so she started sneaking out of the school to dance for customers at a local café. She enjoyed the attention and applause. A boy called Paco introduced her to the café owners, who asked her to come back and entertain their customers. Paco became her first lover when she was only twelve years old. He not only took her virginity, but also took the money the café owners paid her to dance. He wouldn't be the last man to use her to line his pockets.

When school officials found out what she'd been doing, they locked her in her room at night to stop her from getting out. Despite her tender age, Nina clearly wasn't easily intimidated, because she took the first opportunity to escape and run away with Paco. The young couple fled to Lisbon, but it didn't take the police long to find them and bring Nina home. She constantly argued with her mother, who eventually threw her out. She went straight back to Lisbon and searched for Paco. While she was there, the man in the next hotel room introduced himself. He was a theater director. He'd heard her singing and liked her voice so much that he invited her to perform at his theater. She was too young to sign a contract, but when she explained that her father was dead and she couldn't ask her mother to sign for her, the director let her sign the contract herself.

STAGE DEBUT

Nina's first appearance at the theater was a huge success. Inevitably, many of the men who flocked to see her vied for her attention and company. The first was a wealthy banker prepared to pay whatever it took to have her. He offered her a private residence of her own and as much money, jewels, and fine clothes as she wanted. But he insisted that she must leave the theater. And he told her she could do it legally with a clear conscience, because her contract was worthless—she was underage when she signed it. She left the theater and moved into her new accommodation. Life was sweet, but with little to do and no admiring audience, she soon got bored. She craved younger company, especially Paco's. She made her escape from the easy life and chased after Paco, who was now in Barcelona. One night, she went to the opera. The men in the audience couldn't take their eyes off the beautiful stranger. One of the men who gathered around her was Paco, stunned to find that the beauty attracting all the attention was his little Nina. They moved into a flat together, and with Paco's help, she found work at the Palais de Crystal. However, Paco gambled most of her money away. She realized that she'd have to leave him or he would bankrupt her.

She left to join an opera company touring Portugal. As usual, she was a great success, especially with the men in the audience. One of her admirers was Manuelo Domingo, the heir to a wine-making fortune. He chose a dramatic way to get her attention. He sent the chief of police to kidnap her! It worked. He gave her so much money for whatever she wanted that she was able to salt away a fortune and accumulate quite a collection of jewelry. Her life seemed idyllic. Then one day, the chief of police came to see her again. This time he brought a message from Manuelo's father, who thoroughly disapproved of his son's liaison with Nina and the vast sums of money he was spending on her. She was told to leave the city. When she refused, she was arrested and jailed because she had no identity papers. Another admirer, Count Tirenzo, came to her aid and managed to have her released. The experience taught her to despise men who could buy influence.

She began a relationship with her gallant rescuer, Count Tirenzo. She was content for a while, but inevitably, it didn't last long. The moment she saw an Italian opera singer called Guglielmo performing, she was infatuated with him. The feeling was mutual, and so it wasn't long before the couple married. However, he continued to see other women, and like Paco, he was an inveterate gambler. During a visit to Monte Carlo, she had to settle his gambling debts. On her return to their boarding house one night, she spotted a woman leaving their room. Not only was her husband having an affair with the woman, but he had gambled away the woman's life savings, too. Nina left him and fled to Marseille, where she took lessons in singing in French. After a spell in the hospital with typhoid, she moved into an apartment that yet another admirer, the comte Savin de Pont-Maxence, had rented for her.

It wasn't long before her health and her desire for male company returned. A young Spaniard called Auguste Herero became her next lover, but she kept him secret from her older benefactor, Savin, who was still paying her bills. She found work as a singer at the Palais de Crystal in Marseille. Another young man, the son of a brewer, was pursuing her, too. All went well onstage until one night when some of the audience hissed at her. It was the first time she'd experienced an unappreciative audience, but she soon discovered that the hissing had been arranged by a woman called Felicia, the jealous lover of the brewer's son.

When Auguste and Nina arrived at a club one night and discovered

Felicia there, Nina flew at her and hit her with a chair. The two women had to be dragged apart. Nina was charged with assault, but the case was dismissed. The episode taught her that all publicity, even bad publicity, was good for business. The scrapes she got into attracted even bigger audiences to her stage performances. One of the many people who came to see her was her estranged husband, Guglielmo. He begged for her forgiveness and promised to pay back all the money he had lost at the gaming tables. She took him back and they moved to Paris. However, he showed little enthusiasm for finding work. Nina wasn't working either, and her money was running out. One night, Guglielmo packed his bags and left. She never saw him again.

LA BELLE OTERO IS BORN

Nina's life was about to change dramatically. On December 30, 1889, she performed at a soirée dressed in a toreador's costume. She later posed for photographs in the same costume, a daringly figure-hugging red and gold outfit. She danced for an audience that included influential figures in the Parisian club and theater scene. She was immediately offered three months' work at the Cirque d'Été (Summer Circus). It was called a circus because it had opened as a tent circus, or big top, in 1836, but the original tent was replaced by a stone theater in 1841. Press reviews of Otero's performances there were ecstatic. One newspaper called her La Belle Otero, and the soubriquet stuck. Her fame and her strikingly good looks, a doll-like face framed by dark curly hair atop a tightly corseted hourglass figure, attracted titled admirers like moths to a flame. At the age of twenty-one, La Belle Otero had arrived.

She made such an impression that she was soon receiving invitations to perform in other countries. One of the influential persons who saw her was Ernest A. Jurgens, the manager of the Eden Musée in New York, an odd mixture of waxworks museum and theater. Jurgens had traveled to Europe to find a way of raising money to replace funds he had taken from the Eden. He'd been using some of its box office receipts to fund his own projects. When he saw La Belle Otero, he invited her to return to America with him. In September 1890, they sailed for the United States. She worried about how American audiences would receive her. And her worst fears seemed to have been realized when the audience hissed at the end of her first performance.

But they also threw flowers. She was confused. Did they like her or not? Jurgens reassured her that hissing was a sign of approval in the United States at that time. Press reviews were gushing in their praise.

Predictably, she became Jurgens's mistress. They tried to keep their relationship hidden, but when they had a very public row, the secret was out. When they parted, Jurgens lost his job at the Eden and became a theatrical agent, but he seems to have enjoyed little success. His tendency to treat other people's money as his own sealed his fate. Newspapers reported that his actors were turning up to fulfill bookings he said he'd made, but then found that there was no work for them. Jurgens had taken commissions from the actors, but never made the bookings. In desperation, he appealed to Otero for help in repaying the missing money. She later claimed she had no idea how serious the situation was and so she refused to help. Twelve hours later, he killed himself.

THE SUICIDE SIREN

Otero made enough money in the United States to make her financially secure, but she gambled it all away in Monte Carlo. This didn't concern her, because her many admirers were happy to pay her bills. The vicomte de Chênedollé spent his entire fortune on her and then blew his brains out. In fact, so many men killed themselves over her (at least eight) that she became known as the Suicide Siren.

She received lucrative offers of work all over Europe. While she was working in Moscow, her customary coterie of admirers included Russian aristocracy and royalty. She became the lover of Grand Duke Peter Nikolaevich, grandson of Tsar Nicholas I. He was besotted with her and she was very fond of him. He lavished gifts and money on her, and begged her, "Ruin me, but don't leave me." When their relationship became public knowledge, she was suddenly in great demand at high society parties. While she was in Russia, an Algerian-born cameraman, Félix Mesguich, who worked for the Lumière company, filmed her performing her *Valse brillante* dance. The one-minute film made her one of the world's first film stars. It also got Mesguich thrown out of Russia, because a Russian army officer was shown dancing with Otero. Russians were outraged that one of their revered military officers had been turned into a music hall entertainer. Mesguich was immediately escorted to the border.

When Otero returned to Paris, she finally achieved her ambition to appear at the Folies Bergère. Her performances received rave reviews. Everyone wanted to meet her, including Edward, Prince of Wales, who would later become King Edward VII. He often sent for her to join him and dance for him in the evening. In return, he gave her a hunting lodge near Oise, but he had an ulterior motive for this generous gift. It provided a secluded place for them to meet more discreetly outside Paris.

Her fame spread far and wide, and occasionally in surprising ways. Her breasts are said to have inspired the shape of the cupolas on top of the Hotel Carlton in Cannes—although it could just have been a bit of clever promotion by the hotel.

At lunch one day, she was introduced to an Englishman called Thompson. He begged her to go with him to London the same day. She said she would go with him for a price, because she was supposed to be collecting a large sum of money needed to pay her dressmaker. In addition, her failure to meet her commitments at the Folies Bergère would incur a heavy penalty. He agreed to pay. In fact, she owed her dressmaker and the Folies nothing, so she pocketed the money. After an enjoyable visit to London with Thompson, he asked her to give up the stage and he would pay her way. She accepted his offer and she was soon living in luxury near the Champs-Élysées. However, Thompson proved to be very jealous and possessive.

When she resisted the romantic advances of a young man, he shot himself. Newspaper stories named Otero as the reason for his suicide. Thompson was furious and refused to believe her protestations of innocence. His suspicions seemed to be confirmed while she was away working in Berlin. He put a private detective on her tail, who reported her every move and meeting, including assignations with other men. The next time he left home, he never returned and he stopped paying the bills. Nina would have to return to the stage and earn her living again. She had no difficulty finding work.

While she was working onstage in London, she struck up a friendship with one of the richest men in Britain, the Duke of Westminster. He introduced her to Kaiser Wilhelm II. She spent some time in Berlin with the kaiser, but never felt entirely comfortable with him or with Berlin. She busied herself with offers of work from all over Europe and America. And she collected lovers wherever she went.

Her success as a courtesan and her effect on men made enemies. During a visit to her native Spain, a spurned admirer tried to shoot both of them.

She survived, but he didn't. On another occasion, the mistress of a man who had fallen for Otero shot at her onstage. Each attack made headlines and increased her fame. Even more people wanted to see her. She made professional enemies, too. When she appeared in a production of *Carmen,* singing the lead role, professional singers objected to a music hall performer and courtesan like Otero being hired for the job.

A SIMPLE LIFE

When World War I broke out in 1914, Otero threw herself into raising money for charities. At the end of the war, she thought she was too old to return to her former career and retired from public life. She had saved enough money for her retirement, but she couldn't stay away from the gaming tables. Inevitably, she lost it all. She had to sell everything she owned to settle her debts. By 1941, she was living a simple life as a recluse in a small hotel in Nice.

In the afternoon of April 11, 1965, a chambermaid smelled burning and traced the smell to Otero's room. She knocked on the door, but got no answer. The police were called. When they broke in, they found Otero lying dead on a daybed. She'd suffered a heart attack after putting a pot of food on her gas ring. Newspaper reports of her death referred to her fiery, hot-blooded personality. One called her "the Andalusian volcano." One of the most colorful characters of La Belle Époque and the last of the great courtesans had gone.

LE GRAND TROIS—
OTERO, POUGY, AND D'ALENÇON

La Belle Otero and two other leading courtesans of the day—Liane de Pougy and Émilienne d'Alençon—were known as *Le Grand Trois* and "the Three Graces of the Belle Époque." They were friends and rivals in one of the greatest circuses of the nineteenth century.

LIANE DE POUGY

By any measure, Liane de Pougy had an extraordinary life. She ran away to become a courtesan after her husband shot her, took acting lessons from Sarah Bernhardt, had a lesbian affair with an American writer, and then became a nun!

Her story began in the French town of La Flèche in the Loire Valley. La Flèche was home to a military college established by Napoléon Bonaparte. Liane was born there on July 2, 1869, to Pierre Blaise Eugène Chassaigne and his wife, Aimée Lopez. They named her Anne Marie. She was raised in a nunnery, but its security clearly wasn't watertight, because the sixteen-year-old Anne Marie was able to run off with a naval officer called Armand Pourpe. She married Pourpe when she discovered she was pregnant. She wanted a girl, but the baby was a boy. They named him Marc.

Anne Marie readily admitted that she was a terrible mother, which wasn't helped by brutal beatings from her husband. When his military service took him away to Marseille, Anne Marie amused herself with a lover, the marquis Charles de MacMahon. One day, Armand returned home unexpectedly and found them together in bed. His reaction was typically violent. He flew into a rage, drew his revolver, and shot her, wounding her in the wrist.

Instead of submitting to yet more beatings, and fearing that her husband might kill her, she sold her piano to the first buyer she could find and used the money to run away to Paris. She left her son behind. The little boy was sent to his grandparents in Suez, where he grew up to become a pilot. He was flying by 1912 and must have been one of the first pilots in North Africa. He flew the first airmail delivery between Cairo and Khartoum. At the outbreak of World War I, he joined the French Air Force and served with Escadrille (squadron) N23. He was killed when his plane was shot down by a German fighter near Villers-Bretonneux on December 2, 1914.

Meanwhile, Anne Marie turned to acting to earn a living. Her beauty ensured that she was soon highly sought after as an actress and also as a companion. For a time, she was mistress to a man called the comte (or vicomte) de Pougy. When she left him, she kept his name. She added it to Liane, the pet name given to her by her pleasure-seeking friends. As Liane de Pougy, she was lucky enough to secure an appearance at the famous Folies Bergère. She was the first to admit that she had no talent beyond a few dance steps, so she took acting lessons from Sarah Bernhardt. But it was in vain. Bernhardt's advice to her was, "Display your beauty, but once you are on the stage, you had better keep your pretty mouth shut." While she was appearing at the Folies Bergère, the Prince of Wales (the future British King Edward VII) was in town. Pougy cheekily sent him an invitation to the show she was appearing in, and he accepted. The heady mixture of the Folies Bergère and the heir to the British throne gave her a higher profile and attracted a wider circle of admirers—both men and women. She quickly became one of the most famous women in France. Despite her lack of talent, she amassed a fortune, including several homes, expensive carriages, and an impressive collection of jewelry. Photographs of her show one of the most beautiful courtesans of the demimonde. She was described as tall, slender, and refined, with frightened doe eyes gazing out from below her curly brown hair. In later photographs, the frightened doe-eyed look has gone and she displays a more confident persona.

A Lesbian Affair

One of Liane's admirers was the American writer, Natalie Clifford Barney. In 1899, Barney went to Pougy's home dressed as a page boy, saying that she was a page of love sent by Sappho. Barney's bold approach worked, and the two had a brief relationship, which inspired Pougy's 1901 novel, *Idylle saphique*. The book was scandalous at the time, and a huge success. It was reprinted dozens of times in its first year of publication. Barney wrote her own novel, *Lettres à une connue* (*Letters to a Woman I Have Known*), about the affair. Their relationship broke up amid arguments over Barney's wish to rescue Pougy from her courtesan lifestyle. Pougy declined to be rescued.

In 1910, she married Georges Ghica, a Romanian prince, and so she became Princess Ghica. When the prince's family discovered that he was marrying an older woman who was also a courtesan, they cut him off. The couple stayed together for sixteen years before Georges ran off with a younger woman, a rather bohemian young artist called Marcelle Thiébaut. Liane felt particularly betrayed because she knew Marcelle and thought of her as a friend. Liane and her husband separated. Georges left with Marcelle in July 1926. By November, Pougy's diary records a meeting at her solicitors in

Paris to discuss her divorce. However, by March of the following year, her diary reveals that Georges had returned, and without explanation, they were together again. She had started calling him Gilles, perhaps signifying a new start.

Soon after her husband's death in the mid-1940s, she abruptly abandoned her previous life and joined a convent. She entered the Order of Saint Dominic as Sister Anne-Mary and worked with children suffering from birth defects. A few years later, she had to give up her work due to ill health. She spent her final days in the comfortable surroundings of the Hotel Carlton at Lausanne, Switzerland, where she died on December 26, 1950, at the age of eighty-one. Soon after her death, her memoirs, *Mes cahiers bleu* (*My Blue Notebooks*), were published.

ÉMILIENNE D'ALENÇON

Pougy and Otero wrote their own life stories, but the third member of *Le Grand Trois,* Émilienne d'Alençon, did not. Very little of her story, beyond a few references in Pougy's and Otero's memoirs, seems to have survived. Pougy described d'Alençon as being pretty, with enormous golden eyes, the finest complexion, a proud little mouth, and an oval face. Pougy was entranced by her beauty. She said she spent hours just gazing at d'Alençon.

They were friends but also rivals, and Pougy quickly learned not to trust her. She remembered one incident when both women were due to attend the same dinner. D'Alençon convinced Pougy that it wasn't worth dressing up for, so she was just going to wear a casual dress and blouse. Pougy agreed to dress down in the same way. But soon after Pougy arrived, Émilienne swept in wearing the finest white and gold brocade, festooned with pearls, diamonds, and rubies! Pougy never forgot the incident and never trusted her again.

D'Alençon, a Parisian, had run away from home with a gypsy violinist in the 1880s at the age of fifteen. She studied acting at the Conservatoire de Paris, but she left after a year. She felt more at home performing as a dancer. She made her stage debut at the Cirque d'Été in 1889. She went on to appear at the Casino de Paris, the Menus-Plaisirs, the Folies Bergère, the Scala, and the Théâtre des Variétés. One of her acts involved a troupe of rabbits dyed pink and wearing paper ruffs! There doesn't seem to be any record of what she did with the rabbits.

She counted among her lovers King Leopold II of Belgium and Jacques d'Uzés (son of the Duchess d'Uzés, heiress to the Veuve Clicquot fortune). Jacques d'Uzés's family was so alarmed by his relationship with d'Alençon that they sent him abroad to get him away from her. She had affairs with women, too, including the cancan dancer La Goulue, who was one of Toulouse-Lautrec's favorite subjects, and the British poet Renée Vivien. One of Toulouse-Lautrec's illustrations shows d'Alençon and another dancer preparing for a performance at the Folies Bergère.

Another of her lovers was the industrialist Étienne Balsan. He was also a lover of Coco Chanel, who supplied extravagant hats to d'Alençon for her visits to Longchamps. In 1895, she married a jockey, Percy Woodland, and retired from the stage soon afterwards. In 1922, when she was in her fifties, she almost died in a flying accident. She was taken on a flight in northwest France by an unnamed man identified only as "an impresario." The flight went well, but the landing did not. The plane hit a tree and burst into flames. The impresario was killed and Émilienne was taken to hospital in the nearby town of Livarot with serious injuries. By the early 1930s, she had gambled all her money away and had to sell her property. In her old age, she moved to Nice, where she died in 1946, at the age of seventy-seven.

THE QUEEN OF KEPT WOMEN—
LA PAÏVA

When Katharina Slepzóv picked her way through the attic of Schloss Neudeck in Upper Silesia (Poland today), she stumbled across something extraordinary—the body of her husband's first wife! She had been one of the most successful courtesans of the nineteenth century, known as La Païva.

Esther Pauline Lachmann, the woman who would become La Païva, was born in Moscow's Jewish ghetto on May 7, 1819. Her father, Martin, was a weaver or clothing merchant from Polish stock. It was a difficult time for Jews living in the Russian Empire. They were denied full rights unless they converted to the Russian Orthodox Church, and the places where they were allowed to live were strictly regulated.

At the age of seventeen, Esther married Antoine François Hyacinthe Villoing, a twenty-six-year-old Paris-born tailor. His French nationality seems to have been his biggest attraction, as Esther appears to have had the ambition to see Paris from an early age. When it transpired that Villoing had no intention of moving to Paris, she left him and their baby son and went there herself. Now calling herself Thérèse, she probably turned to prostitution to pay her way. In about 1840, she became the mistress of Henri Herz, an Austrian-born pianist and composer she met on a visit to the spa town of Bad Ems in Prussia. He introduced her to his family and his circle of artistic friends as his wife, although they never married. They had a daughter, Henriette, who was handed over to Henri's family to be brought up by them.

Thérèse was spending Henri's money at such a prodigious rate that he risked bankruptcy. In the late 1840s, he decided to go on a six-month concert tour of the United States to replenish his funds. Thérèse normally traveled with him on his tours, but this time he decided to go on his own. While he was away, his family discovered that he and Thérèse were not married. As a result, she was evicted from their home and the family cut off all financial support. An acquaintance suggested that she should go to London, where noblemen were known to pay women a fortune for their company and favors, so she borrowed some fine clothes and headed for England. The line between a comfortable life and destitution was often narrow, so she is said to have asked a friend, the writer Théophile Gautier, for some chloroform to take with her to end her life if she failed. But she needn't have worried. Almost immediately, she snared Edward Stanley, second Baron Stanley of Alderley, and became his mistress. Lucrative relationships with other wealthy men followed. By the time she returned to Paris, she was no longer short of money.

BECOMING LA PAÏVA

During a visit to the fashionable Baden spa, she met Albino Francisco de Araújo de Païva. Photographs of him show a well-dressed gentleman with muttonchop whiskers. Despite his grand name, he had no title and was not an aristocrat. Nevertheless, he had recently inherited a fortune and he was single, which made him very attractive as a prospective husband. Conveniently, Thérèse's first husband had died of cholera in 1849, leaving her free to marry again. Now calling herself Pauline Thérèse Lachmann, she was the lucky girl who caught Païva's eye. Their romance blossomed, and she married him on June 5, 1851, in Passy, a wealthy area of Paris. Remarkably, soon after the wedding (as soon as the next day, according to one account), she handed her new husband a letter telling him that the marriage was over. It said,

> *You wanted to sleep with me, and you've done so, by making me your wife. You have given me your name, I performed my duty. I have behaved like an honest woman. I wanted a position, and now I have it, but all you have is a prostitute for a wife. You can't take me anywhere, and you can't introduce me to anyone. We must therefore separate. You go back to Portugal. I shall stay here with your name, and remain a whore.*

The ruthlessness she displayed typified her cold, calculating attitude to men, who, to her, were merely sources of money. She kept the considerable sum of money and property that were given to her in the marriage contract. Her husband returned alone to his native Portugal. He killed himself in 1873.

Lachmann was now known as La Païva. In 1852, she attended a party in Paris hosted by the Prussian consul, and there she met the twenty-two-year-old, fabulously wealthy Prussian industrialist Guido Georg Friedrich Erdmann Heinrich Adalbert Henckel von Donnersmarck. She spent months and thousands of francs arranging for their paths to cross again and again all over Europe. Eventually, she got exactly what she wanted: He asked her to be his mistress and promised that if she would say yes, he would share his fortune with her. In fact, she did rather better than becoming his mistress. She had her previous marriage annulled and, two months later, on October 28, 1871, she married Henckel. On their marriage, Henckel gave her the Château de Pontchartrain, an annual income, and millions of francs' worth of gems, including an emerald necklace once owned by the French empress, Eugénie, wife of Napoléon III. La Païva loved jewelry. She said that nothing and no one gave her as much delight as her precious stones. She was reputed to have regularly worn two million francs' worth of gems. One piece, made for her by jeweler Frédéric Boucheron, was a collarette containing more than four hundred diamonds, almost 200 carats in weight. Another stone he bought for her was a 100-carat yellow diamond. Henckel introduced her to business and finance, and she introduced him to pleasure.

At her request, Henckel funded the construction of a grand mansion on the Champs-Élysées in Paris, and it was named after her—Hôtel de La Païva. It had a hand-carved staircase made of gold, marble, and onyx imported from Algeria. One of its baths was said to have had three taps, the third being for milk or champagne! La Païva hosted numerous dinners and parties frequented by prominent writers and artists of the day, including Zola, Flaubert, and Delacroix. Her lavishly furnished home also attracted courtesans from all over Europe, who were hoping to be swept up by a rich aristocrat. Count Horace de Viel-Castel described her as the queen of kept women.

A PAINTED CORPSE!

Time was not kind to La Païva, although in truth she never was a great beauty. Photographs of her show a rather plain or even severe-looking woman. And her copious use of makeup didn't help. She troweled it on! When she was not yet forty, she was described as looking like a powdered and painted old tightrope walker. Ten years later, one observer described her as looking like a painted corpse.

Her health began to deteriorate in 1880. She had put on a lot of weight due to heart disease. Eventually, she was persuaded to leave the hustle and bustle of Paris and go to Henckel's family home, Schloss Neudeck in Upper Silesia, to recover. She never returned to Paris. When she died, on January 21, 1884, her husband couldn't bear to be parted from her. He had her body embalmed and kept it with him. He is said to have cried over it every night. Years later, his second wife stumbled across it while she was looking through an attic in Schloss Neudeck. In 1904, La Païva's mansion at 25 Avenue des Champs-Élysées became the home of the Travelers Club, a network of clubhouses and meeting places for wealthy travelers, and now houses a restaurant. In the early 2000s, it was restored to its former glory by Étienne Poncelet, chief architect of Paris's historical monuments, financed by government grants.

THE LADY OF THE CAMELLIAS— MARIE DUPLESSIS

Marie Duplessis lived for only twenty-three years, but she made such an impression in her short life that Alexandre Dumas fils based his novel *La dame aux camélias* (*The Lady of the Camellias*) on her.

In 1839, Alphonsine Rose Plessis was a pretty little fifteen-year-old girl working in a dress shop in Paris. Despite her youth, she had already suffered a difficult, dangerous, and chaotic family life. She had been born into a peasant family in a tiny village called Nonant in Normandy. Her mother left her violent father and escaped to Paris. But when Alphonsine was eight years old, her mother died and she was sent to live with a relative. While there, she is thought to have lost her virginity to a farm laborer when she was only twelve years old. When her guardian found out, she was sent back to her father, who found her a job as a laundress. She spent all day, every day washing and ironing. Then, when she was about fourteen, her father took her to a friend's house and left her with him. When her employer found out about her living arrangements, she was dismissed. She ran away from home and found herself a job as a maid, but after a few months, her father found out where she was and took her to stay with another man. The authorities started asking questions about Alphonsine and how she was being cared for, so her father collected her and took her to Paris, where he left her with relatives. They found her the job in the dress shop. Her father returned to Normandy and died from syphilis soon afterwards. She was finally free of him.

Her meager pay at the dress shop wasn't enough to keep body and soul together, so she looked for other ways to earn money. Within a few months, she had moved into a new apartment paid for by a Monsieur Nollet, a restaurant owner. He also hired a maid for the apartment, but Alphonsine later discovered that the maid's principal job was to spy on her and report back to Nollet. She told a friend that she had chosen prostitution because it was the only way to achieve the lifestyle she wanted. When her relatives found out, they disowned her.

She was such a pretty girl that men paid her a lot of attention. She was described as thin, pale, beautiful, and elegant, with magnificent chestnut hair that reached the ground. Realizing her potential for parting men from their money, she learned to read and write, and kept up with national and international events so that she could talk to men about them. She was preparing herself for life as a courtesan, not a common prostitute. Some of her clients helped to educate her. The duc de Guiche is credited with transforming her from an uneducated peasant girl into a lady. He wanted her to be his equal, and so he arranged for her to have dancing and piano lessons. He also set her up in a better apartment, enabling her to get away from the prying eyes of Nollet's maid.

It was around this time that she changed her name to Marie Duplessis. It is remarkably similar to the name of her brutal father, Marin Plessis. Girls who turned to prostitution often changed their name—partly to make themselves sound a little more exotic and probably to save their friends and family from shame. A false name that could be shed at a moment's notice was also quite useful for evading the authorities. Despite her modest background, Marie had no difficulty in spending large sums of her lovers' money, driving some of them to the edge of bankruptcy.

Her elegance, tact, and natural refinement meant that she was accepted in polite society when many of her coarser fellow "professionals" were not. She was not foulmouthed or given to drunkenness like many of her contemporaries. She mixed with writers, artists, and politicians, including Alexandre Dumas fils, whose mistress she became in September 1844. He had caught sight of her for the first time during a visit to the theater when she was in the company of another lover. He began an affair with her, but he hated being just one of her many lovers. However, he wasn't wealthy enough to be her sole provider. Tired of sharing her with other men, he ended their liaison in August 1845.

Marie always wore white camellias when she went to the opera to make herself stand out from the crowd, so that she might be noticed by potential lovers. After her death, Dumas based the character of Marguerite Gautier in his novel *La dame aux camélias* on her. A play adapted from the novel inspired Verdi's opera *La traviata*. The same story inspired the 1936 film *Camille,* starring Greta Garbo.

During a visit to Spa in 1845, Marie met the elderly Count Gustav Ernst von Stackelberg. Keen to rescue her from a life of prostitution, because she reminded him of his dead daughter, he offered her a new apartment and whatever income she wanted. She accepted his offer, but she found it impossible to keep to her side of the bargain. Perhaps she found a chaste life less colorful and eventful than her previous life. Or perhaps she wanted to pack as much living as possible into her short life—she was aware that she was suffering from consumption (tuberculosis), and so she was condemned to an early death. More likely, her extravagant spending was outstripping the sums the count was prepared to pay, so additional sources of income were necessary.

In April 1845, she saw a piano recital by the composer Franz Liszt and decided she would befriend him. There are contradictory stories about how they met. According to one account, she spotted him in the foyer of a theater and strode purposefully through the crowd toward him. She sat beside him and started talking to him. They got on well and he attended soirées at Marie's home. He went on to give her piano lessons. He evidently felt more for her than for his other music students, because he would later claim that she was the first woman he loved. They parted after a few months when he had to return to work in Weimar.

When the comte Édouard de Perregaux saw her, he abandoned his current paramour, a courtesan called Alice Ozy, and began a liaison with her. Their relationship was clearly closer and deeper than merely courtesan and client, because on February 21, 1846, they were married in a civil ceremony at the Kensington Register Office in London and she became the comtesse de Perregaux. The marriage wasn't recognized in France, but it didn't last long anyway. They never lived together. Perregaux's spending on Marie quickly exhausted his inheritance. She felt deceived by the disappointingly modest scale of his wealth. Without a fortune for her to spend, he held little interest for her. They separated, and Marie sought other lovers who were better able to pay her bills.

Despite the perilous state of her finances, she gambled recklessly and ran up huge debts. Perhaps she knew that she didn't have much time left. She was coughing up blood. Her condition gradually worsened over the next two years. She visited spas and health resorts around Europe in the hope of finding a cure, but her search was in vain. She consulted several doctors, including a quack who prescribed strychnine! Meanwhile, her money situation had become critical. She had to pawn some of her belongings, and she moved her most valuable possessions out of her home so that creditors couldn't seize them. Most of her lovers deserted her.

In the winter of 1846, she took to her bed and rarely left it. One of her last public outings was to the Palais-Royal in January 1847, when she joined the audience to watch a play. Someone who saw her described her as a shadow of a woman. She was so ill that she had to be carried to her seat, and after fainting, she was carried out again before the end of the play. She died on February 3, 1847, to the sound of bailiffs hammering on her door. Her belongings were sold to settle her debts. Her clothes, furniture, paintings, and even her comb and private love letters were all snapped up by people who had shunned her in life but wanted a piece of her in death.

THE LEGENDARY DEMIMONDAINE— CORA PEARL

In the 1850s, when La Païva was at the peak of her fame and wealth, one of the most spectacularly successful courtesans of all arrived in Paris. She called herself Cora Pearl, but her real name was either Emma Elizabeth Crouch or Eliza Emma Crouch. When she was born in Plymouth, a port on the South Coast of England, in the 1830s or early 1840s, it seemed inconceivable that she would become one of the most notorious courtesans of the demimonde.

The girl who would become Cora Pearl was born into reasonably comfortable circumstances. Her father was a cellist, composer, and music teacher, and her mother was a singer. They performed together onstage in the city's theaters. The young Eliza was educated at a boarding school in Boulogne, where she learned to speak French. She'd been sent away from home after her father deserted the family, and she hated her mother's new lover. Ironically, Eliza's father ran away to America to escape mounting debts, but one of the songs he cowrote, "Kathleen Mavourneen," became a huge hit that crossed the Atlantic and became a popular song during the American Civil War. Sadly, Eliza's father had sold it for only five pounds. If he'd held on to the rights, it would have settled his debts and made him a wealthy man.

When Eliza returned to England at the age of nineteen, she went to live with her grandmother in London and found work as a milliner's assistant. Every Sunday, she was sent to church, chaperoned by a maid. But, according to Eliza's own account, one day the maid wasn't there when she came out of church. Shortly after she set off for home on her own, she noticed that she was being followed by a middle-aged man. They got talking, and instead of going straight home, she went with him to a house near Covent Garden market. After taking a drink she was given, she described her head feeling heavy, and then she fell asleep. When she woke up, she was in bed and the man was lying beside her.

RUNNING AWAY

When Eliza realized what had happened, she was too ashamed to go home. She found lodgings and paid for them with money her seducer had given her. She soon attracted more admirers. One of them, a dance hall proprietor, took her to Paris, but when it was time for him to return to England, she refused to go with him. This is the moment when she left her previous life behind and became Cora Pearl.

Paris, under Emperor Napoléon III, was the center of the civilized world and the most exciting city on earth to be in at that time. A series of suitors introduced Cora to Parisian society. The money they lavished on her enabled her to set up home and entertain in great style. She was famous for her excesses. She hired her own chef to delight her guests with his culinary creations. She spent freely and extravagantly on food, drink, flowers, fireworks displays, and anything else she could think of to keep her guests amused. Her behavior was outrageous, and her guests reveled in it. Cora Pearl really knew how to have fun. At one dinner, she is said to have invited her guests to watch her bathing in champagne. At another, she arranged for herself to be served up to her guests on a huge silver platter, naked, as dessert! Her chef had decorated her body with cream, sauces, flowers, grapes, and meringues, covered with a fine dusting of sugar. At the table, when the cover was removed to reveal her, the guests were momentarily astonished at the sight before them. Then the bolder souls among them reached out and helped themselves to grapes and flowers strategically positioned on their final course.

As her fame, or notoriety, spread, she attracted increasingly important lovers. One of them was Victor Masséna, the duc de Rivoli, with whom she had a six-year relationship. It didn't stop her from having affairs with other men at the same time, notably the Prince of Orange, heir to the Dutch throne. While she was with the duc de Rivoli, she developed a liking for gambling, which almost ruined her. Rivoli finally left her, tired of settling her gambling debts. Another of her lovers, Prince Achille Murat, took her hunting and gave her a horse, the first she had ever owned. She discovered that she was a natural horsewoman. Of course, one horse wasn't enough for her. She built up a stable of dozens of horses along with a fleet of fine carriages. Her habit of taking carriage rides through the parks of Paris started a fashion among Parisian women. They were soon copying her clothes and hairstyles as well as her carriage rides. Genteel women found that they were using the same dressmakers and hairdressers as the courtesans. Cora's love of the limelight had succeeded in bringing the courtesans of the demi-monde out of the shadows. The naïve little girl from Plymouth had come a long way.

IMPERIAL CONNECTIONS

Among Cora's most distinguished lovers was the duc de Morny, the French emperor's half brother. He was one of the most important persons in France, a cultured and intelligent man who had been a soldier, businessman, and government minister. He rose to become head of the *Corps législatif,* the lower house of the French legislature.

When the duc de Morny died in 1865, Cora searched for a new patron to replace him. She found Prince Napoléon, the emperor's cousin. He housed her in a palatial mansion befitting a royal mistress and paid her twelve thousand francs a month. She was also given her own key to his residence. He was a powerful man who was used to getting his way. And he was a dangerous man, because he had the power to have Cora deported if she displeased him. He was known for his many affairs, but he was less happy to allow Cora the same freedom to have other lovers. Initially, she acceded to his wishes, but within a few months, she returned to her old ways, running several lovers at the same time. She needed their money to fund her lavish lifestyle.

Cora was now at the peak of her power, fame, and wealth. She had several valuable homes. Her jewelry alone was worth a million francs. Even so, she never missed an opportunity to acquire more treasure. She played her lovers against one another, telling one how generous another had been, to encourage them to outdo each other in the extravagance of their gifts. And she kept meticulous records of her many lovers and what they had given her. She never allowed herself to become the plaything of just one man and thus maintained control of her life and fortune.

Cora tried every way she could think of to keep herself in the public eye. In 1867, she appeared onstage in Paris in a production of Offenbach's comic opera *Orphée aux enfers*. Her appearance caused a sensation. Her skimpy costume, which left little to the imagination, was studded with diamonds. She retired from her short stage career after only twelve performances, having achieved the desired effect. The diamond-encrusted boots she wore onstage were bought by an admirer for fifty thousand francs.

In 1870, France declared war on Prussia. The war lasted less than a year, but it was disastrous for France and for Cora. France was defeated, marking the end of its Second Empire. There was also a seismic shift in European power, away from France and toward a unified Germany. During the war, Cora opened up her homes for use as hospitals for wounded soldiers, and she paid all the expenses out of her own pocket. When the war turned against France, the emperor and Prince Napoléon fled into exile. Cora arranged to meet the prince in London. She stayed at the Grosvenor Hotel, but when the management discovered who she was—or rather, what her profession was—they asked her to leave.

ONE SHOT TOO MANY

Back in France without her principal financier, she rapidly fell into debt. Soon, she met the man who would solve her money problems, but he would also ultimately lead to her downfall. Alexandre Duval's fortune had come from his family's chain of restaurants. Cora lost no time in spending it. The faster she spent it, the more he gave her. Eventually, he was bankrupt. When his money was gone, she had no further use for him. She cut him off. When he called to see her, her servants saw that he got no farther than her front door. On December 19, 1872, he pushed his way past the servants and searched the house until he found Cora. Then he took out a gun and shot himself in front of her.

Duval survived, but the police decided that France couldn't tolerate the malign influence of this foreign courtesan any longer and ordered her out of the country. She left for Monte Carlo and then moved on to Milan, where she found Prince Napoléon. He supported her for a while, but finally cut off contact and support for her in 1874. She managed to return to Paris, but her days of ostentation and limitless spending were over. Her declining circumstances forced her to sell her mansions, jewelry, and paintings.

In 1881, she made her last visit to Monte Carlo. An English visitor found her sitting on the curb, rain-soaked and crying, having been thrown out of her apartment. He took pity on her and brought her back to his villa. Late in the evening as he sat reading, she appeared in front of him wearing a borrowed dressing gown. She let the gown fall to the floor, revealing that she was wearing nothing underneath. She told him that although she had lost everything else, she wanted to show him that she still had the thing that had made her one of the most famous and desired women in Europe—a beautiful body.

In a final attempt to raise some cash, Cora wrote her memoirs. She changed the names of her lovers, but they were so thinly disguised that their true identities were quickly guessed. On July 8, 1886, just four months after the book was published, Cora Pearl died a painful death from intestinal cancer. She was fifty-one years old and living in a small boarding house. A few of her past lovers paid for her funeral, which was attended by only about twenty persons. She was buried as Emma Eliza Crouch at Batignolles Cemetery in Paris. Her grave was not marked, and its location has since been lost. Thus, her life began and ended in anonymity.

In 2012, on Cora's birthday, February 23, the Grosvenor Hotel in London, the hotel that had thrown her out when she tried to stay there, opened a new suite called The Courtesan's Boudoir—The Cora Pearl Suite. It is furnished and decorated in a style reminiscent of nineteenth-century France, a huge portrait of Cora stares across the room from above the bed, and the bathtub is a replica of Cora's own bronze bath.

ZOLA'S NANA—BLANCHE D'ANTIGNY

Some of the most famous citizens of Paris are buried in Père Lachaise Cemetery. One of its "residents" is Blanche d'Antigny, a circus horse-rider who captivated a nation and inspired a famous novelist.

Blanche was born on May 9, 1840, in Martizay, a village in central France. She was named Marie Ernestine Antigny. When she was seven years old, her father deserted the family and left for Paris with another woman. Later, Marie Ernestine's mother handed her and her two younger siblings over to her sister-in-law and went to Paris to try to find her errant husband. In 1850, she sent for her daughter. Marie Ernestine enjoyed life in the countryside so much that she didn't want to leave, but in the end she was persuaded to join her mother in Paris. Her brother and sister had died, so she enjoyed all the attention of an only child. One of the people her mother worked for, the marquise de Gallifet, helped with the cost of sending her to a convent school attended by children of the well-to-do. Over the next few years, she learned the genteel manners and speech of the upper class. It was here that she became known as Blanche on account of her pale complexion.

Unfortunately, when she was fourteen, the marquise de Gallifet died. There was no one to pay her school fees, so she had to leave the institution that had become her home. Instead, she worked twelve hours a day as a salesgirl in a draper's shop. One evening, she went to a bar with a friend. When her friend left, she stayed on and was seduced by one of the men she met there. He took her to Bucharest, but the novelty of their relationship quickly wore off and she left him. She joined a group of gypsies and worked as a dancer. In due course she left them, too, and is said to have become the mistress to an archbishop and then a prince. She returned to Paris in 1856 and found a job as a horse-rider at the Cirque d'Hiver (Winter Circus). From there, she went on to work as a dancer elsewhere. The artist Paul Baudry saw one of her performances and asked her to pose for his painting *La Madeleine pénitente*. As her fame spread, wealthy and aristocratic admirers came calling. She left the stage and concentrated on her paying clients. And she changed her name to the grander Blanche d'Antigny.

She experienced a unique problem that threatened to rob her of hard-earned income. After she made love, she often fell into such a deep sleep that her companions were able to slip out of bed and make their escape without paying for their pleasure. She solved this tricky matter by sewing her nightshirt to her lover's!

One of her clients was the Russian police chief Nikolay Mesentsov, who lured her away from her aristocratic companions in Paris and took her to Saint Petersburg in 1863. She was soon entertaining Saint Petersburg's leading citizens at dinners in the chief's grand residence.

After more than four years in Russia, she made a serious mistake. Keen to make an impression at a gala, she found the perfect dress to wear. However, this particular dress had been ordered by the empress. Despite this, Blanche was willing to pay whatever it took to get it, and she succeeded. At the gala, she took a seat within sight of the empress, who was so angry that she ordered Blanche's expulsion from Russia. She returned to Paris in 1868 with a fine collection of diamonds, gifts from Russian admirers. And she often wore many of them. She began attracting admirers again. One of the most useful was a banker, Louis-Raphaël Bischoffsheim.

Blanche decided to return to the stage, but this time she had the good sense to prepare by taking acting and singing lessons. She debuted at the Palais-Royal to mainly positive reviews. Well-placed friends in newspapers had previewed her appearance, ensuring appreciative audiences. This appearance led to more roles and enabled her to rent a grander home in which to entertain her many admirers. Her stage costumes often sparkled with diamonds. One theatergoer described her as not so much an actress but more a jewelry shop.

Her twin careers of courtesan and stage performer ran in parallel. Her stage career gave her the publicity that made her more desirable as a courtesan, and her life as a courtesan introduced her to powerful supporters who could further her stage career. One of her many lovers was the composer and librettist Hervé, who gave her parts in several of his productions.

She went on tour in 1870, but was interrupted by the outbreak of the Franco-Prussian War. She returned to Paris in time for the siege of the city. It began on September 19, when German forces encircled the French capital. Instead of bombarding it into submission, they simply waited in an attempt to starve the residents into surrender. During the siege, Blanche opened her home as a hospital. Soldiers were grateful for her care, but the wider public resented courtesans like Blanche, accusing them of distracting politicians, diplomats, and senior military officers at a time of national emergency. The siege went on until January 1871, when the Prussians' patience ran out and they finally bombarded the weakened city, forcing a quick surrender and ending the war.

Blanche resumed her stage career, but she made the mistake of ending her relationship with Bischoffsheim, her very personal banker. He had protected her from her creditors, who now moved in on her. The cause of this uncharacteristically poor judgment was a tenor called Luce. She had fallen in love with him and dismissed the other men in her life to spend more time with him. It was probably the only time she ever loved a man, but it proved to be the beginning of the end for her. Unfortunately, she had less than two years with Luce before he died of consumption in 1873.

While she mourned Luce's death, many of her most valuable possessions were seized by creditors, and she had to sell others to settle her debts. She also had to move out of her palatial residence. She fled to Egypt to escape her most persistent creditors or, according to another account, she left France to escape a scandal that followed the bankruptcy of one of her lovers.

She worked onstage in Alexandria and Cairo, where she had an affair with the khedive, the Turkish viceroy who governed Egypt. She returned to Paris in May 1874, suffering from smallpox, typhoid, or consumption and never recovered. She died at the end of June at the age of only thirty-four, having lost all her money and deserted by her friends. The writer Émile Zola learned of Blanche while researching his book *Nana* backstage at the Théâtre des Variétés in Paris. He subsequently based the character of Nana on her.

2

THE PETTICOAT
BEHIND THE THRONE

The demimondaines of the nineteenth century represented the final flowering of a long tradition of French courtesans and royal mistresses. The French royal court was renowned for its sexual intrigue, especially during the reigns of Louis XIV and XV, but there have probably been mistresses at the court of the French king for as long as there have been French kings. The first officially recognized French royal mistress was Agnès Sorel in the fifteenth century.

AGNÈS THE FIRST

Born in 1422 to a soldier and minor member of the nobility, Agnès Sorel went to work for Isabella, Duchess of Lorraine, whose husband, René I of Naples, was the brother-in-law of King Charles VII of France. Agnes was presented to the thirty-nine-year-old French king when she was twenty. She evidently made an impression on him, because he appointed her lady-in-waiting to Marie d'Anjou, queen of France, and within two years, she was his mistress. She would go on to bear him three daughters. He made her his chief counselor at a time when women's thoughts carried little weight. She encouraged him to sack ineffectual courtiers and engage new advisers who succeeded in rescuing the failing economy. In time, she came to feel invincible, despite opposition from the church and even the rivalry of her own cousin, Antoinette, for the king's affection.

While she was heavily pregnant with her fourth child, she made an ill-advised journey in the depths of winter to Jumièges in northern France to join Charles, who was on campaign. While she was there, she suddenly fell ill and died on February 9, 1450, at the age of only twenty-eight. The official cause of her death was given as "flux of the stomach," but there were rumors that enemies at court had poisoned her. In medieval France, as in many other countries at that time, heirs and courtiers were often impatient for nature to take its course, so they might be tempted to help it along with a draft of poison. Early and unexpected deaths due to natural causes were common, but poisoning was often suspected or alleged. Charles's own son, Louis, who would later become King Louis XI, was hostile to his father, and so he was suspected of poisoning Agnès to eliminate the powerful influence she exercised over him. For many years, her death was thought to have been caused by dysentery, but analysis of her remains in 2005 showed that she was indeed poisoned. When some of her hair and pieces of skin were tested using a technique called X-ray microfluorescence, lethally high levels of mercury were found. While the tests established that mercury poisoning was the cause of her death, it was impossible to tell whether the poisoning was accidental or deliberate. Mercury was a common ingredient in many of the quack remedies taken in the fifteenth century for every conceivable ailment, so she may have inadvertently poisoned herself.

Just over fifty years after Agnès Sorel's death, another king of France, François I, summoned another beautiful woman to court. Her name was Françoise de Foix. She was no stranger to royalty, having been brought up at the English court of Queen Anne. Françoise was already married when the king took her as his mistress in about 1518. Born in the early to mid-1490s, she was engaged to be married to Jean de Laval, Count of Châteaubriant in 1505. She was about eleven years old, and Laval was nineteen. At the age of thirteen, she gave birth to a girl, Anne, who herself would only live to the age of thirteen. Françoise married Laval in 1509, and they were summoned to court seven years later. By then, Françoise was a tall, dark-haired, and cultured woman. The equally cultured king soon noticed her.

Within two years, she was his mistress. He bought her family's acquiescence by promoting the men to senior positions in the army and government. Her husband accepted the situation—he had little choice—but he was never comfortable with his wife's infidelity, even if the "other man" was the king. He took his frustration out on his wife, risking the king's anger. The king's mother, Louise of Savoy, disapproved of her son's extramarital liaison because she disliked Françoise's family. But her displeasure carried little weight with the king, so Françoise remained his official mistress for nearly a decade.

King François was taken prisoner at the Battle of Pavia in 1525. When he was released and returned to the French court, he spotted the young, attractive Anne de Pisseleu d'Heilly and transferred his affection to her. Françoise and Anne vied with each other for the king's attention, but in the end Françoise surrendered and left the court to return to her husband. She died in 1537 amid rumors that her husband had killed her.

Anne de Pisseleu d'Heilly was described as the most beautiful among the learned and the most learned among the beautiful. Her relationship with the king was no obstacle to her marriage, so in 1533, she married Jean IV de Brosse. At the ceremony, the king personally gave her away. As with Françoise, Anne's relatives were ennobled and enriched by the king to buy their cooperation. She remained his mistress until his death from a fever in 1547.

Succeeding kings were happy to continue the tradition of taking mistresses for more than two hundred years. When the privilege, ostentatious wealth, and decadence of the French royal court was swept away by the French Revolution, the citizens who replaced the kings were just as likely to take mistresses. Napoléon Bonaparte's wife, Joséphine de Beauharnais, had served as the mistress to several politicians before she met Napoléon. After she married Napoléon, both of them had lovers. While Napoléon was away with his troops, she started an affair with a Hussar lieutenant, Hippolyte Charles. Two years later, Napoléon joined the game by starting an affair with Pauline Fourès, the wife of one of his cavalry officers. He went on to have several more affairs, including a long-lasting liaison with Maria Walewska, whom he called his "little Polish wife." The husbands of women taken as lovers by kings and emperors of France usually accepted the situation, but the husband of one of Napoléon's mistresses, Virginia Oldoini, Countess of Castiglione, was so angry at her behavior, having spent a fortune on her, that he divorced her.

THE GREAT POX

In the 1490s, at about the time when Françoise de Foix was born, a frightening disease plagued Europe. It was a killer and it was spread by sex. It was the scourge of the courtesans and royal mistresses, as well as their clients and lovers. Its symptoms were similar to those of smallpox. Ulcers formed all over the body. It was known as the great pox to distinguish it from smallpox, but we now know it as syphilis. It's a bacterial infection caused by a bacterium called *Treponema pallidum*. No one knows conclusively where it came from or when. It may have originated in some form in the Americas and was brought to Europe in the 1490s by Christopher Columbus's crew. Alternatively, it may already have existed in Europe, but went unrecognized until the 1490s. Recent evidence seems to indicate the former.

A study of syphilis cases in the *American Journal of Physical Anthropology* in 2011 found no reliable evidence for syphilis in Europe before 1492, when Columbus voyaged to the Americas. About fifty skeletons have been found with signs of syphilis that appear to predate Columbus. However, they come from coastal areas. Skeletons from coasts can be difficult to date accurately by the radiocarbon method, because the individuals probably ate a lot of seafood. This can contain very old carbon from deep upwelling seawater, and can cause errors in radiocarbon dating. It's called the "marine reservoir effect." When these skeletons' data were adjusted to take account of the marine reservoir effect, the dates all moved to later than 1492.

The first syphilis epidemic in Europe occurred in 1495. The 2011 report suggests that one of Columbus's sailors may have contracted a bacterial disease similar to syphilis, perhaps something like yaws, a disease that was endemic in the Americas, but it then mutated into a different form that was transmitted by sex. When it reached Europe, wars were raging across the Continent, providing ideal conditions for spreading the disease. The first outbreak occurred among French troops attacking Naples in 1495. Hundreds of prostitutes traveling with the troops may have been infected with syphilis by Spanish mercenaries in the pay of the French king, Charles VIII. These mercenaries may have included sailors who had returned from the New World with Columbus or prostitutes infected by them. When Charles disbanded his army, the soldiers and their accompanying prostitutes dispersed all over Europe, and syphilis went with them. It spread throughout

Europe and beyond, making syphilis one of the first global diseases. By 1500, only five years after the initial outbreak, it had reached China. Holy Roman Emperor Maximilian I declared it a punishment from God.

Syphilis has changed over the centuries. In the fifteenth century, it developed faster in the body and was more lethal than it is today. When it appeared in Europe, sufferers died a few months after infection. Today, without treatment it can take more than twenty years to run its course.

Fifteenth- and sixteenth-century physicians and quacks tried all sorts of herbal and other remedies in an attempt to cure it, but nothing worked. One of the most widespread remedies was mercury, leading to the saying, "A night in the arms of Venus leads to a lifetime on Mercury." But mercury is highly toxic. Its effects on the human body include tooth loss, ulcers on the skin and in the mouth and throat, nerve damage, and ultimately death.

One of the more distressing consequences of syphilis was facial disfigurement. A sufferer's nose could collapse. Some victims wore false noses to conceal the damage. In the sixteenth century, a surgeon called Gasparo Tagliacozzi developed a procedure to rebuild the nose using the victim's own flesh. He took a flap of skin from the arm and grafted it onto the face. But the flap couldn't be cut away from the arm to form a new nose until new blood vessels had grown into it from its new position on the face. Patients had to have their arm strapped up to their face for weeks before it could be cut free.

A treatment for syphilis was not found until 1910, when a compound of arsenic known as Salvarsan was found to have some success. However, Salvarsan wasn't totally effective, so syphilis sufferers were sometimes deliberately infected with malaria! The reasoning was that a high fever sometimes appeared to cure syphilis, and malaria produces fever, so malaria was thought to be a cure for syphilis. Once the syphilis was dealt with, the malaria could be treated with quinine. Antibiotics finally provided an effective cure in the 1940s. However, syphilis has not been beaten. In fact, it's making a comeback. Bacteria have an unnerving habit of evolving new strains that are resistant to antibiotics, and syphilis is no different in this respect. Antibiotic-resistant syphilis is on the increase.

CONTRACEPTION

The arrival of syphilis may have prompted the invention of the condom in Europe. There is some evidence that condoms may have been used in the ancient world, but they were unknown in Europe until the sixteenth century. The Italian anatomist and physician Gabriele Falloppio, after whom the fallopian tubes are named, was the first European to describe a condom. He made condoms from linen and soaked them in an unspecified cocktail of "chemicals." Then he tested them on 1,100 men, none of whom contracted syphilis. By Casanova's time (the eighteenth century) condoms were being worn to prevent pregnancy as well as infection.

The term "condom" appeared in the seventeenth century, but the origin of the name is not known with any certainty. According to one story, the Earl of Condom was King Charles II's physician. The king had countless mistresses and wanted something to protect him from syphilis. Lord Condom suggested using an oiled sheath made from a sheep's intestine, and the invention was named after him. However, there is no reliable evidence that Dr. Condom ever existed. Because of the shame associated with their use, condoms were often nicknamed after a nation's enemies. In England they were known as "French letters," while in France they were called "*capotes anglaises*" (English overcoats).

Prostitutes and courtesans generally tried to avoid getting pregnant, because pregnancy reduced their earning potential. Whether or not their clients wore condoms, women often took their own precautions. A common method involved wearing an internal sponge soaked in lemon juice or vinegar. Prostitutes and courtesans were aided in their avoidance of pregnancy by poor fertility and potency caused by ill health, inadequate diet, rampant untreated infections, and the effects of lead poisoning. Lead was commonly used to make water pipes, cooking utensils, and drinking vessels. It was also a constituent of paint, and, amazingly, powdered lead was used to sweeten wine. The effects of chronic lead poisoning include reduced sperm count, miscarriage, premature birth, low birth weight, and developmental problems in babies.

Royal mistresses and concubines weren't so concerned with avoiding pregnancy, because it could be the route to lifelong wealth and influence.

Kings and emperors usually provided generously for their illegitimate children and bought off their mothers with noble titles.

QUEEN IN ALL BUT NAME— DIANE DE POITIERS

At a jousting tournament to celebrate the second marriage of King François I in 1530, his twelve-year-old son, Prince Henry, surprised everyone by addressing his salute not to the new queen, but to his mentor, Diane de Poitiers. His lance carried Diane's ribbon, not the queen's. Although she was twenty years older than the young prince, she would soon be his mistress.

Diane de Poitiers was born just before midnight on New Year's Eve 1499, to an aristocratic family. One of her ancestors was King Louis IX. She was named Diana after the goddess of the hunt, because her father was a keen hunter. When she was six years old, her mother died. Anne de Beaujeu, the most powerful woman in France, agreed to take charge of her education. Anne was related to two French kings. She was the eldest daughter of Louis XI and the sister of Charles VIII. She had acted as Charles's regent, reigning on his behalf until he was old enough to rule in his own right. It was a rare privilege for Diane to be brought up in such a noble household. She became one of Anne's maids of honor and was schooled in the manners and traditions of the royal court. She was being prepared for an advantageous marriage.

AN ARRANGED MARRIAGE

When Diane was fifteen years old, she was told who her husband was to be. The man chosen for her was Louis de Brézé. His mother was Charlotte de France, the illegitimate daughter of King Charles VII and his mistress, Agnès Sorel. Charlotte had been murdered by her husband, Jacques de Brézé, when he discovered her in bed with her lover. He killed the lover, too! It was a frenzied attack. The couple were slashed with more than a hundred sword cuts. Unfortunately for Jacques, Charlotte was the half sister of King Louis XI. Louis was so furious at her murder that Jacques was condemned to death. He managed to save his neck by handing over all his possessions to the king. When the next king, Charles VIII, came to the throne, he annulled the verdict and restored Jacques's titles and property.

Louis de Brézé was wealthy and powerful, but he was also said to be ugly, and at fifty-six, he was old enough to be the teenage Diane's grandfather. Nevertheless, she accepted her fate and married him on March 29, 1515, with the king and queen in attendance. Soon after her marriage, she was appointed lady-in-waiting to the queen. When she wasn't needed at court, she spent her time at her family home, the Château d'Anet in Normandy. The king and court often visited Anet to go hunting in the forests nearby. Diane became an accomplished horsewoman and often joined the hunts.

At the age of seventeen, she gave birth to her first child, a girl they named Françoise in honor of the king. Three years later she had another daughter, Louise. In 1524, her father, Jean de Poitiers, was found guilty of treason and sentenced to death for his part in a plot to depose the king. On the appointed day, he was brought to the place of execution. He knelt at the headsman's block and waited for the ax to fall, but nothing happened. He knelt there for half an hour, expecting to die at any moment, but the king finally reprieved him. The crowd of onlookers who had gathered to watch him die probably felt cheated of their day's entertainment. His death sentence was commuted to life imprisonment.

A PRINCE'S LOVE

By the time Diane's husband died, in 1531, she had already made an impression on the young Prince Henry. When his father, the king, was captured at the Battle of Pavia in 1525 and taken to Spain, he was released on condition that the six-year-old Prince Henry and his older brother would go to Spain in his place to encourage the king to stick to the peace treaty that had been negotiated. Amazingly, the deal was accepted. It was Diane who kissed and hugged the young boy as he left. He spent three years in captivity in a foreign land, among strangers, starved of affection, before he was able to return to France. In 1533, he married Catherine de Médicis. Of course, it was an arranged marriage. Catherine's hand had been offered to him by her cousin, Pope Clement VII, who was keen to form an alliance with France.

Initially, it was the king, not Prince Henry, who seemed to be warming to Diane. He often went hunting with her, earning her the displeasure of his mistress, Anne, duchesse d'Etampes. Coincidentally (perhaps), rumors about Diane's lasting beauty began to circulate at court. It was said to be due to witchcraft. The unmarried Diane was now in great danger, because if a charge of witchcraft could be proved, she could be burned at the stake. To everyone's surprise, it was the shy, quiet Prince Henry who defended her.

The fourteen-year-old prince grew closer and closer to the thirty-three-year-old Diane until they became lovers. Their relationship didn't cause any concern at court, because Henry was not destined to be king. His older brother, the dauphin, would inherit the throne. Then in 1536, as the king and his sons prepared for war against the Holy Roman Emperor, the dauphin fell ill and died. Now it was Henry who would be king. And he needed an heir. However, year after year, his wife, Catherine, failed to do her duty and produce a son for him. It would be ten years before she gave birth to a boy. She then produced another nine children in rapid succession. But it was Diane whom Henry was devoted to. Catherine knew it and despised her. She stored up her hatred and grudges and waited for an opportunity to deal with Diane.

The young prince became King Henry II of France on March 31, 1547, when his father, François I, died. Diane continued to exercise great influence over him, because he trusted only her. It was Diane, not his queen, who accompanied him on his royal visits to French towns and cities. Local dignitaries kissed Diane's hand, not the queen's. Diane was queen in all but name. He even let her write some of his official correspondence and sign it on his behalf.

When Catherine married Henry, she had expected him to give her the grand Château de Chenonceau in the Loire Valley as a coronation gift. Instead, he gave it to Diane. In 1548, he had a gold coin struck with Diane's face on it. It was the first time any French king had honored his mistress in this way. However, despite his devotion to Diane, he still managed to have three illegitimate children by three different women—Filippa Duci, Lady Janet Stewart, and Nicole de Savigny.

A DEATH PREDICTED

The seeds of Henry's demise were sown by the marriage of his daughter, Élisabeth de Valois, to King Philip II of Spain in 1559. The wedding festivities included jousting contests. Henry, a keen horseman, intended to take part. The superstitious Diane begged him not to compete, because an astrologer had predicted his death. The famous seer Nostradamus had been consulted and confirmed the prediction. However, Henry refused to withdraw.

After winning several rounds, he faced the comte de Montgomery, Gabriel de Lorges. The two men, on horseback and dressed in full armor, charged toward each other at a gallop. They lowered their lances until each pointed straight at the other horseman. Both lances were on target and broke on impact as they were designed to do. The king slumped forward and had to be helped down from his horse. When his helmet visor was opened, his face was covered with blood. The visor had not been closed properly. This had been noticed and he was warned about it, but he had continued regardless. Splinters of wood from the broken lance had gone through the opening in the visor and had pierced his right eye and throat. He was operated on immediately.

The queen saw her opportunity to isolate him from Diane. Over the next few days, Diane pleaded to be allowed to visit him, and Henry was asking for her, but the queen refused to let her go to him. Henry developed a fever and died on July 10, 1559, twelve days after the accident. As soon as he died, the queen took her revenge on the woman who had stolen her husband. She demanded the return of jewels the king had given Diane. And when Henry was buried, Diane was not allowed to attend the funeral. The home the king had given her, the Château de Chenonceau, was seized, too. And, finally, she was banished from court.

DEADLY DRINKABLE GOLD

Diane de Poitiers died on April 22, 1566. She was buried in a chapel at the Château d'Anet, but she didn't rest in peace. Her grave was desecrated during the French Revolution, and her remains were thrown into a common grave outside the château's walls. The grave was investigated in 2009, and

Diane's remains were identified. When samples were analyzed, high levels of gold were found in her hair. She was known to have taken a tonic called drinkable gold that was believed to preserve youth. Far from keeping her young, it may have killed her.

Henry II was succeeded as French king by his son, François II, but he reigned for only seventeen months before he died at the age of sixteen. The next king, Charles IX, came to the throne at the age of only ten and didn't live much longer than François—he died at the age of twenty-three. His only mistress was Marie Touchet. They were almost the same age. She was born in 1549, he in 1550. She was not an aristocrat, but that didn't seem to discourage the king. In 1573, when he had been on the throne for thirteen years, she bore him a son, his only son, Charles de Valois. When the king died the following year, his illegitimate son was brought up by his successor, Henry III, who also granted Marie a pension. She had another child, a daughter, Catherine Henriette de Balzac, who would later become the mistress of Henry IV. Marie Touchet died in her late eighties in 1638.

THE PURSUIT OF PLEASURE— NINON DE L'ENCLOS

In Marie Touchet's final years, a new courtesan, Ninon de l'Enclos, was becoming the talk of the Paris salons. Her name was Anne, but she was nicknamed Ninon by her cavalry officer father, Henry. She became a famous Parisian courtesan, independent thinker, and patron of the arts.

Ninon was born in about 1620 in the Marais district of Paris. Her parents were very different from each other, and their marriage was unhappy as a result. Her mother, Marie-Barbé de La Marche, was a devout Catholic, whereas her father was a libertine who subscribed to the Epicurean approach to life. Epicureanism, named after the Ancient Greek philosopher Epicurus, contended that pleasure is the greatest good. Ninon preferred her father's beliefs. When she was twelve years old, she told him that from then on, she would be a boy. He humored her by having boys' clothes made for her. He also gave her a boy's education. Soon afterwards, she also decided that religion was an invention of man. Despite her mother's best efforts, Ninon's course in life was already set.

In her teens in the 1630s, her father was sent into exile because of a duel fought over another man's wife. Ninon was sent away to live in a convent, because her family couldn't afford the dowry that would have assured her of a good marriage. But after a year, she determined to take control of her life and live it on her own terms. She made the decision to leave the convent and go to Paris to live an independent life as a courtesan. Fortunately, she'd had a good education, she spoke several languages, and she was well read—useful assets for a courtesan. She became a popular figure on the Paris social circuit, where she was famous for her mastery of the lute and clavichord. Prominent literary figures, including Cyrano de Bergerac and Molière, attended her salons. Wealthy men, including the king's cousin, pursued the attractive, well-educated, talented, and unmarried Ninon. Her first lover was Gaspard de Coligny.

After her mother's death followed by her father's death shortly afterwards, Ninon lived openly as a courtesan. She invested her small inheritance wisely, giving herself an income for life and the independence that came with it. Cardinal Richelieu was one of her first pursuers. He offered fifty thousand crowns for one night in her company. She took the money, but sent another courtesan, Marion Delorme, in her place. Her clients included statesmen, aristocrats, and clergymen, but her determination to keep control of her life meant that she never became a *royal* mistress. She was associated with a series of prominent Frenchmen, including the duc d'Enghien (later known as the Grand Condé), the marquis de Villarceaux, the marquis de Sévigné (and his son, Charles), the duc de La Rochefoucauld, Abbé François de Châteauneuf, and Canon Nicolas Gédoyn, who was more than fifty years younger than Ninon! She was such an acknowledged authority on her chosen profession that men and women sought her advice on love and lovemaking.

CONDUCT UNBECOMING

Ninon's lifestyle as a serial mistress attracted unwelcome attention from the authorities, resulting in her imprisonment in the Madelonnettes Convent in Paris in 1656, on the orders of Queen Anne of Austria, the French regent. The convent had been established for the confinement of women accused of misconduct. The exiled ex-queen Christina of Sweden visited Ninon and was so impressed with her that she appealed to the chief minister of France, Cardinal Mazarin, to have her freed.

She was keen for her views to be more widely known. A pamphlet called *La coquette vengée* (*The Coquette Avenged*), published in 1659, is thought to have been written by her or influenced by her ideas. In it, the writer discusses the possibility of leading a virtuous life without the need for religion. A few years later, in the late 1660s, Ninon abandoned her life as a courtesan and concentrated on promoting the arts. One of her close friends at this time was Françoise d'Aubigné, who would later become Madame de Maintenon, the mistress and then second wife of Louis XIV.

Ninon was renowned for her wit and her beauty, even in her old age. When she was sixty-five, she was said to be as beautiful as she was in her twenties. Young men still pursued her. However, one of her breathless admirers was to die as a result of tragic circumstances. Her many liaisons resulted in the birth of two sons. One, the chevalier de La Boissière, served with distinction in the navy. The other, unaware that Ninon was his mother, fell hopelessly in love with her. She tried to repel his advances, but he wouldn't be deterred. In the end, she had to tell him that she was his mother. The young man was so horrified that he ran outside and killed himself by falling on his sword.

Ninon was still being courted by men when she was in her eighties. When she died in 1705, her will bequeathed some of her money to a young boy called François-Marie Arouet, to buy books. He was her lawyer's son. He is better known as Voltaire. Could it be that a gift from a notorious courtesan inspired his lifelong love of books and writing?

AT THE COURT OF THE SUN KING

Louis XIV, also known as the Sun King because he took the sun as his emblem, was one of the most sexually incontinent French monarchs. He had a voracious appetite for women. He had plenty of time to amass a veritable army of mistresses because he reigned for more than seventy-two years, the longest reign of any monarch of a major European country. He came to the throne when he was only four years old, so his mother, Anne of Austria, ruled on his behalf as queen regent with the assistance of Louis XIII's chief minister, Cardinal Mazarin, until he came of age. The first of his many mistresses, Catherine Bellier, was engaged by his mother to take his virginity in 1652, when he was fourteen years old. The task was successfully accomplished, proving that the royal "equipment" was in full working order, and Bellier was rewarded with an estate and a pension.

Louis got his first taste of romantic love with a young Italian beauty called Marie Mancini. She was one of seven nieces of Cardinal Mazarin. He had brought his nieces to Paris to arrange advantageous marriages for them. His services weren't entirely altruistic, because their marriages strengthened his position and made him very well connected among the nobility. The girls, whose dark Italian complexion contrasted with fashionably pale Frenchwomen, were known as the Mazarinettes.

French and English noblewomen worked hard on their pale complexions, unwittingly risking their health in the process. Much of the makeup they used was toxic. Paleness was highly prized, because it demonstrated that its possessor didn't have to work outside, as most people did at that time, and could spend all day indoors. It indicated wealth and status. Women, in particular, were keen to show that they didn't have to work for a living. They made their face unnaturally pale by applying makeup containing white lead. It also covered blemishes in the skin caused by disease and infection. On top of the white lead foundation, lips received a red blush from vermilion (mercuric sulfide). Mercury and lead are both highly toxic. Eyes were given an extra gleam by using a drop or two of belladonna (also known as deadly nightshade because of its poisonous nature) to dilate their pupils. Even relatively low lead levels in the human body cause neurological problems, leading to shortened attention span, learning difficulties, and lower IQ. Lead is particularly dangerous to children, who may suffer stunted growth and, in extreme cases, fatal brain damage. Mercury also has harmful effects on the brain and nervous system. Belladonna causes blurred vision and sensitivity to bright light.

THE MAGNIFICENT MAZARINETTES

As upper-class women with dark Mediterranean complexions, the Mazarinettes were an exotic curiosity to the French court. Louis spotted the first of them, Marie Mancini, in 1656, while he was visiting her dying mother.

He appreciated Marie's honesty and found that he could speak freely to her. Their relationship was romantic, but it wasn't consummated. Their closeness worried courtiers, who felt that Marie was not a suitable bride for a king of France. The queen mother convinced Cardinal Mazarin of the importance of a dynastic marriage, so he agreed to separate the couple. Marie was taken away to La Rochelle while the cardinal concentrated on negotiations with Spain over a potential marriage between Louis and the Spanish infanta, Maria Theresa. She was a much more fitting match, because the marriage would calm the turbulent relations between the two countries by uniting their royal houses.

Unknown to the cardinal, Louis and Marie stayed in touch. They were secretly sending letters to each other. When the cardinal found out, he put pressure on both of them to put France first and accept the inevitable, which they eventually did. To make sure the affair was over, the cardinal even arranged for another of his nieces, Olympia, to distract the king and take his mind off Marie. After extensive negotiations, Louis eventually married Maria Theresa on June 9, 1660. The following year, Marie Mancini was married off to an Italian prince, Lorenzo Onofrio Colonna, to get her out of the way. Lorenzo expressed great surprise when he discovered that his bride was a virgin. He said he did not expect to find such innocence among the loves of kings.

CAPTURING THE KING'S HEART

Barely two years into his marriage, Louis began an affair with his brother's wife, Henrietta, Duchess of Orléans. Louis's mother disapproved of their liaison, so the lovers came up with a plan to make it look as if Louis had moved on to pastures new. Feigning an affair with one of Henrietta's unmarried ladies-in-waiting would enable him to visit Henrietta without raising suspicions. Unfortunately, the ruse didn't go entirely according to plan, because the king fell for the pretty, blue-eyed, blond-haired lady-in-waiting, Louise de La Vallière. She tried to end their relationship after she heard sermons delivered by the court preacher, Jacques-Bénigne Bossuet, condemning the king's immoral behavior. Racked with shame and guilt, she ran away to a convent with the king in hot pursuit. He must have been very persuasive, because she not only returned to court, but also went on to have four children with the king. The first two died in infancy, and the other two died in their teens. By the time Louise had their fourth child, the king had noticed his next conquest, Françoise-Athénaïs de Rochechouart de Mortemart.

Françoise-Athénaïs, who had become the marquise de Montespan by marriage, made sure she was seen at court, because she had embarked on a mission to seize the position of official royal mistress. She was strikingly beautiful and also aware of current political events, making her a prime candidate for royal mistress. Several aristocrats courted her, unsuccessfully, because she had her sights on a greater prize. Her opportunity to seize the top job came when the queen and Louise de La Vallière were both pregnant by the king. They needed someone to keep the king amused at private social gatherings. Despite their suspicions of the marquise de Montespan, they asked her to entertain the king and she agreed. They thought they could dispense with her services a few months later when they were able to resume their customary duties, but they had underestimated her. She made such an impression on the king that she replaced Louise as *maîtresse-en-titre*. The king and the marquise went on to have seven illegitimate children together.

A POISONOUS AFFAIR

Madame de Montespan's reign as the king's favorite ended in about 1680 with a scandal called *L'affaire des poisons* (Affair of the Poisons). After a series of poisoning cases, a number of fortune-tellers, alchemists, and aristocrats were arrested and charged with witchcraft and poisoning. The king was so alarmed, especially when some of his own courtiers were implicated, that he established a commission, La Chambre Ardente, to investigate those who were charged. Anyone of note whose husband or wife had died, or even just fallen ill, came under suspicion. There were stories of terrified aristocrats grabbing handfuls of jewels and cash before hurrying across the border to escape. Hundreds of people were arrested. Many of them were tortured to encourage them to name others. In the end, sixty-five were imprisoned for life and thirty-six were executed.

In 1679, one of those arrested was Catherine Deshayes Monvoisin, also known as La Voisin. Under torture, she accused dozens of people. Several of their interrogations implicated Madame de Montespan. She was accused not only of buying aphrodisiacs from La Voisin and taking part in Black Masses to ensure the king's continued interest in her but also, when they failed to produce the desired result, of buying poison with which to take her revenge on the king. Montespan was never brought to trial, but La Voisin, lacking friends in high places to protect her, was burned at the stake as a witch on February 22, 1680.

Although no charges were brought against Madame de Montespan, *L'affaire des poisons* caused a rift between her and the king that never healed. They remained on good terms, but her time as *maîtresse-en-titre* was at an end. Unwittingly, she had already given the king's next lover a helping hand. When she met Françoise d'Aubigné, she liked her so much that she persuaded the king to pay her a pension. D'Aubigné's husband had died and she was preparing to move to Portugal to take up an appointment as the queen's lady-in-waiting. The pension enabled her to stay in Paris.

THE SUN KING'S WIFE?—
MADAME DE MAINTENON

Françoise d'Aubigné's life was unusual, even by the standards of the seventeenth century. This provincial girl, who was almost thrown overboard from a ship in the mid-Atlantic, became the uncrowned queen of France.

In 1627, Constant d'Aubigné was serving a prison sentence in Bordeaux. He was evidently quite a charmer, because he somehow managed to get the prison governor's sixteen-year-old daughter, Jeanne de Cardilhac, pregnant. They were quickly married to save face, but Jeanne was still disowned by her family. When Constant was released from prison, he took her to Niort, where their baby was born. The baby boy was named Constant after his father. The elder Constant was soon in trouble again and back in prison. Jeanne had their second child, a boy called Charles, and with Constant in prison yet again, she had a third child, Françoise, on November 27, 1635. Constant senior was Protestant, a descendant of Huguenots, but Jeanne was Catholic. Their daughter, Françoise, was baptized as a Catholic, but her father insisted that she was brought up as a Protestant.

With her father in prison and unable to support the family, Françoise was taken in by her aunt Louise, Constant's sister. Meanwhile, her mother took the two boys to Paris. She was unable to find enough work to support herself, but she refused to follow the usual road trod by many a provincial woman coming to the capital. She didn't turn to prostitution. As a result, she was declared bankrupt.

A CLOSE SHAVE

When Constant was released from prison, he revealed a dramatic plan to improve the family's prospects. He intended to leave France for the Caribbean to make his fortune. He somehow raised the cost of the passage and set sail with his family in September 1644. The voyage was pretty grim. Most of the passengers fell ill, including Françoise. She was struck down by a fever and became so ill that her parents thought she had died, but just as the crew was about to consign her body to the sea, her mother noticed a tiny movement, a flicker of life. She wasn't dead after all. Moments before being dropped into the ocean, she was pulled back into the ship and revived. Against the odds, she recovered.

Two months after Constant and his family left France, they arrived in Martinique. From there, they moved on to a tiny island called Marie-Galante, where Constant planned to establish a plantation. Leaving his family on the island, he returned to France, where he successfully secured the position of governor of Marie-Galante and any other island he could grab for France. After a short reunion with his family in the Caribbean, he left for France again, but this time he didn't return. He vanished. Jeanne had little choice but to bring her family back to France. When she searched for her feckless husband, she discovered that he had died a month earlier. He appeared to have been trying to escape from his financial troubles by running away and adopting an alias when illness overwhelmed him.

Madame de Neuillant, the mother of Françoise's godmother, came to the family's aid. She arranged to have Françoise schooled in a convent. The rebellious teenager didn't enjoy the experience. She thought it was little better than a prison. However, she eventually came to like the convent and the nuns who cared for her, especially when she was given some responsibility for teaching the younger girls. She was devastated when she learned that she'd have to leave because her fees were not being paid anymore. She returned to live with Madame de Neuillant and earned her keep by working on the family estate.

When Françoise was sixteen years old, Madame de Neuillant took her to Paris with the intention of getting rid of her by marrying her off. There, Françoise met the writer Paul Scarron. They started writing to each other. He liked her and wanted to help the attractive but penniless girl, so he offered to pay for her to enter a convent or alternatively he would marry her. Given her past experience, convent life held no attraction for her, so although Scarron was twenty-five years older than she and crippled with rheumatoid arthritis, Françoise married him. In doing so, she gained a protector and independence from Madame de Neuillant, and he gained a nurse and companion. She now found herself mixing with Scarron's friends, who included the great writers and artists of the time, and the noblemen and -women who sought their company. Over the next few years, Scarron became increasingly disabled and obese until he died on October 6, 1660.

Scarron died in debt and left no will, so Françoise was left with little more than the clothes on her back. She had to rely on the charity of friends to put a roof over her head. The queen mother was persuaded to pay her a pension, which made her financially independent for the first time in her life.

AN IDEAL GOVERNESS

Unknown to Françoise, events at the court of Louis XIV were about to take her life in a new direction. The king's favorite, Madame de Montespan, was pregnant for the third time. She faced the unappealing prospect of coping with an ongoing series of royal bastards, so she was in urgent need of a governess to take charge of them. She remembered the widow Scarron, an independent woman, genteel, discreet, not part of the nobility, not at court—in short, an ideal person with whom to hide the king's indiscretions. She gave Françoise the job together with a generous income and her own staff. When her brood and the staff who helped look after them outgrew her home, the king bought a bigger house for her. He also started calling in to see his illegitimate children.

During these visits, he got to know Françoise and inevitably started thinking of her as more than a governess. On seeing how caring and loving she was with her young charges, he is reported to have said, "She knows how to love. There would be great pleasure in being loved by her." In 1673, he increased her pension. In fact, he tripled it. When he publicly acknowledged paternity of his illegitimate children, there was no need to hide them away anymore, so he asked Françoise to give up her home and move to the palace of Saint-Germain-en-Laye, where his court was based. At the beginning of 1674, she moved to the palace, which was also the home of the king's current mistress, Madame de Montespan. Even with his wife and mistress under the same roof, he pursued the thirty-eight-year-old Françoise. After months of resistance to his approaches, she finally suspended her religious reservations and worries about her reputation. By November 1674, she was his mistress. Her euphoria at being chosen by the king didn't last long when she saw him continue with a relentless series of casual affairs with other women.

One of his many infatuations was an eighteen-year-old girl called Marie-Angélique de Scorailles. She arrived at court in 1678, as maid of honor to Princess Elisabeth Charlotte von der Pfalz, known as Liselotte. Marie-Angélique was less than half the king's age. While courtiers privately expressed their embarrassment at the king's behavior, pursuing a girl the same age as his son, they also acknowledged that she was probably the most beautiful woman ever to grace the Palace of Versailles with her presence. She enjoyed the high life at court—the fine gowns, the jewelry, and the ornate carriages drawn by impeccably groomed horses. However, her grip on the king's affections was short-lived. Inevitably, she became pregnant. Unfortunately, her baby was stillborn, and she sustained such serious injuries during the delivery that it was impossible for her to have sex thereafter. The king dispensed with her services and paid her off in the customary manner by making her a duchess. Marie-Angélique, now the duchesse de Fontanges, died soon afterwards at the age of only nineteen from tuberculosis, poisoning, or complications arising from the delivery of her baby. Suspicions that she might have been poisoned by Montespan as part of *L'affaire des poisons* scandal helped to end Montespan's relationship with the king.

THE MAKING OF A MADAME

With Montespan and Marie-Angélique both out of the picture, Françoise was now the king's unrivaled favorite. Louis had been so impressed by her hard work with the royal bastards that he rewarded her with enough money to buy the estate of Maintenon. Then he gave her the title to match, marquise de Maintenon. She was also given a new job, Second Mistress of the Robes to the dauphine, the wife of the king's only surviving legitimate son. Montespan was incandescent with rage that a woman she considered to be so far beneath her, a former paid servant, had replaced her in the king's affections.

In 1682, Louis moved his court and government from the cramped quarters at Saint-Germain-en-Laye to Versailles, a hunting lodge that he had rebuilt as a grand palace befitting a great king of France. He had moved his court out of Paris because of a series of rebellions called the Fronde early in his reign. The French people and nobility alike resented what they saw as the "foreign rule" of their country during the king's minority by Anne of Austria, who, despite her title, was Spanish, and the Italian-born Cardinal Mazarin. *Fronde* means "sling," referring to the slings rebels used to hurl stones at their opponents' windows. The rebellions attempted to limit the power of the king and his court, but unlike a similar rebellion in England, they were unsuccessful. Louis defeated the rebels and emerged from the Fronde even stronger than before.

When he moved the court to Versailles, Françoise moved with him. Montespan was still at court, too, still a royal mistress, but her time was past. In July 1683, the forty-five-year-old queen suddenly fell ill with a fever. It may have been caused by a boil or a growth (some reports say a tumor) that had developed on her arm. Despite (or possibly because of) the attentions of the royal physicians, she deteriorated rapidly and died on July 30. Within four days of her death, the king was "consoling himself" with Françoise at Fontainebleau. She had been worried that the queen's death might drive him back into the arms of Madame de Montespan, but it was Françoise he chose.

A ROYAL MARRIAGE?

The king decided not to endure another dynastic marriage. He considered marrying Françoise, but horrified advisers counseled him against it. It is thought that a secret marriage ceremony did take place sometime between the end of 1683 and the winter of 1685, although there is no official record of it and, because of her low social status, she was never crowned queen. As she aged, Françoise succumbed to painful rheumatism and felt weary in the face of an endless stream of visitors and correspondents who expected her to intercede with the king on their behalf.

The king's health began to give concern in 1715. Now that he was well into his seventies, his legs were increasingly painful. He had been suffering from gout for some time. Then one leg developed gangrene. It was obvious to the royal physician, Dr. Fagon, that the Sun King's life was drawing to a close. Françoise saw him for the last time on August 30. Two days later he was dead. Françoise spent her remaining years at École de Saint-Cyr, a girls' boarding school she had established in 1684. It was unique in that it was the only girls' school in France that was not a convent. She lived there quietly, gradually fading from people's memory. At the beginning of April 1719, she took to her bed with a fever. After a few days, she seemed to be improving, but on the fifteenth, her condition rapidly worsened and she died.

She was buried in the chapel at Saint-Cyr, but she didn't lie in peace for long. During the French Revolution, workmen discovered her grave while they were converting the chapel into a hospital ward. They broke her coffin open and pulled her body out. They dragged it through the streets and intended to burn her as a witch, but during the night, the body was rescued by supporters and reburied in secret. In 1802, her body was taken from its hiding place and a new burial ceremony was held, when she was buried in the courtyard at Saint-Cyr. It was in the way by 1816, so it was disinterred once again and kept in a storehouse. In 1836, it was reburied in a new marble sarcophagus. By 1890, the sarcophagus was in the way, so her body was disinterred once again. This time her remains underwent an autopsy to confirm that they were indeed those of Madame de Maintenon. That done, they were reburied in the Saint-Cyr chapel. But the chapel and grave were badly damaged by an air raid during World War II, so the remains were moved yet again, this time to the chapel at Versailles. Finally, in 1969, the remains of Françoise d'Aubigné, Madame de Maintenon, were returned to Saint-Cyr and buried under a black marble slab in the chapel's central aisle.

LOUIS XV'S MISTRESSES

The Sun King outlived his son and grandson, so in 1715, he was succeeded by his five-year-old great-grandson, who became Louis XV. Until he was old enough to take power, the Duke of Orléans ruled as regent. In his twenties, the new king carried on the family tradition by starting his own impressive collection of mistresses, including four women who were sisters! The first of the sisters to charm the king was Louise-Julie, comtesse de Mailly.

Born in 1710, the same year as the king, she became Louis's mistress in 1738, with her husband's permission. In the same year, her younger sister, Pauline-Félicité, visited court and quickly seduced the king. She became pregnant by him, but she died while giving birth. She was replaced by her younger sister, Marie-Anne. At first, she rejected the king's advances, because she already had a lover. To help the king, a friend, the duc de Richelieu (great-nephew of the more famous Cardinal Richelieu) had Marie-Anne's lover sent to Italy as a soldier in the hope that he might be killed in action. He was indeed wounded, but inconveniently he survived and returned home. Next, Richelieu had him sent to Languedoc, where he had arranged for a young lady to seduce him. She delivered the goods, resulting in passionate letters between the two. Of course, Richelieu made sure that Marie-Anne saw the letters. It achieved the desired effect. She abandoned her lover and turned all her attention to the king.

In return for her services, Marie-Anne demanded a title, an income, a grand house, and the expulsion of her sister from court. The besotted king agreed to it all. Marie-Anne became the duchesse de Chateauroux. Unlike Louise-Julie, who had no interest in politics, Marie-Anne interfered in affairs of state at the highest level. She persuaded the king to take personal command of his army's involvement in the War of the Austrian Succession (1740–48). Controversially, he took Marie-Anne with him. While he was away with his forces in 1744, he fell gravely ill. When it looked like he was dying, he did what kings often did to ease their entry into paradise. He prepared to meet his maker by ending his relationships with his mistresses and confessing his sins. In fact, he survived, but Marie-Anne did not. She caught a chill and died in December of the same year. The king consoled himself with yet another of the family's sisters, Diane-Adélaïde. But just a few months later, one of the most famous royal mistresses of all was diverting the king—Madame de Pompadour.

DESTINED FOR GREATNESS?— MADAME DE POMPADOUR

The woman who would become Louis XV's favorite was born Jeanne-Antoinette Poisson to a middle-class family at the end of December 1721. She later claimed that when she was nine years old, a fortune-teller predicted that she would one day become the king's mistress and that her mother's response was to embark on an ambitious program of training and education to prepare Jeanne-Antoinette for her future role. It sounds a little too good to be true. In any case, she took lessons in singing, playing the clavichord, art, poetry, conversation, and fashion. In 1741, she was married to Charles-Guillaume Le Normant d'Étioles. Her marriage launched her into the fashionable salons of Paris. The salons had developed at the end of Louis XIV's reign. The aging king no longer amused his inner circle of courtiers and friends, so they started meeting in each other's homes, away from court.

Jeanne-Antoinette was such a hit in the salons that her name began to circulate at court. It was an opportune time. The king's confidants thought he needed a new mistress to raise his spirits, and Jeanne-Antoinette, Madame d'Etioles, was perfect for the job. However, a lowborn commoner like Jeanne-Antoinette could not be presented to the king . . . at least, not officially, so arrangements were made for them to meet unofficially. The forthcoming marriage of the dauphin in February 1745 provided the perfect opportunity. The celebrations would include a number of masked balls. The king and Jeanne-Antoinette could attend in disguise and meet unnoticed by gossipmongers. They did—he as a yew tree and she as the goddess Diana—and the king was entranced by her.

FULFILLING THE PROPHECY

The married twenty-three-year-old was the king's mistress within a month. It wasn't acceptable for the king's mistress to be a commoner, so she was given the title of the marquise de Pompadour, Pompadour being the name of an estate the king had bought for her. Now, she could be presented to the king officially and publicly. She had fulfilled the fortune-teller's prophecy of fourteen years earlier (if it really happened), but despite her aristocratic title, she was still considered to be a commoner by courtiers, who consequently disapproved of her and resented her closeness to the king. One by one, they plotted against her—opposition to her focused on the dauphin, who loathed Pompadour and sided with his mother, the queen—but Pompadour got the better of them and grew more powerful and indispensable to the king.

One reason Pompadour lasted so long at court was her good relations with the queen, who said, "If there must be a mistress, better her than any other." She also put a lot of effort into keeping the king happy. She entertained him with dinners and accompanied him on tours and hunts. She hosted suppers for him and invited his close friends, including women whose company he enjoyed. The king trusted her so much that he listened to her advice and opinions on all sorts of issues, ranging from military affairs to foreign policy and the appointment of ministers—who therefore owed their positions to her, and so her power increased with every appointment. Diplomats and politicians consulted her in the hope of winning her support and reaching the king's ear. In 1755, Austria sought her help with negotiations that led to the Treaty of Versailles. The treaty formed a defensive alliance between France and Austria. France hoped it would ensure peace in a restless Europe, but it actually resulted in France being drawn into the Seven Years' War (1754–63). The conflict raged across Europe, North America, South America, West Africa, and India. It was disastrous for France, which lost its North American colonies to Britain and almost bankrupted itself. Madame de Pompadour was blamed for this reversal of France's fortunes, in part because it would have been treason or at the very least social suicide to blame the king.

Her fate was inextricably linked with the king's. At the beginning of 1757, she thought her life of luxury and privilege was over. As Louis left the Palace of Versailles to climb into his waiting carriage, a man burst through his guards and ran up to him. The intruder was arrested, initially because he had failed to take his hat off in the king's presence. The king thought the man had struck him, but then realized that he was bleeding from a wound in his side. He had been stabbed. He was carried back into the palace, convinced he was dying. He resolved to give up his mistresses and lead a more saintly life with his wife if God spared him. For more than a week, there was no news of his condition. Pompadour was not allowed to visit him. She feared the worst and contemplated an abrupt end to her reign as *maîtresse-en-titre*. But she held her nerve, and after eleven days she learned that the king had survived and she was still "the favorite." In fact, the wound had been quite superficial and the king's life was never in danger. He quickly forgot about his "deathbed resolution" to lead a better life. His would-be assassin, Robert-François Damiens, fared less well. Damiens, a domestic servant, was tortured horribly with molten lead to make him reveal the names of his accomplices, but there were none. Damiens had acted alone. He was condemned to death by dismemberment. He was to be quartered by horse. His four limbs were tied to four horses, whose job was to set off in different directions and tear his body apart. However, the horses failed in their duty. To placate impatient spectators, the executioner, Charles-Henri Sanson, severed Damiens's limbs with an ax. His remains were then burned.

COPING WITH RIVALS

Like that of other royal mistresses, Pompadour's position was constantly under threat from up-and-coming new mistresses who could supplant her. In 1761, she was alarmed to learn that another of the king's mistresses, Anne Coupier de Romans, was expecting his child. Coupier was young and beautiful. Pompadour was forty-two, but looked much older because she had been in poor health for some time. She was suffering from tuberculosis and coughing up blood every day. Her spies kept her informed of the king's meetings with Coupier, whose baby, a boy, was born on January 13, 1762. However, Coupier made the mistake of demanding too much from the king. He eventually tired of her and had her sent away from court into exile. He never recognized her son as his.

Another minor mistress, Marie-Louise O'Murphy (also known as La Morphise), had made the same mistake several years earlier. Born in 1737, she was the daughter of an Irish soldier-turned-shoemaker who settled in Rouen with his French wife. When her father died, her mother took her to Paris. When she was about twelve years old, the infamous Venetian libertine Giacomo Casanova spotted her while he was visiting her actress sister. He described her as "a pretty, ragged, dirty little creature." Nevertheless, he had a nude picture of her painted by his friend, the artist François Boucher. This picture, or perhaps another painting of her by a German artist, was seen by the king's valet and procurer, Dominique Guillaume Lebel. News of it reached the king, who summoned Marie-Louise to court and recruited her as one of his mistresses. She was sixteen and the king was forty-three.

In no time, she was pregnant. There were rumors that the king planned to recognize the baby as his and promote La Morphise to chief mistress. However, she lost the baby and almost died in the process. The following year, before her seventeenth birthday, she gave birth to a girl, Agathe-Louise de Saint-Antoine, the king's illegitimate daughter. The king showed no interest in the little girl. She was taken from Marie-Louise and brought up in a convent. She would later die during her own first pregnancy. In 1755, Marie-Louise made the disastrous error of trying to unseat Madame de Pompadour as the king's favorite. Like Coupier, she was dismissed from court and married off to get rid of her.

Pompadour's health declined in the spring of 1764. She succumbed to pneumonia and resigned herself to death. She spent her last days at Versailles with the king at her side until near the end. She made her final confession on April 14 and died on the following evening. She had been the king's chief mistress for nineteen years. Deprived of the love and companionship of his favorite, the king descended into a melancholy gloom that lasted five years until a successor to Pompadour arrived at court—Madame du Barry.

Pompadour is mainly remembered today for the hairstyle named after her, the pompadour—with the hair swept up high off the forehead and piled on top of the head. It was widely copied by Frenchwomen during Pompadour's lifetime, and revived in the nineteenth century by the fashionably curvaceous Gibson Girls. It was back in fashion again in the 1940s. In the 1950s, men got in on the act, copying Elvis Presley's pompadour. The teddy boys who appeared in Britain in the 1950s probably didn't realize that they owed their trademark hairstyle to a French king's mistress.

A Peasant at Court— Madame du Barry

While Madame de Pompadour lived out her days in comfort, surrounded by the opulent excesses of the French court, her successor had an altogether different fate. Madame du Barry, one of the most famous French royal mistresses, ended her days pleading with her executioner for just another moment of life.

Madame du Barry's story begins with the birth of a little girl called Jeanne Bécu on August 19, 1743, at Vaucouleurs in northeast France. Her mother, Anne, was a seamstress who never revealed the name of Jeanne's father. The prime suspect was a monk, Jean-Baptiste Gomard de Vaubernier, for whom Anne had worked. Three years later, she became pregnant again. This time the father was probably a government official, Monsieur Billiard-Dumonceaux. Anne's second child was a little boy she named Claude. A few months later, when Jeanne was four years old, Anne moved to Paris. She stayed with her sister, who worked as housekeeper to the king's librarian. Sadly, Claude died before his first birthday.

Anne and her daughter then moved into the household of Monsieur Billiard-Dumonceaux with his Italian mistress, Francesca. (She was also known as the courtesan Madame Frédérique, for whom Anne was put to work as a cook.) Anne evidently didn't care much for her life as a cook, or perhaps Francesca grew tired of sharing her home and perhaps her husband with another woman, because as soon as a potential husband for Anne came along, she and her daughter left. Billiard-Dumonceaux appears to have been in favor of the marriage, because he offered the suitor, a widower called Nicolas Rançon, a job as a storekeeper and offered to pay for young Jeanne's education in a convent.

When Jeanne left the convent nine years later, the pretty fifteen-year-old quickly found work as an apprentice hairdresser. It wasn't long before she was her employer's mistress and moved into his home. Six months later, when he fled to escape his debts, she went to work as a companion to a rich widow. She had to leave after a few months, because she was causing friction in the family by attracting too much attention from the woman's married sons. She moved on to work at a fashion house run by Madame Labille and her husband. Their customers included noblemen and their mistresses. Before long, the pretty milliner's assistant was attracting attention there, too. She was noticed by a procurer called Jean-Baptiste du Barry. He took her under his wing and introduced her to his aristocratic clients. Her life as a courtesan had begun.

She had been calling herself Jeanne Vaubernier, after the man she believed to be her father, but Du Barry gave her a new name, Mademoiselle Lange. She wore fine gowns and jewelry, and mixed with noblemen. One of her early clients was the marshal of France, le maréchal duc de Richelieu, a distant relative of Cardinal Richelieu. Meanwhile, Du Barry's son, Adolphe, worked as a page at Versailles and later served in the King's Infantry. The young Du Barry entertained Jeanne with stories about the customs and habits at court, which would serve her well in the future. In 1768, she was introduced to the most powerful man in France, Étienne-François, comte de Stainville, duc de Choiseul. Unlike most men, he was not attracted to her at all, but while she was visiting him at Versailles, she was spotted by the king, Louis XV. The king's chief mistress, Madame de Pompadour, had died in 1764. Several replacements procured by the king's valet, Lebel, had come and gone. As soon as Louis saw Jeanne, he summoned her to meet him.

GET HER MARRIED!

As the queen lay dying, the king spent his first night with Jeanne. However, the illegitimate daughter of a seamstress was not a fitting mistress for a king of France. Louis didn't know that Jeanne was lowborn and unmarried until Lebel finally told him. Far from rejecting her, he instructed Lebel to get her married to an appropriate husband without delay to make her acceptable in royal circles. The chosen man was Du Barry's drunken brother, Guillaume. He met his bride for the first time on the day of their sham wedding—September 1, 1768. Jeanne was now Madame du Barry.

With his new companion to amuse him, the king was more cheerful than he'd been for a long time. But behind his back, ministers were outraged by the installation of a peasant prostitute as a royal mistress. She couldn't be seen publicly with the king until she was officially presented at court, so she spent a lot of time alone and bored. She was so lonely that her procurer sent his sister, Claire-Françoise, known as Chon, to befriend her and keep her company. Her presentation at court couldn't be done by just anyone—it had to be done by a titled lady. However, there was a distinct shortage of noble ladies who were prepared to be associated with Madame du Barry. Finally, Madame de Béarn was bribed to do the job, but she dropped out at the last moment. A second presentation had to be canceled when the king was badly injured by a fall from his horse. When he recovered and Madame de Béarn was persuaded to overcome her reluctance, a regally dressed Madame du Barry was presented to the king on April 22, 1769. She became his official mistress the next day and moved into an apartment above his. Jean-Baptiste du Barry was ecstatic. He had borrowed and spent a fortune transforming

Jeanne into a king's mistress, and now that his protégée, Madame du Barry, and his sister were both at the heart of the court, he expected to recoup it all and more.

As the king's favorite, Madame du Barry made friends and enemies at court in equal measure. The king's chief minister, the duc de Choiseul, and his sister, Béatrice de Gramont, who had hoped to become a royal mistress until Madame du Barry's arrival, were bitter enemies. The dauphin's wife, Marie Antoinette, also disapproved of her, and many of the other grand ladies at court ignored her. But she wasn't short of supporters either. One of them was the duc d'Aiguillon, who in turn was an enemy of Choiseul. D'Aiguillon benefited when, on Madame du Barry's advice, the king reorganized the government and appointed him foreign minister. In contrast, Choiseul's career went into decline, not just because of his opposition to Madame du Barry, but also because of his support for the losing side in a series of military and political disputes. He was finally dismissed when Madame du Barry discovered that he was siding with Spain in a dispute against Britain that risked drawing France into another war against the king's wishes. She brought the matter to the king's attention, sealing Choiseul's fate.

Madame du Barry was also winning friends by her kindness to others. When the comte and comtesse de Louerne were sentenced to death for killing an official and a bailiff who were trying to evict them from their home because of unpaid debts, Madame du Barry heard of their plight and pleaded with the king to pardon them. Friends advised her not to bother the king with such a trivial matter, because she had no chance of success. However, the king was so impressed that the first favor she asked of him was for the benefit of someone else and not herself that he agreed to issue a pardon. She used her influence again when she heard about a young woman found guilty of infanticide and sentenced to be hanged after failing to report the birth of a stillborn baby. She wrote a letter to the chancellor of France, who pardoned the woman. She also helped to save the life of a soldier who had deserted because of homesickness and was sentenced to death. One of the soldier's officers appealed for help to his commanding officer, who happened to be the duc d'Aiguillon. He advised the officer that Madame du Barry might be able to help. She succeeded in persuading the king to pardon the soldier.

SETTLING ACCOUNTS

However, Madame du Barry drew increasing criticism because of the extravagance of her spending. When Jean-Baptiste du Barry finally presented his accounts to the king for his expenditure on her, the bill was eventually paid but he was told to leave Paris, probably because he reminded the king of Madame's disconcertingly humble origins. The king paid her a monthly sum of 200,000 livres, rising to 300,000 livres. One livre was equivalent to about 350 francs in the 1990s. When the franc was replaced by the euro, the exchange rate was set at 6.56 francs to the euro, giving the livre a value of more than fifty-three euros. So, in the 1770s Madame du Barry was receiving about 16 million euros, 13 million pounds sterling, or 22 million U.S. dollars *a month*. Even so, her spending was so outrageous that she still managed to incur debts. One sizable call on her income was Jean-Baptiste du Barry, who often reminded her that her drunkard of a husband was still alive and might not be dissuaded from claiming his marital rights, causing severe embarrassment to the king, if Madame failed to settle Jean-Baptiste's debts. In other words, he was blackmailing her.

She was also beginning to use her influence to settle scores and benefit friends and family. When the baron de Breteuil failed to show her the respect she thought she warranted, she pressured the duc d'Aiguillon to have him dismissed from his ambassadorial position in Vienna and replaced by an inept diplomat who happened to be one of her supporters. She also had her nephew, Adolphe du Barry, appointed as an equerry to the king.

In the early 1770s, the king was now in his sixties and beginning to feel his age. He feared for his future. He was increasingly concerned about his fate in the afterlife and the need for repentance before his death. In April 1774, when he was sixty-four years old, he began to feel unwell while he was staying at Le Petit Trianon, a small château in the grounds of the Palace of Versailles. He was known to be something of a hypochondriac, so those close to him weren't unduly worried. But for once, this wasn't a false alarm. His condition worsened. He grew increasingly feverish. It became obvious that he was genuinely ill, but his physician assured Madame du Barry that he would soon recover. The royal surgeon heard of the king's indisposition and insisted that he should be moved to the palace, which he said was the proper place for a king to be ill! A common treatment at that time was bleeding—opening blood vessels to drain blood. The king was bled, but far from helping him, it weakened him even further. By then, it was clear that he was suffering from smallpox. Despite the risk of infection, his daughters sat with him during the day and Madame du Barry took their place at night. When the king realized he was dying, he ordered Madame du Barry to leave and assured her that she would be looked after. A couple of days later, he was finally ready to make his confession. As a condition of saving his soul, he reluctantly agreed to order the detention of Madame du Barry. Louis XV died on May 10, 1774. To minimize the spread of smallpox, his body was hastily buried and anyone who had been in contact with him during his illness was placed in quarantine. The late king's daughters developed the disease, but they survived.

Madame du Barry was taken under armed guard to the abbey of Pont-aux-Dames and held there for a year. On her release, she moved into a new home bought for her by the duc d'Aiguillon. The following year, she was given permission to return to the Château de Louveciennes, which the king had given her. Soon afterwards, she had a love affair with a near neighbor, a married Englishman called Henry Seymour. However, they were both so possessive and jealous of each other that the affair was doomed. Seymour ended it by returning a miniature of Madame du Barry that she had given him with the words "Leave me alone" written at the bottom. Even before she parted from Seymour, she had begun a relationship with the duc de Brissac. She finally seemed happy and content, and was still beautiful in her early forties.

REVOLUTION!

In 1789, rioting broke out in Paris. The revolution had begun. The first aristocrats had already met their deaths at the hands of the mobs, and their heads were being paraded on pikes. Brissac was detained briefly at Le Mans, but then released. However, he made the mistake of going to work at court as commander of the king's guard and was seized by revolutionaries at the Tuileries in Paris and taken to Orléans. He quickly realized that he was doomed and made his will. He was transported to Versailles with other prisoners in open carts, attracting jeers and abuse from angry mobs along the way. The only place that was thought to be secure enough to hold prisoners safely was the former zoo at the Palace of Versailles. They were to be locked in cages the animals had occupied. However, the mob stopped the carts before they reached their destination. While the guards stood by, refusing to intervene, the prisoners were attacked. Brissac was dragged out of his cart, killed, and beheaded. His head was then delivered to Madame du Barry.

In 1793, Madame du Barry herself was arrested, suspected of helping aristocrats to escape from the revolutionaries. She was put on trial. Witness after witness denounced her. She was quickly found guilty and sentenced to death, the sentence to be carried out the following morning. As the verdict was read out, she fainted and had to be carried back to her cell. In an attempt to save her life, she gave a statement listing the jewelry, gold, and silver she had buried in the grounds of her estate at Louveciennes, together with their locations. She thought her honesty would be rewarded with a more lenient sentence, but she was wrong. Later that morning, December 8, 1793, she was prepared for execution. Her hair was cut to give the guillotine blade a clean passage through her neck, and her hands were tied behind her back. She was so distressed that she had to be carried to the guillotine. As she was strapped down, she begged the executioner, *"Encore un moment, monsieur le bourreau, un petit moment"* ("Another moment, Mr. Executioner, just a little moment"). But she wasn't granted another second. Without delay, the blade fell and her executioner shouted, *"Vive la révolution!"* The last of the French royal favorites had gone. Her body, like many of those who died on the guillotine, was thrown into a trench in the Madeleine Cemetery and covered with quicklime to speed its decomposition.

A Deadly Mistress— Madame La Guillotine

The execution machine that took Madame du Barry's life and thousands of others during the French Revolution was proposed by a man who opposed the death penalty. Dr. Joseph-Ignace Guillotin wanted the death penalty to be abolished. He proposed the famous decapitation machine named after him as a more humane killing method that he hoped would lead to the end of state execution altogether.

Before the guillotine, several execution methods were used in France, including burning at the stake, decapitation with a sword or ax, dismember-ment by horse, hanging, and breaking on the wheel. The choice of execution method depended on the crime and the status of the convict. Execution by breaking wheel involved tying the condemned man to a cartwheel and then smashing his limbs with an iron bar. Some victims survived for hours or even days before they finally died of shock and blood loss. If the victim was "lucky," he would be shown mercy—the executioner would administer coups de grâce (blows of mercy). He would strike the victim's chest, smashing his rib cage, to hasten death. Alternatively, after the victim's limbs were smashed to pieces, he might be strangled to end his suffering.

Louis XVI banned the breaking wheel as excessively brutal, so the National Assembly searched for another method that could be used for all condemned criminals whether of noble birth or not, both men and women. Inspired by decapitation machines in use elsewhere, Dr. Guillotin devised a new machine designed to end life as quickly and painlessly as possible. His proposal was initially rejected, but the continuing desire for a less barbaric execution method revived interest in the guillotine. After some improve-ments were made by engineers, it was accepted. The first guillotine was built by a German engineer, Tobias Schmidt, and tested on animals and human corpses. A weighted blade slid down between two fourteen-foot-high (four-meter) uprights.

The first execution by guillotine was carried out on April 25, 1792, on a highwayman called Nicolas Jacques Pelletier. From then on, the guillotine was the only execution method used in France. On July 27, there was an "imperfect operation" of the guillotine when the blade failed to fall smoothly. It jammed because the wooden runners it ran down between had swollen. The problem was solved by using metal runners instead. By the end of the French Revolution, in 1799, about fifteen thousand people are thought to have been executed by guillotine. Convicted murderers were still being sent to the guillotine as recently as the 1970s. The last person to be executed by guillotine in France was Hamida Djandoubi in Marseille, on September 10, 1977. France finally abolished the death penalty in 1981.

The often-repeated story that Dr. Guillotin was himself executed by the machine named after him is untrue. He died of natural causes in 1814. A Dr. Guillotin was indeed executed by the guillotine, but it was a different person.

Dr. Elliot's Wayward Wife— Grace Elliott

Unlike Madame du Barry, Grace Dalrymple Elliott was a courtesan and royal mistress at the French court who managed to escape the guillotine despite her support for the French royal family, but she had a close shave—literally.

By the time Grace Dalrymple was born in Scotland in the 1750s, her parents had already gone their separate ways. She was brought up by her mother, Grizel, in her maternal grandparents' house. When she was eleven years old, her mother died and she was sent to live with her father, Hew. He packed her off to a convent school in France to finish her education. She returned to Britain at the age of sixteen and joined her father in London. This was something of an inconvenience for him, because he was about to move to the West Indies to take up a government position and didn't want a young daughter in tow. The answer was to marry her off, so that she would be someone else's responsibility.

The man who stepped up to the plate to take on young Grace was a wealthy doctor, John Elliott. They were not well matched in any sense. He was more than twice her age. She was young, tall, elegant, and vivacious. He was older, short, unattractive, and a bit of a bore. Nevertheless, they married on October 19, 1771. He bought a new house in Knightsbridge, London, for his new wife and filled it with servants.

Going to Court

Dr. Elliott was a workaholic, never turning down an opportunity to make another penny, so Grace was probably left alone at home a lot. At some point, the doctor appears to have become suspicious of how his young wife was spending her time. He interrogated his servants about her and discovered that she had made the acquaintance of Arthur Annesley, Lord Valentia, a young rake about town. Elliott immediately evicted Grace from their Knightsbridge home and began divorce proceedings. He also instituted civil proceedings against Valentia for the offense of criminal conversation. In the nineteenth century, an Englishman's wife was treated in law as his chattel, his personal property. Any man who seduced a married woman could be said to have deprived her husband of his property rights, and so the husband could claim compensation for this loss. And the compensation claims were astonishing for the time—often more than ten thousand pounds and sometimes more than twenty thousand, equivalent to millions of pounds or dollars today.

Elliott won his case against Valentia and was awarded compensation of twelve thousand pounds. Meanwhile, the divorce took two years to work its way through the courts and Parliament, finally being signed off by King George III in 1776. As part of the settlement, Elliott agreed to provide Grace with an annuity of two hundred pounds a year for the rest of her life. Lord Valentia was not prepared to leave his wife for Grace, and her father had died just before the divorce proceedings began, so she was now on her own. She needed a protector. Her knight in shining armor came in the shape of George James Cholmondeley, Marquess of Cholmondeley.

Cholmondeley and Grace had been lovers since they met at a masquerade ball in January 1776, two months before her divorce was finalized. He was known as a handsome, fun-loving ladies' man. They were such an attractive couple that there were frequent rumors of their impending marriage. However, Cholmondeley's family became increasingly unhappy with his liaison with the notorious divorcée. They didn't consider her to be a suitable addition to their family. Grace didn't have a title and wouldn't bring any significant property or money with her to the Cholmondeley family. Cholmondeley's great-uncle, Horace Walpole, was particularly opposed to Grace. Coincidentally, his doctor was none other than Dr. John Elliott. Walpole probably heard unflattering stories about Grace from Elliott, which is likely why he was so set against her joining his family. That sealed Grace's fate. The relationship finally foundered in 1779.

Grace's reaction was to take herself off to France in search of new admirers to support her. Her name had already been linked with French noblemen visiting London, including Louis XVI's brother, the comte d'Artois. In France, she attracted the attention of Philippe, duc de Chartres, one of the wealthiest men on the Continent. For a time, she was the queen bee of his harem of lovers. But in 1781, she suddenly returned to England. The comte was known to be somewhat fickle, so it may be that he had simply tired of his English paramour. There were also reports that she had returned to London in the company of her old love, Lord Cholmondeley.

She arrived in the English capital just as the heir to the throne, the Prince of Wales, was ending his latest affair of the heart. He looked around for a new love interest and he saw Grace Elliott. Their relationship lasted just a few months at most. Then Grace discovered that she was pregnant. She insisted that the father was the Prince of Wales, but rumors suggested that there were at least four other candidates, including Cholmondeley. The baby, born on March 30, 1782, was christened Georgiana Augusta Frederica Elliott. Cholmondeley agreed to take responsibility for the child, but inevitably there were rumors that he'd done so at the suggestion of the real father, the Prince of Wales. The mystery of Georgiana's father was never resolved. She was brought up with the Cholmondeley children.

Whatever the truth about Grace's reunion with Cholmondeley, it didn't last long. She returned to France in 1784 to resume her liaison with the staggeringly wealthy Philippe, but this time, she had to share him with his current favorite, Agnès de Buffon. It was a small price to pay, considering the lifestyle he could provide for her. But events beyond their control would interrupt Grace's charmed life. France was heading for a massive convulsion. The country was bankrupt. The tax system heavily penalized the poor but afforded endless exemptions to the nobility. Discontent spread through the lower classes. The king tried to flee in 1791, but was caught and arrested. The monarchy was abolished in 1792. The king and queen were executed the following year. Their heir, Louis-Charles, who should have become King Louis XVII on his father's execution, was incarcerated in a medieval fortress in Paris called the Temple, where he disappeared. There were rumors that he had been freed by royalists, prompting the appearance of a string of pretenders claiming to be the missing heir. But recent genetic tests on the preserved heart of a young boy who died in the Temple confirmed that it was Louis-Charles who died there—he hadn't escaped. Soon after the king and queen were executed, Grace's former lover, Philippe, took his last journey to an appointment with Madame La Guillotine. This period of mass executions is known as the Reign of Terror, or simply the Terror.

RISKING EVERYTHING

The French royal family and aristocracy had supported Grace financially, and now she wanted to repay their loyalty, but she risked everything in the process. She made several visits to Spa and Brussels, apparently acting as a courier for members of the royal family. Unwisely, she made no secret of her support for the royal family. Inevitably, her home was searched by revolutionaries, and suspicious letters were found.

Despite the great danger she was in, she risked her life to save the governor of the Tuileries Palace. The palace had been attacked by revolutionaries, and hundreds of royal guards were killed. The governor, the marquis de Champcenetz, survived by playing dead. Grace received a message saying that he was in hiding in Paris and appealing for her help. She managed to smuggle him out of his hiding place and bring him back to her home. From there, she smuggled him out of Paris. But after another visit by revolutionaries, more incriminating letters were found and Grace was taken for interrogation. She was released, but then received news that the revolutionaries were on their way to arrest her. She fled from her home to Meudon, where she thought she was safe, because she was beyond the jurisdiction of the Paris officials. But local officials seized her and took her to prison. Every morning, the names of those to be executed were read out. Morning after morning, Grace's name was not among those announced. Then one morning, she was on the list. However, the architect of the Reign of Terror, Robespierre, was himself executed on August 6, 1794, bringing the Terror to an end. Grace was saved at the last possible moment. Her hair had been cut in preparation for decapitation. But as soon as Robespierre was executed, many of the prisoners, including Grace, were released.

She returned to England sometime between 1798 and 1802. Georgiana didn't appear to welcome her mother's return, because she had dropped the Elliott surname and instead adopted the name Seymour. Despite her beauty and connection with the Cholmondeleys, Georgiana didn't marry until she was twenty-six, quite old for the time. She married Lord William Charles Augustus Cavendish-Bentinck, equerry to the Prince of Wales and son of the Duke of Portland. She died in 1813, at the age of thirty-one. The following year, Grace returned to France, where she didn't face so much disapproval as in England. And there she disappeared from the public record until her death at around the age of seventy in Ville-d'Avray, near Paris, on May 15, 1823.

NAPOLÉON'S "LITTLE POLISH WIFE"— MARIE WALEWSKA

The French monarchy was swept away by the Revolution, which brought Napoléon Bonaparte to power. Bonaparte is quoted as saying, "The man who lets himself be ruled by a woman is a fool!" The woman most famously associated with Napoléon is his wife, Joséphine de Beauharnais, but there were other women in his life. One was a Polish countess called Marie Walewska.

As Marie Laczynska, she was born into an old and influential Polish family on December 7, 1786. Her family had lost most of its estates when Prussia seized part of Poland in 1772. Marie was brought up on the family farm at Kiernozia. In 1792, Russia invaded Poland, signaling the beginning of the Polish-Russian War. Marie's father volunteered for service in the army. The fighting lasted for only two months and ended in capitulation by Poland, which was carved up by its enemies. Two years later, discontent among army officers at Poland's military collapse led to an uprising and renewed fighting against Russian forces. When Marie was just eight years old, her father was killed at one of the last military confrontations of the rebellion, the Battle of Maciejowice. The uprising ended in defeat for the Polish army.

Marie was educated at home with her two sisters. One of her tutors was a Frenchman, Nicolas Chopin, who would later father the famous composer Frédéric Chopin. When his job in Poland came to an end, he welcomed the offer of work as a tutor to Marie and her sisters instead of returning to France, which was descending into the Reign of Terror and full-blown revolution. When Marie was thirteen, she was sent to the Convent of Our Lady of the Assumption in Warsaw to finish her education. She enjoyed the bustle of the city and the company of girls her own age.

She was described by those who met her as beautiful, with large blue eyes, a sweet expression, and long blond hair worn down to her waist. And now at the age of sixteen, she was well educated, too. Her family looked forward to marrying her to someone who might be able to help with their debts. The first man she took a shine to was a handsome young soldier she met at a ball. However, when she found out who he was, she was horrified.

She hadn't heard his name when they were introduced. From his accent, she thought he might be Swedish. In fact, his name was Suvorov. He was not only Russian; he was also related to Field Marshal Alexander Suvorov, who had commanded the Russian army at the Battle of Maciejowice, where her father was killed. The young Suvorov pursued Marie and wanted to marry her, but she refused to see him again.

The match finally chosen for her was Count Athenasius Colonna-Walewski, a wealthy landowner. At the age of sixty-eight, he was fifty-two years older than she. Nevertheless, her family pressured her into going ahead with the marriage because they didn't want to risk losing a second wealthy suitor. Marie and the count were married on June 17, 1804. Almost exactly a year later, she gave birth to Antoni Rudolf Bazyli Colonna-Walewski.

In 1806, Napoléon's inexorable progress across Europe brought him to Poland. Poles eagerly awaited his arrival, hoping he would restore Poland's lost territory and return the country to its former glory. He had promised them as much if they fought with France. A small advance guard of French troops prepared the way for Napoléon, who arrived in Warsaw on horseback on December 18.

AN EMPEROR SMITTEN

Over Christmas, Marie was working in Warsaw's hospitals, looking after wounded soldiers being brought back from the front, where Napoléon's forces were engaging Russian troops. The weather was so bad that fighting had to be suspended for the winter. In the New Year, the city threw a ball to welcome Napoléon. And it was here that he set eyes on Marie Walewska for the first time. He was instantly captivated by her and made a point of finding out who she was.

When another ball was held, he sought her out and danced with her. Two other officers who showed rather too much interest in her were soon posted to far-flung units. In the days that followed, Napoléon repeatedly sent Marie flowers and requested her company, but she declined out of respect, if not love, for her husband. The emperor wasn't used to being refused. He held a formal dinner and invited Marie and her husband. They couldn't fail to attend without causing offense. When they arrived, Marie found that she had been seated opposite the emperor, who gazed at her throughout the dinner. Afterwards, he sent her a letter that once again requested her company, but this time he said, "Your country will be so much dearer to me if you take pity on my heart." The implication was clear—refusing the emperor could jeopardize her country's future prospects.

She relented and agreed to see him, but their first meeting went badly. Marie sobbed continually until Napoléon sent her home in the early hours of the morning. He persevered and sent her more letters and gifts until she finally surrendered and became his mistress. Suddenly, everyone who was anyone wanted to meet Marie or just see her because of her elevated status as the emperor's lover.

Their time together was interrupted by an unexpected Russian attack on French forces in East Prussia. When Napoléon left to take command of his army, he sent a message asking Marie to join him. He didn't want his wife, Joséphine, to find out that he was sharing his headquarters with his mistress, so Marie was smuggled in. She spent six weeks hidden in his rooms at the Finckenstein Palace, then in West Prussia. She later described them as the happiest weeks of her life and told a friend that she felt like Napoléon's wife during this time. Indeed, Napoléon called her his "little Polish wife." When the weather improved and fighting resumed, Marie was smuggled out of his headquarters again. She had hoped that her affair with Napoléon would result in him looking kindly on Poland when the fighting was finally over, peace treaties were agreed, and borders were redrawn, but she was disappointed. Napoléon made peace with Russia, which was allowed to keep its Polish territories. He returned to Paris as Napoléon the Great, conqueror of Europe.

At Christmas 1807, he finally sent for Marie to join him. She was installed in a house on the rue de La Houssaye with her own staff. But he was so busy that he rarely had time to see her. Early in 1808, he had to leave for Spain. Marie quickly tired of Paris on her own and left for Poland. Soon after she arrived, Austrian troops invaded her homeland. Napoléon sent urgent messages to Poland insisting that Marie should be protected. Austria was eventually defeated and Marie was able to travel to Vienna to be with Napoléon. Then the very thing that Napoléon's wife had dreaded happened. Marie discovered that she was pregnant. As soon as Napoléon was told, he realized that he could father children and so his childless marriage with Joséphine was not his fault. He had yearned for a son and heir who could inherit his continental empire. He wanted to establish a new dynasty of European rulers. He blamed his childlessness on Joséphine and began divorce proceedings against her. However, he knew that if his heir was to be recognized internationally, the boy's mother would have to be from royal stock. A Polish countess wasn't grand enough. He decided that a fitting bride would be the tsar's sister, Grand Duchess Anne. But he'd have to make it worth Russia's while to give up the grand duchess to him, so in return for her hand in marriage, he was prepared to see Poland disappear forever to make way for Russian expansion.

THE END OF THE AFFAIR

When Marie discovered his marriage plans, she realized that her time as the emperor's mistress was over. Napoléon's negotiations for his Russian bride failed. Instead, he married the Archduchess Marie Louise of Austria. They married on April 2, 1810. Marie learned of the wedding when she read about it in a newspaper. Just over a month later she gave birth to a boy, Alexander Florian Joseph Colonna-Walewski. In September, Napoléon invited Marie to Paris. She was given a home, a villa near Boulogne, and a monthly income of ten thousand francs—more than a high-ranking military officer could expect to earn in a year. He paid frequent visits to see his son. In March of the following year, Napoléon's wife gave birth to a boy.

Poland went to war for France again in 1812. Russia had hoped to form an alliance with Austria and Poland to push France back. The tsar indicated that Poland's reward for switching sides might be Polish independence, but the Poles were offended by Russia's attempt to buy them off. Poland stuck with France despite Napoléon's continued evasion on the matter of Polish territory and independence. As events moved inexorably toward war, Napoléon, fearing that he might not survive another war, signed a document providing generously for Marie and her son. The boy was also created a count of the French Empire.

In June 1812, with the war under way, Marie returned to Poland to help Napoléon mobilize Polish support. She also asked her elderly husband for a divorce. Her motive was probably financial. Legally, she was jointly responsible for her family's debts, which were rising. Divorcing her impoverished husband ended her responsibility for his debts. The court accepted her claim that she had been coerced into marriage and had suffered extreme mental cruelty, so the marriage was dissolved.

Napoléon's Russian campaign was a disastrous failure. As his forces advanced across Russia, the Russians constantly withdrew after destroying everything that might be of use to Napoléon's troops. This scorched-earth tactic left Napoléon's troops without essential supplies, which had to be delivered over longer and longer supply lines. The Russians even burned Moscow soon after the French entered the city. Then the Russians refused to negotiate a peace treaty. After five weeks, with the Russian winter closing in, Napoléon simply turned his troops around and left. His Grand Armée had been annihilated. Between the bitterly cold Russian winter, disease, and battle casualties, only about forty thousand of the half million troops who invaded Russia survived.

THE EMPIRE COLLAPSES

With resurgent Russian forces now approaching Poland and seeking revenge, it was no longer safe for Marie to stay there, so she left for Paris. Prussia now joined forces with Russia and declared war on France. Austria later joined the alliance. And now England was fighting the French in Spain. Napoléon's great continental empire was collapsing around him. By March 1814, Paris itself had fallen and the tsar rode triumphantly down the Champs-Élysées. Napoléon abdicated and accepted exile on the island of Elba, between Italy and his birthplace, Corsica. He assumed his wife and son would go with him, but they didn't. His wife, Marie Louise, took their son with her to Austria. Napoléon was in such despair that he tried to kill himself by taking poison. Marie rushed to him at Fontainebleau, but her requests to see him went unanswered.

He recovered from his suicide attempt and left France for Elba, accompanied by some of his troops. A guard of four hundred had been agreed, but so many troops wanted to go with him that it had to be increased to a thousand. He sent letters to his wife and Marie, pleading with them to visit him on Elba and to bring his sons with them. Marie agreed. When she arrived, she and her son, Alexander, were taken to a house in the hills, where Napoléon met them. However, some of the islanders had spotted Marie and assumed she was the empress. If news got out that it was actually Marie, it could spoil any chance of his wife joining him on the island, so she was spirited away one evening after dark. In fact, his wife, Marie Louise, had no intention of seeing him again. She was now the lover of Count Adam Albert von Neipperg, a general in the Austrian army. He had been given the task of escorting her to Aix-les-Bains, where she intended to take the waters before moving on to Elba. His secret mission was actually to prevent her from reaching Elba. Within a few weeks, they were lovers and the empress abandoned plans to visit Napoléon.

When the new French king, Louis XVIII, returned from exile in May 1814, he stopped payment of the money due to Napoléon for his upkeep according to the Treaty of Fontainebleau. Unable to pay his servants or guards, Napoléon escaped from the island at the end of February 1815 and landed on the French coast near Antibes with his troops. More troops joined him as he headed for Paris. He entered the city on March 20. The king fled into exile again. However, Napoléon's reign lasted only one hundred days. An alliance of European countries including Britain, Prussia, and the Netherlands set out to remove him from power once and for all.

Napoléon went on the attack. On June 18, 1815, more than 70,000 French troops faced 118,000 coalition troops near Waterloo in present-day Belgium. Napoléon was defeated by forces commanded by the Duke of Wellington and Field Marshal Blücher. Just before the battle, he met Marie—mainly, it seems, to give her financial advice. The next time she saw him, he was busy burning state papers at the Elysée Palace.

FINAL EXILE

Napoléon tried to escape to the United States, but he was captured and exiled on the Atlantic island of Saint Helena. Just before he left for the island, he met Marie for the last time. They met at his former wife's home, the Château de Malmaison. Joséphine had died from pneumonia the previous year. Marie offered to go to Saint Helena with him, but he refused. In need of protection and support, Marie married Count Philippe-Antoine d'Ornano, who had fought with Napoléon and was his second cousin. They were married in Brussels on September 7, 1816, and went to live in Liège. Nine months later, she gave birth to a healthy baby boy, but her own health, already weakened by kidney disease, quickly declined. She died on December 11, 1817, at the age of only thirty-one. Napoléon would never hear of Marie's death. On Saint Helena, his health deteriorated until his death on May 5, 1821. His remains were returned to France in 1840. Two days after he died, a death mask was molded from his face. Several copies were made from this original. In 2013, one of these masks was sold at auction in London. The owner, a descendant of the senior British chaplain on Saint Helena, had kept it in his attic for years. It was expected to fetch up to sixty thousand pounds. The auctioneer's hammer fell at 170,000 pounds.

Napoléon's cause of death was the subject of rumor and conjecture for nearly two hundred years. An autopsy soon after his death put his death down to stomach cancer. However, when his body was examined later, it appeared to be very well preserved, raising suspicions of arsenic poisoning, because arsenic is an excellent preservative. Tests in 1961 did indeed find high arsenic levels in the emperor's hair. However, a review of the evidence carried out in 2007 by a team of American, Swiss, and Canadian research-ers confirmed stomach cancer as the most likely cause of death. Even if Napoléon had been treated today, his cancer was so advanced that he would likely have died within a year.

According to Marie's wishes, her heart was buried in the d'Ornano crypt at Père Lachaise Cemetery in Paris and the rest of her body was buried in her family's crypt in Kiernozia.

3

THE ANCIENT WORLD

Although the most famous courtesans were French, courtesans, concubines, and royal mistresses have probably existed in many parts of the world for almost as long as human civilization itself. The earliest recorded examples date from more than 2,500 years ago in Greece, India, and China.

Courtesans in Ancient Greece inspired writers, influenced generals, and infatuated statesmen. Greek men often married after the age of thirty, so young men turned to "professional women" for sexual experience. And it was socially acceptable. Prostitution was legal and taxed by the state. As usual, there was a hierarchy. At the bottom were common prostitutes called *pornai,* giving us our word "pornography." Above them were *auletrides,* or "flute girls," who were primarily musicians, but often available for sex. At the top of the tree were courtesans known as hetaerae, meaning "companions." The rather complex relationships in Ancient Greece were summed up by Demosthenes when he said, "We have hetaerae for pleasure, *pallakae* [concubines or slaves] to care for our daily bodily needs and *gynaekes* [wives] to bear us legitimate children and be faithful guardians of our households." Unlike most Greek women in antiquity, the hetaerae were educated. They were also skilled in dance and music. They were the only women allowed to take part in symposia, drinking parties where men discussed the issues of the day. No respectable Greek woman would be allowed to attend a symposium, or would want to attend.

India's courtesan culture emerged at about the same time as that in

Ancient Greece, around the sixth century B.C. It grew out of the tradition of families donating girls to local temples to serve the gods, primarily as dancers. In time, some of these dancers performed to entertain people and formed relationships with wealthy patrons.

In Ancient Rome, the lives of women were just as strictly controlled as in Greece and India. Roman women were not citizens, and they had few rights. Only adult free men could be citizens. Women lived under the guardianship of their father or husband. They gained more freedom later in the Roman Empire. Eventually, they could own land and run businesses, but they still couldn't hold public office or work in government. Prostitution was accepted throughout the Roman Empire, but adultery was not. However, as usual, there was a double standard that favored men. While adultery was never acceptable for women, powerful men could take their pleasure with slaves, prostitutes, or actresses as long as they were discreet. Prostitutes called meretrices had to register with the authorities and pay tax. Despite their official recognition, they were not allowed to give evidence in court, and freeborn men were not allowed to marry them. There were also unregistered prostitutes called *prostibulae*.

Halfway round the world in Ancient China, the courtesans who plied their trade there were, like those in the rest of the ancient world, rarely recorded in the official histories of the time. And their stories often became embroidered with myth and legend, so it's difficult to know how much of the tales written about them, or by them, are true.

CINDERELLA AND OTHER GREEK TALES

One of the earliest Greek hetaerae was called Rhodopis. Very little is known about her. She was mentioned as a hetaera in Herodotus's *Histories,* nine books detailing Ancient Greek history, politics, and traditions. Born in Thrace in the sixth century B.C., Rhodopis probably wasn't her real name. It means "rosy cheeks," and so it was probably a nickname or professional alias. Her real name has been lost. She was the property of a Samian man called Xanthes, who took her to the city of Naucratis in Egypt during the reign of Pharaoh Amasis II (570–526 B.C.). There, a merchant called Charaxus of Mytilene, the brother of the Greek poet Sappho, saw her being sold in a slave market. Charaxus instantly fell in love with her and bought her. According to some accounts, he married her. Sappho didn't approve of her and attacked her in poetry. The object of the attack is named as Doricha, which might have been Rhodopis's real name.

One tale inspired by her life is thought to be the first telling of the Cinderella story. It goes like this: Rhodopis had an Egyptian master. Although he was kind, Rhodopis was treated badly by his other servants and slaves, who made her work hard. Her master gave her a pair of slippers. While she was bathing, an eagle swooped down and picked up one of the slippers. The bird flew away with it. Later, it dropped the slipper, which fell into the pharaoh's lap. It was such a fine slipper that the pharaoh thought its owner must be a very beautiful woman. He searched for her by ordering women to try the slipper on. Eventually, he found Rhodopis. The slipper was a perfect fit and she was able to produce its twin. The pharaoh made her his queen. However, this story is likely to be an invention of later writers such as Strabo (ca. 64 B.C.–ca. A.D. 4) and doesn't appear to be based on fact.

In Ancient Greece, only the wealthiest men could afford a hetaera. One hetaera, called Neaira, is said to have been bought by two men, Timanoridas and Eukrates, for the equivalent of eight years' pay for a skilled worker. They bought her from the brothel-keeper who had owned her since childhood. When it was time for one or both of the men to get married, they sold her to a man called Phrynion, who took her from Corinth to Athens. She escaped from him and ran away to Megara. There, she met a man called Stephanos, who brought her back to Athens. When Phrynion learned that she was back in Athens, he tried to reclaim her as his slave, but he failed. Stephanos and Neaira lived together happily for several years until an old opponent of Stephanos, Apollodorus, launched a lawsuit against Neaira. He claimed that she, a non-Athenian, was living illegally with an Athenian as his wife. Stephanos and Apollodorus had crossed swords in court several times. Frustratingly, the outcome of this case isn't known.

Another hetaera, Aspasia, was uncharacteristically outspoken for a Greek woman. Born in Miletus (an Ionian Greek colony on the coast of present-day Turkey) in about 470 B.C., she had an unusually good education for a girl, at the insistence of her father, Axiochus. In about 445 B.C., she moved to Megara in Greece, where she opened a brothel. Soon afterwards, she moved to Athens to try to make her fortune as a hetaera. Eventually, she was noticed by the statesman, general, and governor of Athens, Pericles. He is said to have been attracted by her beauty, intellect, and political wisdom. Although Pericles divorced his first wife to be with Aspasia, he couldn't marry her, because she was a hetaera and a metic (a non-Athenian living in Athens). Both of these barred her from marrying an Athenian like Pericles—ironically, because of laws introduced by Pericles himself.

Greek women were supposed to stay very much in the background, not seen or heard, subservient to their menfolk. But Pericles consulted Aspasia as if she were his equal. Her habit of speaking her mind earned her enemies. And people disapproved of Athens's first citizen openly keeping a non-Athenian lover. Her influence on him was resented. She is said to have written some of his speeches. Despite widespread criticism, Pericles stood by her and publicly defended her. He announced to Athenians, "If you wish to take Aspasia away from me, then take my life as well." She was blamed for Athens's role in a war between Samos and Miletus in 440 B.C., when Pericles sent a fleet of ships to suppress Samos, supposedly at the behest of his Milesian partner, Aspasia. In the same year, she bore him a son, who was named after him.

Aspasia was also accused of causing the Peloponnesian War. The war, between Athens and Sparta (431–404 B.C.), was sparked by the growing power of Athens, which threatened other Greek states, principally Sparta. Distrust between the two turned to open hostility and then war, which ultimately resulted in Athens's defeat. At the end of the first year of the war, Pericles made a speech to honor the dead. This famous funeral oration is said to have been influenced by Aspasia, or even written by her.

During the war, Athens was ravaged by a plague epidemic that claimed the lives of tens of thousands of Athenians, including Pericles. As his health worsened, with both his legitimate sons dead, he asked for an exemption to the law so that his son by Aspasia could be legitimized. The plague finally got the better of him and he died in 429 B.C. Athenians took pity on Aspasia after Pericles' death and granted her son full citizenship.

Socrates, Plato, Cicero, Xenophon, and Athenaeus are said to have been fans of Aspasia. She may have inspired the main character in *Lysistrata,* a comedy by Aristophanes about an outspoken woman. She established a school for Athenian girls, where she encouraged the students to seek a broader education than the sewing, weaving, dance, and music that they were expected to learn.

Aspasia took a new partner, Lysicles, and had a son by him. But Lysicles, a general, was himself killed in action just a year after Pericles' death. By 406 B.C., Aspasia's other son, the young Pericles, had risen to the rank of general. In the same year, the Athenian fleet fought the Spartan fleet at the Battle of Arginusae. The Athenians won the battle, but two thousand of their sailors drowned because a storm prevented ships from rescuing the crews of dozens of damaged and sinking ships. The eight generals who had commanded the ships were put on trial. Two of them fled, but the others, including the young Pericles, were found guilty and executed. No one knows whether Aspasia was still alive when her son was executed. She had disappeared from the historical record by then.

Another hetaera, Thaïs, was unknown to history until she burst on the scene in 330 B.C. As the mistress of one of Alexander the Great's generals, the Macedonian commander Ptolemy I Soter, she accompanied Alexander on his military campaigns. When Alexander captured Persepolis, the capital of the Persian Empire, he celebrated his victory with games, feasts, and sacrifices to the gods. During one feast, Thaïs gave a speech that prompted Alexander to burn down Persepolis as a final insult to the Persians. Alexander and Thaïs threw the first torches.

One of the most famous and wealthiest courtesans of Ancient Greece, Phryne, was born in about 371 B.C. in Thespiae, a city in Boeotia in Central Greece. Phryne wasn't her real name. She was born as Mnesarete, but her yellowish complexion earned the nickname Phryne, meaning "toad." Her beauty inspired several famous works of art, including Apelles' painting *Aphrodite Anadyomene* (*Aphrodite Rising from the Sea*) and the statue of *Aphrodite of Knidos,* by Praxiteles, who was also her lover.

She is famous for the novel way in which a court case against her was settled. According to one account, she was tried for being disrespectful to the Eleusian Mysteries (initiation ceremonies for the cult of Demeter, the goddess of the harvest). She had taken off her clothes and walked naked into the sea in front of thousands of people who had congregated to witness the ceremonies. This was such a serious offense that she faced the death penalty if found guilty. When it looked like the case was going against her, her defender, Hypereides, pulled her robe down, baring her breasts! And it worked! The judges, presumably all men, felt unable to condemn such an elegant and graceful beauty.

Phryne had so many wealthy lovers that she amassed a great fortune. She is said to have offered to pay for the city walls of Thebes to be rebuilt after their destruction by Alexander the Great . . . on condition that the words "Destroyed by Alexander, rebuilt by Phryne the courtesan" were carved into them. The town's elders declined her offer. However, some historians think that this and other colorful stories about Phryne were the inventions of over-enthusiastic historians and biographers in antiquity. There is no doubt, though, that she was one of the most beautiful, famous, and wealthy courtesans of Ancient Greece.

Hetaerae sometimes competed with each other for influential clients. One of Phryne's rivals was Lais of Hyccara. Born in Hyccara (modern Carini), Sicily, she was offered one thousand drachmas for a night of her company by the Greek statesman Demosthenes, but when she saw him, she demanded ten thousand drachmas! The philosopher Diogenes must have presented a more attractive prospect, because she is said to have given herself to him for nothing! One of her lovers, Hippostratus, took her to live in Thessaly. The Thessalian women were so jealous of her that they lured her to the temple of Aphrodite and stoned her to death.

India's Dancing Girls

In parts of Ancient India, there was a tradition known as *nagarvadhu,* which means "bride of the city"—in other words, an official prostitute. Nagarvadhu was a coveted title that women competed for. There was no taboo or shame attached to it. A *nagarvadhu* charged a great deal of money for her services, and so was only within the grasp of the richest men.

India also has a long tradition of temple dancing. The temple dancers were called *devadasis*. They were dedicated from childhood to the service of a deity or temple and had a very high status, second in importance only to a temple's priests. A wealthy temple might have hundreds of devadasis. Royalty and noblemen who supported the temples were privy to their dances and rituals. They wanted dancers to entertain them in their palaces, giving rise to another class of dancers called *rajadasis*. While devadasis danced to honor a god or temple, *rajadasis* danced for entertainment. Kings and princes sometimes formed relationships with the girls.

All of the famous courtesans of Ancient India began as dancers or *nagarvadhu*. One of the best known was Amrapali. She is said to have been discovered as a baby under a mango tree in Vaishali, a city in Bihar, in about 500 B.C. Her name, Amrapali, means "found in a mango grove." She was renowned for her beauty and grew up to become a dancer and courtesan. When the king of Vaishali, Mahanaman, saw Amrapali dancing, he desired her so powerfully that he murdered her husband-to-be, Pushpakumar, and appointed her as his court dancer. She also became his mistress. When the king of a nearby state, Magadha, attacked Vaishali, Mahanaman sent an army to meet him in battle. While all the men were away fighting, a stranger visited Amrapali. He asked her to dance for him and stayed with her for several days. When he prepared to leave, he asked her to go with him, but she refused because she was the city's official dancer. He revealed that he was Bimbisara, the king of Magadha, whose army was attacking Vaishali. She pleaded with him to end the war. And he did. He left and took his army with him. Soon after this, Amrapali met the Buddha and, as a result, renounced her position as courtesan to the king and became a Buddhist.

CHINA'S CONCUBINES

In Imperial China, there was a long tradition of emperors keeping concubines. Some emperors kept hundreds or even thousands of them. However, there was a serious downside: a concubine's fate was often closely linked to that of her emperor. When Emperor Qin Shi Huang, the first emperor of a united China, died in 210 B.C., some of his concubines were sealed inside his massive tomb complex to serve him in the afterlife. The emperor is said to have been poisoned by mercury pills given to him by his alchemists and court physicians to make him immortal.

Stories of courtesans in Ancient China have been passed down through the generations, but without official records of their lives, it isn't clear whether they are fact or fiction. One account of a woman called Du Shiniang is typical of many. During the reign of the Ming dynasty's Wanli Emperor (1572–1620), Du Shiniang was sold to a brothel in Peking (Beijing) after her father died. Her family had been quite well-off, so she was educated in music and dance, making her more attractive to the brothel's wealthier clients. Du was eventually able to buy her way out of the brothel so that she could marry the son of a local official. However, after they were married, the young man had second thoughts. Fearing his father's reaction to his marriage to a courtesan, he sold Du to another man. She was so shocked by her husband's betrayal that she killed herself by jumping into a river.

Four women known as the Four Beauties were famous for their influence on emperors and kings. The first of the Four Beauties, Xi Shi, was said to have been so beautiful that when she leaned over her balcony, fish in a pond below her would forget how to swim. She was born in 487 B.C. or 506 B.C. (sources differ) and lived in Zhuji, the capital of the state of Yue. When Yue was defeated in a war with another state, Wu, an official suggested sending beautiful women to King Fuchai of Wu to distract him from state business. Xi Shi was one of the women selected for this mission. King Fuchai was so entranced by her that he neglected his duties. Instead, he busied himself with building a new palace for Xi Shi and another woman, Zheng Dan, who had accompanied her. He called it the Palace of Beautiful Women. He neglected his duties to such an extent that the state went into decline. In 473 B.C., the king of Yue attacked and defeated the Wu army.

The second of the Four Beauties was Wang Qiang, also known as Wang Zhaojun. She was said to be so beautiful that birds would fall from the sky when they saw her. She was born in about 50 B.C. in a small village, Baoping, in the west of China. When she was about fourteen years old, she was chosen to be a concubine by the Han dynasty emperor Yuan. He presented her as a gift to the nomadic Xiongnu people in the north of China, leading to an improvement in relations between the two peoples. She had at least three children with the Xiongnu king. When he died in 31 B.C., she asked to be allowed to return home. However, she was told to stay and observe the Xiongnu custom that she should marry the new king. She is thought to have died as a Xiongnu consort in about A.D. 8.

The third of the Four Beauties, Diaochan, is said to have had an affair with a general called Lü Bu in about A.D. 190, which resulted in Lü Bu turning against his warlord, Dong Zhou, and killing him. Lü Bu and Dong Zhou did exist and Lü Bu did kill Dong Zhou, but the part of the story involving Diaochan doesn't seem to have any factual basis. Her story appears in a part-fact, part-fiction book called *Romance of the Three Kingdoms,* written by Luo Guanzhong in the fourteenth century.

The fourth beauty was Yang Yuhuan. She was born in 719 in Yongji, the daughter of a census official. When the great Tang emperor Xuanzong's favorite concubine died, he decided that he wanted Yang to replace her. Inconveniently, she was already married to his son, Prince Li Mao, but this didn't deter the emperor. He got around it by making her a Taoist nun and giving her a new name, Taizhen. It was almost as if she had become a new person. Then he made her his concubine under her new name and gave his son a new wife. In 745, he made Priestess Taizhen his official imperial consort with the highest possible rank, called Guifei—hence the name by which she is usually remembered, Yang Guifei. In 755, one of the emperor's generals, An Lushan, started a revolution. The emperor, Xuanzong, fled toward Chengdu in Sichuan (Szechwan today), but the imperial guards traveling with him rebelled and arrested him. They demanded, among other things, the death of his consort, Yang Guifei. Eventually, to save himself, he acquiesced to their demands and ordered her to be taken to a nearby Buddhist shrine and strangled. The emperor was forced to watch. It didn't save his crown, though. Within days, he was deposed and replaced by his son. Today, Emperor Xuanzong's palace at Huaqing Hot Springs, with Yang Guifei's bath, is a major tourist attraction about 40 kilometers from the ancient capital, Xian.

In the seventh century, just before the time of the fourth beauty, one concubine rose to the very top and became empress of China. She even founded her own dynasty, albeit a very short-lived, one-emperor dynasty.

Wu Zhao was a concubine at the court of Emperor Taizong. She was expected to have children for the emperor, but she was childless. When an emperor died, his childless concubines were often sent to a temple to become Buddhist nuns. When Emperor Taizong died in 649, the twenty-five-year-old Wu was sent to a temple and expected to be confined there for the rest of her life. However, she somehow left the temple and returned to the imperial palace. According to one account, the new emperor's mother did not want her son, Emperor Gaozong, to be influenced by his favorite concubine, Xiao, so she arranged for the pretty Wu to be brought back from the temple to serve once again as a concubine and hopefully distract the emperor from Xiao. According to an alternative account, Wu never left the palace. Whichever story was the truth, the emperor's mother got her way. Wu quickly overtook Xiao as the emperor's favorite.

This time she bore the sons the emperor wanted. She is said to have strengthened her position by framing the empress for the death of Wu's daughter in 655. The young girl was strangled. There are suspicions that Wu may have killed the girl herself. The empress could not prove her innocence and her problems grew worse when she was accused of witchcraft. The emperor had her removed as empress and replaced by Wu. Now with the power of an empress, Wu began removing, demoting, and sometimes executing officials and rivals who had opposed her.

Five years later, the emperor suffered an illness that may have been caused by high blood pressure or possibly a stroke. It could even have been the result of poisoning by the ruthless Empress Wu. She took control of the empire from the incapacitated Gaozong. At imperial meetings, she sat hidden behind a curtain so that she could hear everything that was said and advise the emperor.

When Emperor Gaozong died in 683, he was succeeded by his (and Wu's) son, Li Xian, who became Emperor Zhongzong. Wu was still in control of the empire as dowager empress and regent. Zhongzong made the mistake of disobeying his mother. As a result, he reigned for only six weeks before he was deposed and exiled. He was replaced by another of Wu's sons, Li Dan, who became Emperor Ruizong. But Wu was still in control. Now, she didn't bother to hide behind a curtain at imperial meetings. She ruled openly. In 690, she took the throne herself and pronounced herself Empress Wu Zetian, the first ruler of the new Zhou dynasty. During her reign, she changed the state religion from Taoism to Buddhism. Then in 705, during a period of ill health, her opponents moved against her. She was deposed by her exiled son, Emperor Zhongzong. She died peacefully later the same year at the age of about eighty. The Zhou Dynasty she created ended with her death.

ANCIENT ROME

In Ancient Rome, the purpose of marriage was to produce legitimate heirs to inherit a family's property and wealth. Adultery, especially adultery by women, threatened this by making the identity of a child's father uncertain. Adultery by a woman was a crime in Ancient Rome, but adultery by a man was not a criminal act so long as the man's illicit partner was not a respectable woman, so slave girls, actresses, prostitutes, and other low-status women were fair game. Augustus Caesar, founder and first emperor of the Roman Empire, introduced laws that made adultery punishable by exile. Later laws required a husband who discovered that his wife was guilty of adultery to divorce her immediately. But these laws didn't trouble important and powerful Romans. Mark Antony, whose most famous mistress was Cleopatra, also had a Roman mistress, an actress known as Cytheris. She moved on from him to Marcus Junius Brutus, who would later become famous as one of Julius Caesar's killers. After Brutus, she had a relationship with the soldier, politician, and poet Cornelius Gallus. She inspired four books of his poetry.

The poet Catullus had a mistress called Clodia, the sister of the Roman politician Publius Clodius. Clodia was never far from one scandal or another. In 63 B.C., she married her cousin, Quintus Metellus Celer. When he died four years later, she was suspected of being involved in his death. Later, another of her lovers, Marcus Caelius Rufus, was accused of trying to poison her. At his trial, he was successfully defended by Cicero, a bitter enemy of Clodia's brother. Nothing more was heard of Clodia.

The Roman Empire disintegrated in A.D. 476 when Romulus Augustus (also known as Romulus Augustulus) abdicated in favor of the Germanic warrior Odoacer, but the eastern part of the empire continued as the Byzantine Empire, and this is where one of the most powerful women of the ancient world emerged—Theodora. She was a child prostitute who became a courtesan and then an empress.

Theodora was born in about A.D. 500. Her birthplace is unknown, but several writers and historians have suggested that she could have been born in Syria, Cyprus, or Paphlagonia, an area on the south coast of the Black Sea (in modern Turkey). Her father worked as a bear trainer in Constantinople. He looked after the bears and other animals that entertained the crowds between chariot races at the Hippodrome. Her mother was a dancer and actress. As a child, she worked in a Constantinople brothel and as an actress. By her teens, she was the mistress of a Syrian government official called Hecebolus. She accompanied him to Pentapolis in modern Libya, where he had been appointed governor. Four years later, he abandoned her, so she made her own way back to Constantinople. In her twenties, while she was working near the emperor's palace, she caught the eye of his nephew, Justinian. It wasn't long before she was his mistress, but they were forbidden from marrying because of a law preventing a patrician from marrying an actress. Justinian's solution was to have the law repealed. Theodora married Justinian, who became emperor on his uncle's death in 527. Theodora was now the most powerful woman in the empire.

When a rebellion called the Nika revolt broke out in Constantinople in 532, Theodora gave a speech that inspired Justinian to stay and fight instead of running. And he won. Then she and Justinian rebuilt much of Constantinople, which had been ravaged by the revolt, making it one of the greatest cities of the empire. One of the dozens of churches they built is the world-famous Hagia Sophia.

Theodora's elevation from child prostitute to empress was a remarkable transformation, but in the fourth century, a courtesan called Thaïs went one better. She became a saint. Thaïs led a pious life in Alexandria in Roman Egypt until she was orphaned. When she'd spent her inheritance, she embarked on a life as a courtesan to earn a living. Men were said to have ruined themselves by spending all their money on her, and her many lovers fought over her. But when she was challenged by a desert hermit about her sinful behavior, she repented. She burned her belongings and fled to a monastery, where she did solitary penance. She was sealed inside a tiny cell, leaving a small window in the door to let the nuns pass food in to her. After three years, believing she had finally earned forgiveness, she left the monastery. Just fifteen days later, she was found dead. She was transformed into a saint because of her instant and total repentance.

❧ 4 ❧

HONORED COURTESANS

After Ancient Greece and Rome, the next great flowering of courtesan culture occurred in Venice. Once the wealthiest city in Europe, Venice stood at one end of the Silk Road and dominated Mediterranean sea routes. A large proportion of the goods and materials bound for Europe from the east passed through Venice, generating enormous fortunes in taxes and duties. As the city's wealth grew, its merchants, traders, and nobility competed with each other to build ever grander homes and palaces.

But by the sixteenth century, Venice was in decline. It had lost control of the Adriatic Sea to the Turks, depriving it of access to the Mediterranean. Moreover, its traditional trading routes were increasingly being bypassed by new trade routes between Europe and the Americas across the Atlantic Ocean, and around Africa by sea to India and the Far East. Venice's days as a great European trading gateway were coming to an end.

As the city's wealth declined, more and more families were unable to afford the huge dowries payable on the marriage of their daughters. Women with little prospect of marriage were faced with two options: They could enter a convent and resign themselves to a life of contemplation and abstinence shut away from the rest of society. Or they could earn their living from the oldest profession. The numbers of prostitutes in Venice soared. They serviced the many visitors who were still attracted to the city by its great art, music, and literature. Where merchants once gathered to trade, travelers now sought entertainment and pleasure. By the end of the sixteenth century, Venice had as many as twelve thousand officially registered courtesans, and many more unregistered prostitutes, out of a population of only 150,000.

THE COURTESAN POET— VERONICA FRANCO

As prominent figures of their time, courtesans were favorite subjects for artists. In 1575, an artist called Jacopo Comin painted the portrait of a beautiful Venetian woman. She wears a fine crimson gown embroidered with silver thread and decorated with pearls. The front of her bodice lies open, revealing a linen undergarment called a *camicia*. Her clothing, especially her scandalously low neckline, points to her place in Venetian society. The artist, Jacopo Comin, is better known as Tintoretto. A handwritten note on the back of his painting identifies the subject as Veronica Franco, probably the most famous and sought-after Venetian courtesan.

Franco was born in 1546 to a family of *cittadini originari* (original citizens), native-born Venetians who formed the city's professional and government class. Her father, Francesco, could afford tutors for his three sons. As a rule, women were not educated, but Veronica was allowed to attend her brothers' classes and receive the same education. She could read and write at a time when fewer than 10 percent of Venetian women were literate and their only education concerned how to be an obedient wife. When Franco was sixteen years old, she was married to a physician, Paolo Panizza, but the marriage failed and they separated before her eighteenth birthday. By the age of about twenty, her life had taken a dramatic turn. She was listed in *Il Catalogo di tutte le principal et più honorate cortigiane di Venetia* (*The Catalog of All the Principal and Most Honorable Courtesans of Venice*). It was a directory of more than two hundred of Venice's most desired courtesans. It listed their names, addresses, procuresses, and how much they charged for their services, along with their portraits.

Franco's procuress was her own mother, Paola Fracassa, who was herself a courtesan. It wasn't unusual for daughters to follow mothers into the profession. Educated and trained by her mother, Franco quickly joined the ranks of the highest class of Venetian courtesans, the *cortigiani onesti* (honest, or honored, courtesans). It raised her above the ranks of the lower-class *cortigiani di lume* (courtesans of the light), who plied their trade in the inns and brothels of Venice, especially near the Rialto Bridge. While the high-class *cortigiani onesti* were almost indistinguishable from noblewomen, common prostitutes were easier to identify. The government encouraged them to bare their breasts in public in an attempt to "convert" Venice's many homosexual men. An area around a bridge that became known as the Ponte delle Tette (the Bridge of the Breasts) was notorious for this.

AT THE KING'S PLEASURE

In July 1574, the twenty-two-year-old Henry of Valois visited Venice on his way to France to be crowned King Henry III following the death of his sickly brother, Charles IX. The Republic of Venice judged that a fitting gift would be a night with its most desirable courtesan. Henry was carried into the city in a fine galley rowed by four hundred oarsmen. He entered through a triumphal arch designed by Palladio. After a sumptuous meal and an opera specially written for the occasion, he was presented with the infamous directory of courtesans and invited to make his choice. He chose Veronica Franco.

Courtesans like Franco vied with each other to dress in the finest clothes and wear the most brilliant gems, befitting their high-class companions. It became so difficult to distinguish courtesans from respectable women of substance that sumptuary laws were passed to limit the sort of clothes courtesans were allowed to wear. Sumptuary laws were passed all over Europe, ostensibly to protect people from bankrupting themselves by spending too much money on extravagant clothing, but in fact their purpose was to maintain class differences and stop people from lower classes looking like they belonged to a higher class. However, most Venetian courtesans ignored these laws. The richly dressed courtesans had become such a visible expression of Venice's wealth, and they were so important to the city's success as a magnet for travelers, that the sumptuary laws weren't often enforced. Even when they were, they could usually be circumvented by the payment of bribes.

PLAGUE

In 1575, Venice suffered a terrible plague epidemic. Plague was endemic in Europe from the fourteenth to seventeenth centuries, and Venice had suffered frequent outbreaks. As a busy seaport, it was vulnerable to all sorts of infectious diseases brought in by sailors and merchants. At that time, doctors had no answer to plague. In the absence of any effective treatment, the only way to prevent infection was to avoid all contact with sufferers. In an attempt to protect the city from an earlier outbreak, Venice had established the world's first isolation hospital on the island of Santa Maria di Nazareth (Lazzaretto Vecchio today). It became known as a lazaretto after the biblical character Lazarus. More lazarettos were established on other islands. Ships arriving at Venice were led to decontamination areas, where the crews were questioned about the ports they had visited. If there was any sign or suspicion of disease, the passengers and crews were quarantined for forty days before being allowed to enter the city. Meanwhile, the ships' cargoes were offloaded and treated to try to remove any trace of disease. Plague deaths on Santa Maria di Nazareth are thought to have reached five hundred a day during the 1575 outbreak. More than 1,500 skeletons were unearthed there in 2007 by archaeologists, who expect to find thousands more.

One of the strangest sights in Venice during plague outbreaks were the *pizzicamorti*. They were people who had the unenviable task of searching the city for bodies. If someone hadn't been seen for a while, the *pizzicamorti* would break into their home in case they had died. They were instantly recognizable because they wore a mask with a long birdlike beak. The beak was filled with aromatic herbs. At a time when people thought disease was spread by foul air, sweet-smelling substances were thought to give some protection against infection.

Another common belief was that plague was spread by vampires. A skeleton found on another of Venice's lazaretti, Lazzaretto Nuovo, had a brick forced between its jaws. This was done in the hope that it would stop the corpse from eating its shroud and coming back to life as a vampire. The belief that some bodies were vampires is thought to have originated from the sight of bodies bloated with gas moving as if alive, with blood seeping from their mouths, when mass graves were opened for reuse.

In 1575, plague spread rapidly through the densely populated city.

Anyone who could leave fled to safer places. Those who remained did what they could to isolate themselves from each other. Many of Venice's courtesans found themselves out of work. There was a widespread belief that the courtesans' sinful ways were responsible for the plague, which was thought to be a punishment from God. Despite all the protective measures, about fifty thousand people, one third of the city's population, were dead by the time the epidemic finally subsided in 1577.

WITCHCRAFT

In 1580, Franco was accused of heresy by her sons' teacher, Ridolfo Vannitelli. It is said that Vannitelli made the allegation out of revenge for Franco's suspicions that he may have stolen items from her home. He accused her of using magical incantations to reveal the identity of the thief, a serious charge that brought her to the attention of the Inquisition. He also branded her a prostitute and accused her of eating meat on Fridays. Catholics were required to abstain from eating meat on Fridays as an act of penance in memory of Christ's death on the cross. Eating meat on Fridays represented a serious breach of church law.

Franco was put on trial by the Holy Office of Venice, accused of practicing witchcraft and magic. When she was interrogated by the Inquisitor, she readily admitted performing the incantations. However, she claimed they were not heretical, but simply popular superstitions suggested by friends and neighbors, and they did not involve invoking the devil. She managed to convince the court of her innocence.

PATRON OF THE ARTS

Franco maintained an interest in art and literature throughout her life and often attended meetings of writers and artists. She hosted some of these meetings in her own home. As a poet, she was a protégée of Domenico Venier, an influential Venetian politician and literary figure. She became a prominent member of his literary circle.

Franco wrote two volumes of poetry in terza rima—literally "third rhyme," a verse form with a three-line rhyming structure. And in 1580, she published a volume of letters, *Lettere familiari a diversi (Familiar Letters to Var-*

ious People), including those she wrote to the French king, Henry III, and the artist who painted her portrait, Tintoretto.

Some of her writings suggest that she enjoyed her work as a courtesan:

> *Lying alongside you, tenderly*
> *I would have you taste*
> *the delights of love that I know so well.*
> *And I could give you such pleasure*
> *that you would find yourself satisfied*
> *and even more completely in love.*
> *I become so tender, so charming*
> *when I find myself in bed with a man*
> *who makes me feel loved and appreciated*
> *That my pleasuring exceeds all former delights,*
> *and however tight had seemed the knot of love*
> *it becomes tighter still.*

However, this could have been written as an advertisement for her services rather than a genuine expression of her pleasure. She tried to dissuade friends from letting their daughters become courtesans. She wrote to one friend:

> *I want to show you the hidden precipice toward which you are heading,*
> *shouting as loud as I can, so that there is time to avoid it. . . . To make*
> *yourself prey to so many men at the risk of being swindled, robbed, killed, to*
> *have one man take away from you everything you've acquired from all the*
> *others for so many years, along with how many other dangers of injury and*
> *horrible contagious diseases. To eat with another's mouth, to sleep with*
> *another's eyes, to move according to another's will, obviously sailing*
> *headlong toward the shipwreck of everything you possess, as well as your*
> *life . . . Consider the consequences, look at what happens to the countless*
> *women in this profession . . . your daughter herself will abandon you when*
> *she realizes how you have exploited and ruined her.*

In 1577, she persuaded the Venetian authorities to establish a home for unmarried mothers and prostitutes.

DECLINE AND FALL

Franco lost most of her wealth and possessions during the 1575 plague epidemic. She left Venice during the epidemic and returned to find that her home had been broken into and looted. Her tax records for 1582 showed that by then she was living in part of the city where destitute prostitutes lived.

She died on July 22, 1591, at the age of only forty-five after twenty days of an unidentified fever. She was survived by two children, another four having died in infancy. Her life story was told in *The Honest Courtesan,* by Margaret Rosenthal (1992), and she was played by Catherine McCormack in the film *Dangerous Beauty* (1998), based on Rosenthal's book.

TANTALIZING TULLIA—
TULLIA D'ARAGONA

Veronica Franco wasn't the first superstar poet-courtesan in Italy. She was following in the footsteps of a woman called Tullia d'Aragona. Unlike Franco, Tullia left no one in any doubt of her feelings about her profession. She wrote, "If you knew the servility, the vileness, the depths and inconstancy of such a life, you would blame anyone . . . who said it was a good one and excused it. And anyone who helps a young girl, foolish enough to be pushed into such a life, to get out of it is saving her from misery."

For much of her life, she divided her time between writing and servicing her clients. She was born in about 1510 in Rome, where her mother, Giulia Campana (also known as Giulia Ferrarese), was a courtesan renowned as one of the most beautiful women of her time. Tullia didn't inherit her mother's strikingly good looks. She is described as being too tall, thin, lacking her mother's sensual curves, with a long face, hooked nose, and large mouth. However, Tullia was well taught by her mother, and her intelligence, wit, fashion, sparkling eyes, and proficiency in seduction more than compensated for her modest appearance.

Officially, her father was Constanzo Palmieri d'Aragona, but there are suspicions that Campana's marriage to Constanzo was a sham to preserve the reputation of Tullia's real father—Costanzo's cousin, Cardinal Luigi d'Aragona, an illegitimate grandson of Ferdinando d'Aragona, king of Naples.

When Luigi died in 1519, Tullia's mother took her to Siena. Nothing more is known about her until she turned up in Rome in 1526 with a man called Filippo Strozzi, a member of a prominent family of bankers and politicians. This appears to mark the beginning of her career as a courtesan, while she was still in her teens. Strozzi was so besotted with her that he neglected his job and had to be summoned back to Florence to save him from her influence. She moved from city to city, plying her trade—Rome, Venice, Bologna, Florence, Adria, Ferrara, and Siena. She was popular among writers and philosophers. They dedicated poems to her and encouraged her to write and to publish her own work. In addition to poetry, she wrote a book called *Dialogue on the Infinity of Love,* based on her conversations with several of the men she knew. She had a devoted following among her admirers and clients.

In 1535, she went to Adria with her mother for the birth of a baby girl, Penelope. It isn't clear whether Penelope was Tullia's daughter or sister. On January 8, 1543, Tullia married Silvestro Guiccardi. The marriage was an advantage to someone in her line of work. It enabled to her work without having to live in the district set aside for prostitutes or being constrained by any of the laws and regulations applying to prostitutes. Getting married bought her a measure of respectability. For a man who could accept a courtesan's lifestyle, a woman like Tullia was an attractive spouse—she was financially independent, a good companion, knowledgeable about the topics of the day that interested men, and skilled in seduction.

Italy didn't exist as a single unified country at that time. It was a collection of separate states and kingdoms that were often at war with each other. By 1545, the region around Adria was in such turmoil that Tullia fled to Florence and sought the protection of its ruler, Cosimo I de' Medici. However, she was charged with refusing to wear the style of clothes that prostitutes in Florence were required to wear. Luckily Cosimo I de' Medici was a patron of the arts, and so he granted Tullia an exemption from the law because of her poetry. In return, she dedicated her next book to him and dedicated other works to his wife.

In 1548, she returned to her birthplace, Rome. At about this time, she gave birth to a boy, Celio. Celio's father is unknown. It wasn't Tullia's husband, because he had died. She then wrote the earliest known epic poem by a woman, "Il Meschino, altramente ditto il Guerrino" ("The Unfortunate, also Called Guerrino"). It was published four years after her death, in 1556.

PAPAL MISTRESSES

The pope ruled territories called the Papal States between the eighth century and 1870, when the last Papal State, Lazio, was incorporated into a unified Italy. After that, the pope had no geographic territory. The Vatican City State was created in 1929 by Benito Mussolini to address this. Vatican City is the smallest independent state in the world, and the only example of an entire state existing within a city, Rome.

Today, the pope is celibate, but that was not always the case. Several early popes were married before they took holy orders or were elected pope. They include Pope Adrian II in the ninth century, Pope John XVII in the eleventh century, and Pope Clement IV in the thirteenth century. Several others had illegitimate children before taking holy orders. These include Popes Pius II and Innocent VIII in the fifteenth century and Popes Clement VII and Gregory XIII in the sixteenth century.

Several popes had mistresses before they were elevated to the papacy. Rodrigo Borgia, who became Pope Alexander VI in 1492, had multiple mistresses. One of them, Vannozza dei Cattanei, bore him four children, including the infamous Lucrezia and Cesare Borgia. Alexander was also one of a handful of popes who continued to keep mistresses even after they were elevated to the papacy. He was accused of rigging his election as pope by spending a fortune bribing cardinals for their votes. He proved to be one of the most corrupt popes, known for lavishing honors on his relatives. Giulia Farnese was his mistress while he was pope, earning her the nickname of "the pope's whore." She had a daughter, Laura, and claimed that the pope was the girl's father. However, she may have made the claim to improve the girl's marriage prospects. She earned the pope's displeasure by leaving Rome without his permission to visit her dying brother. She eventually gave in to his demands that she should return, but she was captured by invading French troops. The pope had to pay a ransom of three thousand scudi for her release.

The scandal of the pope and his mistress resurfaced in 2007 when a painting that once adorned Pope Alexander VI's bedroom wall came to light. It shows the Child Jesus being held by two disembodied hands, while a third hand touches his foot. Some experts believe the painting to be a small part of a larger work of art that showed the pope kneeling in front of the Virgin Mary and Child Jesus. They believe that the two hands holding the child belong to the Virgin Mary, and the third hand belongs to the pope. The painting, a fresco, was hacked off the pope's bedroom wall when he died, because the face of the Virgin Mary was said to be that of his mistress, Giulia Farnese.

In the tenth century, Pope Sergius III was accused of having an affair with a woman called Marozia, although the accusation was made by his enemies, and so it may not be true. Marozia was married to Alberic I, Duke of Spoleto. She is said to have given birth to the pope's child, a boy who later became Pope John XI. The fact that the boy, Alberic's eldest son, entered the church instead of inheriting his father's title might indicate that he was illegitimate, and so he could indeed have been the pope's son, but we will never know the truth one way or the other. Popes John X and John XII in the tenth century and Benedict IX, who was elected pope three times in the tenth and eleventh centuries, were also accused of having affairs.

5

MEANWHILE IN
BRITAIN . . .

While France and Italy were setting the pace in Europe, British monarchs were no slouches on the wrong side of the blanket either. Very little is known about English royal mistresses before the fifteenth century. Women were rarely written about at this time. References to their lives generally have to be gleaned from accounts of their husbands, fathers, lovers, or children. King Henry I, who reigned from 1100 to 1135, had more than twenty illegitimate children, but the identities of most of his mistresses are unknown. From these murky times a thousand years ago until the twentieth century, most English kings had multiple mistresses. One exception was Richard III, the last Plantagenet king of England and the last English king to die in battle. He is thought to have had only one mistress, whose name may have been Katherine Haute.

The monarchs who followed him were not known for their mistresses until the arrival of Charles II in 1660. He returned from exile in France and the Dutch Republic, which was enjoying a golden age. In the seventeenth century, the Dutch Republic was one of Europe's most powerful nations, with an extensive overseas empire. Its citizens included some of the most important and significant scientists and artists of the century, including Christiaan Huygens, Antonie van Leeuwenhoek, Rembrandt, Vermeer, and Frans Hals. When Charles returned to England, he brought continental customs and attitudes with him, including the French custom of taking royal mistresses. The most famous of his mistresses was a feisty little orange-seller and actress, Nell Gwyn. Charles's successor, James II, was even more promiscuous, having at least eleven mistresses.

In the eighteenth century, the first three monarchs of the Georgian era took few mistresses, but George IV made up for their deficiencies in this respect. He had at least nine mistresses, including one who blackmailed him and another whom he married, illegally. George's successor, William IV, was a very unusual British king in that he had a happy marriage. He hadn't expected to inherit the throne, but did so at the age of sixty-four because his older brothers died without legitimate issue. Before he became king, he lived as the Duke of Clarence for twenty years with an Irish actress called Dorothea (or Dorothy) Bland, better known as Dora Jordan. They had ten illegitimate children, five boys and five girls. When their relationship came to an end in 1811, she was given custody of the girls and a financial settlement on condition that she didn't resume her stage career. When poverty eventually did force her back onto the stage, William took the girls away from her. She left for France to escape her creditors and died there in poverty in 1816. Two years later, William married Princess Adelaide of Saxe-Meiningen and is not known to have had any further mistresses.

THE MERRIEST MISTRESS—
JANE SHORE

Edward IV was king of England between 1461 and 1470. He had multiple mistresses, but one of them stood out from the others. Medieval kings and princes generally hunted for their mistresses among women of their own social class. But Jane Shore was an exception. She was not remotely noble or royal, yet she was the one mistress the king said he truly loved.

Elizabeth Lambert was born into a family of merchants in the Cheapside area of London sometime between 1445 and 1450. King Henry VI was on the throne. It was a turbulent time. Henry's armies had been defeated in France and driven out of Normandy. There was trouble at home, too. England would soon be torn apart by a civil war that became known as the Wars of the Roses—a war for the throne of England between two royal houses, the House of York and the House of Lancaster, that lasted more than thirty years.

Elizabeth Lambert was used to seeing upper-class people in her father's shop. She studied their behavior and how they spoke. And the customers noticed her. She was said to be a beautiful child, so much so that she was nicknamed "the Rose of London." When she was old enough to marry—twelve in the fifteenth century—her father was keen to find a suitable match for her. He chose a fellow merchant, William Shore. The marriage probably took place in the late 1460s. Shore was about fifteen years older than his wife. She was now Elizabeth Shore, but she is known as Jane today, thanks to a playwright who mistakenly called her Jane in the seventeenth century.

An Appeal for Help

Jane was never happy in her marriage and eventually appealed to a church court called the Court of Arches to have it annulled. The grounds for the annulment were that after living together for the regulation three years, her husband was impotent and incapable of consummating the marriage, and therefore it wasn't really a marriage at all. The Court of the Arches dismissed her case, so she appealed to the court of the apostolic see in Rome, the church's highest ecclesiastical court. Pope Sixtus IV took pity on her and asked the bishops of Hereford, Sidon, and Ross to hear her case. The three bishops considered the case and granted an annulment on March 1, 1476. Cases like this cost a fortune and were normally out of the question for someone in Jane's position. It isn't known who paid her costs. One possibility is King Edward IV, who had won the throne in battle in 1471. The bishop of Hereford was known to be acquainted with the king. He may have appealed to the king on her behalf for help with the cost. Whatever the truth, her affair with the king began the same year. No one knows how they met.

King Edward had married Elizabeth Woodville in 1463. The reason for the marriage is a bit of a mystery. Kings usually married to form powerful alliances with countries, regions, or families that could support the king and country in time of war. But Edward's marriage to Elizabeth Woodville added nothing to the power, wealth, or security of the king or the country. He may have married for love or lust, which would have been very unusual for an English king at that time. He kept the marriage secret, but when his advisers started discussing the matter of whom he might choose for a wife, he had to admit to them that he was already married. Aristocrats and commoners alike were appalled by his irresponsible behavior. He was faithful to his wife for only a short time. He couldn't resist a pretty girl, but he also did his duty as king—he and his wife had ten children. He is reputed to have had many mistresses, but he quickly tired of them and passed them on to courtiers with a handsome payment to calm their displeasure.

The queen tolerated his mistresses, as queens usually did. However, most royal mistresses were married aristocrats who knew how to behave in royal circles. Jane was a commoner, and therefore a greater risk to the monarchy. She could embarrass the king or blackmail him, or—horror of horrors— she might actually want to marry him! An English king (or even an heir to the throne) marrying a commoner is still worthy of note and press comment in the twenty-first century; in the fifteenth century, it was unimaginable. So, following the annulment of Jane's marriage, the queen was less inclined to tolerate her.

A MISTRESS LOVED

Jane doesn't seem to have been ambitious for personal power, and she didn't interfere in politics as some other royal mistresses did. The king probably set her up in a house of her own somewhere close to one of his palaces. And he seems to have loved her. He described her as the merriest of his concubines. Sir Thomas More, Henry VIII's lord chancellor, mentioned her in his book, *The History of King Richard III,* written in the early 1500s. He said of Edward IV's mistresses, "the merriest was this Shore's wife, in whom the king therefore took special pleasure. For many he had, but her he loved."

While some mistresses encouraged intrigue at court to divide courtiers and advance their own position, Jane seems to have been a peacemaker and calming influence on the king. Sir Thomas More wrote,

> *She never abused to any man's hurt, but to many a man's comfort and relief. Where the king took displeasure, she would mitigate and appease his mind; where men were out of favor, she would bring them in his grace; for many that had highly offended, she obtained pardon. Of great forfeitures, she got men remission. And finally, in many weighty suits, she stood many men in great stead, either for none, or very small, rewards.*

Her appeal wasn't just her beauty. By all accounts, she was witty without being too talkative. Sir Thomas More said she was "ready and quick of answer, neither mute nor full of babble."

The late 1470s and early 1480s were the happiest and most comfortable time of Jane's life. She was her own woman, with all the material advantages that the love of a king of England afforded her. But her fortunes changed dramatically in 1483. On April 9, the king died suddenly and unexpectedly, just a couple of weeks short of his forty-first birthday. The cause of his death is unknown, but it seems to have been a fever of some sort. He hadn't given any thought to the consequences of his death. In particular, he hadn't made any provisions for Jane. As soon as the king was dead, Lord Hastings, who had been the king's lord chamberlain, rushed to her side. He had been a secret admirer, but had kept his distance out of deference to the king.

The king was succeeded by his young son, now King Edward V, but he would never be crowned. The new king was only twelve years old, so Richard, Duke of Gloucester, was appointed as his Protector. Richard was expected to rule until the boy was old enough to take the reins of power. However, Richard showed a ruthless streak from the start. He stopped the queen, Elizabeth Woodville, from seizing power by having several of her relatives and supporters arrested and executed. He then had the new king and his nine-year-old brother, the Duke of York, taken to the Tower of London. They were never seen alive again. They are remembered as the Princes in the Tower. Richard then accused Hastings of conspiring against him with the queen's family and Jane. Hastings was immediately beheaded. Richard then seized the throne and had himself crowned as King Richard III.

The only close relative of the queen whom he hadn't been able to neutralize was her son from her first marriage, Thomas Grey, Marquess of Dorset. He had fled to France after a failed rebellion against Richard. The king claimed that Jane had been Dorset's mistress, so if he couldn't seize Dorset, he would take his revenge on Jane instead. He had her arrested and taken to prison. He ordered the bishop of London to make her perform public penance. She had to walk around the city carrying a candle and wearing only her kirtle (petticoat). Crowds gathered to watch her walking past in what amounted to fifteenth-century underwear. Far from condemning her to the status of a harlot, as Richard had expected, her dignity won her praise and admiration. Richard was furious and had her sent back to prison. His mood wasn't improved by the next development in the extraordinary life of Jane Shore.

A Surprise Proposal

The king was surprised when he was informed that Jane had received a proposal of marriage while she languished in prison. The surprise was the identity of the man who wanted to marry her. It was none other than the king's own solicitor, Thomas Lynom! The king wrote to his chancellor, John Russell, bishop of Lincoln, and instructed him to change Lynom's mind. But Lynom was determined. The king eventually relented and allowed the marriage. There is no record of when or where they married, but Thomas Lynom appears in wills made by Jane's older relatives, so he clearly did join her family. Very little is known about Thomas and Jane's lives after this point, other than that they had a daughter. Thomas lost his position as the king's solicitor after Richard was killed at the Battle of Bosworth Field in 1485. He died around 1518.

Thomas More's writings contain references to Jane in her old age. He reports that she reached her seventies, but was reduced to begging for money from former friends and acquaintances because of poverty. Her husband doesn't appear to have made any provision for her, perhaps because he wasn't able to after he lost his position as the king's solicitor. Jane is thought to have died around 1527.

The Ten Mistresses of Henry VIII

King Henry VIII is famous for his six wives, but less well known is the fact that he had at least ten mistresses. Two of his mistresses became queens in their own right, and one of them caused a seismic shift in English history.

Henry hadn't expected to become king. It was his older brother, Arthur, who was the heir to the throne. Arthur had married a Spanish princess, Catherine of Aragon, in 1501 to form a strategic alliance between England and Spain against France. Six months later, they both fell ill. Catherine survived, but the fifteen-year-old Arthur died. At only ten years of age, Henry unexpectedly found himself heir to the throne. The alliance between the two countries' royal houses was so important that Catherine was persuaded to marry her dead husband's brother, Henry. A marriage like this, between a man and his brother's widow, was forbidden by the church. However, Catherine testified that her marriage to Arthur had never been consummated, and so the pope granted a special dispensation allowing her to marry Henry. The fact that, on the morning after his wedding, Arthur had called for ale because "I have been this night in the midst of Spain," suggesting that the marriage was indeed consummated, was quietly forgotten.

Henry's first mistress was probably Lady Anne Hastings, one of the queen's ladies-in-waiting. His affair with her began in 1510, just a year after his marriage to Catherine. At the English court, husbands were often content to let their wives conduct affairs with a king, because the husband and relatives stood to benefit from the arrangement. But Anne's husband, Lord Hastings, was so angry when he found out about her affair with Henry that he took her away from court to a convent sixty miles from London and had her held there. Interfering with a king's love life was usually a recipe for disaster, but Hastings appears to have retained the king's loyalty, because Henry made him Earl of Huntingdon a few years later. Meanwhile, Anne returned to court and appears to have resumed her affair with Henry, because he gave her a very expensive gift made of thirty ounces of silver gilt in 1513. In the same year, Henry invaded France. When he wasn't commanding his troops, he appears to have had an affair with a French-woman called Étienette de La Baume.

By about 1514, he was back in England and rumored to be "entertaining" three ladies-in-waiting—Jane Popincourt, Elizabeth "Bessie" Blount, and Elizabeth Carew. Popincourt had been brought to England from France to tutor Henry's sisters, and possibly Henry himself, in the French language. Her unremarkable liaison with Henry ended in 1516 when she returned to France. She had been a few years older than Henry, but Bessie Blount was a mere child of eleven when she arrived at court in 1512. She worked as a maid of honor to the queen. Two years later, Henry invited the now thirteen-year-old Bessie to dance with him when the queen was unable to partner him because she was pregnant. The young girl was said to be a talented dancer. Bessie became pregnant by the king in 1518. The baby, a boy, was born the following year and named Henry FitzRoy (FitzRoy is an Anglo-Norman name meaning "son of the king"). Soon after the boy's birth, the affair between Henry and Bessie ended. Very little is known about Henry's affair with the third lady-in-waiting, Elizabeth Carew, beyond the fact that he gave her a series of unusually expensive gifts, indicating a particular closeness beyond that of mere friend or employer. At about this time, he is also thought to have had a fling with a woman known only as Mistress Parker.

THE BOLEYN GIRLS

Then Henry turned his attention to the two sisters who would change everything—the Boleyn girls, Mary and Anne. Their father, Sir Thomas Boleyn, was a courtier and diplomat. Their mother, Lady Elizabeth Howard, was lady-in-waiting to Elizabeth of York and then to Catherine of Aragon. The Boleyn family home was Hever Castle in Kent, but they also owned Blickling Hall in Norfolk, and this is probably where Mary and Anne were born. Another form of the Boleyn name, Bullen, is still common in Norfolk today. Mary was born first, in 1498, and her sister, Anne, followed about three years later. The fifteen-year-old Mary Boleyn worked as a maid of honor to Henry VIII's sister, Princess Mary. When Princess Mary sailed for France to marry the uncharacteristically virtuous French king, Louis XII, Mary Boleyn went with her.

Princess Mary was widowed in 1515, just three months after her marriage, and returned to England. Mary Boleyn stayed in France and became a lady-in-waiting to the new French queen, Claude. At about the same time, her father was appointed ambassador to France. Her sister, Anne, was also in France at this time.

Mary quickly acquired a reputation as a girl who knew how to enjoy herself between the sheets. There were rumors that she was involved in several affairs, perhaps even one with the new king, François I. Whatever the truth of the matter, she returned to England in 1519 and became a maid of honor to Henry's queen, Catherine of Aragon. In 1520, she married William Carey, a courtier who was very close to the king. One of their wedding guests was King Henry himself. He clearly thought well of young Mary, because within a few months he had recruited her as his latest mistress. The liaison continued in secret for about five years until 1526. During this time, Mary had two children. One of them, named Henry, was said to have resembled the king.

Tragedy struck two years later, when Mary's husband suddenly died of an ailment known as the sweating disease or sweating sickness. It was a mystery illness that swept through England and Continental Europe in a series of epidemics beginning in 1485. It may have been brought to England by French mercenaries fighting for Henry Tudor (who became King Henry VII) at the end of the Wars of the Roses. Victims often died within a few hours of developing the first feverish symptoms. Epidemics of the disease always occurred in the summer and came to an end with the onset of winter. It may have been spread by ticks or lice, which flourished during the warm summer months and died out in winter. The disease vanished in the sixteenth century as quickly as it had appeared. It has not been seen in England since then, although a similar ailment known as "the Picardy sweat" appeared in France between 1718 and 1874.

In 1534, Mary secretly married William Stafford. She probably kept it secret because of her new husband's poor prospects as a lowly soldier and second son. However, when she became pregnant, her family found out what she had done. They were so angry that they disowned her. She also managed to offend her sister, Anne, and get herself banished from court. Considering the fate that awaited Anne, Mary was probably lucky to be excluded from the intrigue at court. She outlived her parents and sister, and died in her forties on July 19, 1543.

Meanwhile, in 1522, Anne Boleyn had been summoned to England from France to settle a dispute between the Boleyns and another family, the Butlers. The Boleyns and the Butlers both claimed the title of Earl of Ormond and the estates that went with it. It was decided that Anne should marry her cousin, James Butler, to unite the two families and settle their rival claims. However, the marriage negotiations came to nothing. Anne found a position in the service of the queen. With her French-inspired fashion, graceful style, ability to play the lute, conversational skills, sparkling personality, and elegance on the dance floor, she was described as the perfect courtier. Men pursued her and she enjoyed their attention.

MAKE ME QUEEN

Her most ardent admirer was King Henry VIII. He wanted her for his mistress from the spring of 1526, when she was in her midtwenties and Henry was about ten years older. However, unlike her sister, she resisted his attempts to seduce him. She made it clear that she would be his companion but not his lover . . . unless he made her his queen. It was quite an ambitious demand, but she'd set Henry's impressive codpiece aquiver and he was determined to have her. Henry assumed Pope Clement VII would agree to annul his marriage to Catherine, who had outlived her usefulness to him by failing to produce the male Tudor heir he was desperate for. She had given birth to six children in eight years and three of them were boys. However, two of the boys lived for just a few hours, and the third died after a few weeks. One of the girls was lost due to miscarriage, and another lived for just a few days. Only one of the six children survived infancy. She would grow up to become Queen Mary I.

Henry claimed that Catherine's failure to produce a surviving male heir was because their marriage contravened God's law (because Catherine had been his brother's wife). He quoted a passage from Leviticus, saying that it was a sin for a man to lie with his brother's widow, to support his claim. In May 1527, Cardinal Wolsey opened a secret trial to test Henry's case. It was so secret that even the queen didn't know about it. Wolsey asked the pope to accept that the special dispensation given by the previous pope, allowing Henry to marry his brother's widow, was void because it contradicted Bible text. He also wanted the pope to allow the decision on Henry's situation to be made in England, not in Rome. Wolsey could then ensure that the king got his way. The pope did allow the matter to be decided in England, but he refused to let Wolsey adjudicate alone. A papal legate, Cardinal Lorenzo Campeggio, would assist him. On instructions from the pope, Campeggio delayed giving his decision for as long as possible. In the middle of 1529, he suspended the case and returned to Rome, never to return. The reluctance of the pope and his legate, Campeggio, to reach a decision was due to their wish to avoid offending the Holy Roman Emperor, Charles V, who also happened to be the nephew of Catherine of Aragon. Henry was furious.

The crisis was almost resolved in 1528 when Anne fell ill with the sweating sickness during the same epidemic that killed her brother-in-law, William Carey. Henry sent his own physician to care for her and she recovered.

When Catherine realized what Henry was up to, she protested loudly that she was the only legitimate queen of England. The public sided with her. They saw her as a faithful wife and rightful queen who was being cast aside so that the king could put his mistress on the throne. But Henry was determined to have Anne.

In 1530, she gave him a book by William Tyndale called *The Obedience of a Christian Man and How Christian Rulers Ought to Govern*. It was this that gave Henry the idea of becoming head of the church in England in place of the pope. However, Tyndale, who also produced a famous English translation of the Bible, opposed Henry's divorce from Catherine and his proposed marriage to Anne, earning him Henry's anger. When he fled to Europe to escape the king's wrath, Henry asked the Holy Roman Emperor to arrest him and return him to England. Charles declined on the grounds that he had no evidence against Tyndale on which to extradite him. Eventually, Tyndale was betrayed and arrested in Antwerp. In 1536, he was tried for heresy and found guilty. He was sentenced to death. He was executed by strangulation and then his body was burned at the stake. Tyndale's Bible would later form the basis of Henry's Great Bible, the first authorized edition of the Bible in English, published in 1539.

On February 11, 1531, Henry forced the Catholic Church in England to accept him as its head. A few months later, he banished Catherine from court. In 1532, Thomas Cranmer was appointed archbishop of Canterbury, with the pope's approval. The following year, Cranmer declared Henry's marriage to Catherine invalid, leaving the way open for him to marry Anne. There is some doubt about the precise date of their marriage. There is some evidence that they married secretly on November 14, 1532, immediately after their return from a visit to King François I of France. Whether or not this wedding actually happened, there was certainly a wedding ceremony on January 25, 1533, followed by a coronation just over four months later, making Anne Boleyn queen of England. By then, she was already pregnant.

When the pope learned of the marriage, he excommunicated Henry, whose position as head of the newly established Church of England was soon confirmed by the Act of Supremacy in 1534. One advantage of this course of action was that taxes on ecclesiastical income formerly paid to the pope were now paid to Henry. Next, he eyed the valuable land and property owned by the church, leading to the dissolution of the monasteries and the redistribution of their land to the nobility. The extra income this provided enabled Henry to build coastal defenses and warships against a feared invasion by European powers to return England to the Roman Catholic fold. It was the beginning of the Royal Navy, which eventually grew to become the world's most powerful navy, enabling England to establish and defend the biggest empire the world had ever seen.

Brain Damage

On the advice of physicians and astrologers, Henry and Anne confidently expected their baby to be a boy, but on September 7, 1533, Anne gave birth to a girl. The arrival of a girl was such a great disappointment to the king that he canceled celebrations being prepared for the birth of his son and heir. Ironically, the little girl whose birth was considered to be such a failure and disappointment would grow up to become one of England's greatest monarchs, Queen Elizabeth I. At least four more of Anne's pregnancies ended in miscarriage or stillbirth. While she was pregnant, Henry took other mistresses, including Anne's own cousin, Mary Shelton, and a young lady-in-waiting called Jane Seymour. In January 1536, a few days after Henry suffered an accident while jousting, Anne miscarried her latest pregnancy. The baby would have been a boy.

Henry's accident was so serious that he is thought to have suffered brain damage bad enough to cause a change in his personality. The generous and generally happy king became cruel and vicious after the accident. He'd already had a serious jousting accident in 1524 when he'd failed to close his visor securely and was struck in the face by his opponent's lance. The 1536 accident was even more serious. The forty-four-year-old king was thrown from his horse, which then fell on him. He was unconscious for two hours. In addition to a suspected brain injury, the accident aggravated earlier leg injuries, which plagued him for the rest of his life. He never went jousting again. His weight ballooned. Suits of armor made for him and still in existence today show that his waist measurement grew from thirty-two to more than fifty inches and his weight reached about twenty-eight stones (nearly four hundred pounds).

The accident and Anne's latest miscarriage seemed to mark the end of the marriage as far as Henry was concerned. He was already homing in on his next lover, Jane Seymour. He embarked on an exit plan from his marriage with ruthless efficiency. He appointed a committee to examine Anne's activities for any behavior that could be considered treasonous. It wasn't difficult to make enemies at court, so the committee soon found people to testify against her. A court musician and a dancer were arrested and tortured on the rack until they confessed to committing adultery with her. Then three knights were arrested on the same charge. She was even accused of incest with her brother and conspiracy to kill the king. Multiple charges were laid against her in the hope that at least one of them would stick.

KILLING A QUEEN

On May 2, 1536, Anne was arrested and taken to the Tower of London. She is said to have been so distressed that she collapsed shortly after her arrival. On May 15, she was put on trial for adultery, incest, and high treason—namely, plotting the king's death so that she could marry one of her alleged lovers. It was more theater than trial. The four men accused of adultery with Anne were found guilty and sentenced to death by beheading. Then Anne and her brother were found guilty and sentenced to death by burning at the stake. Henry showed them "mercy" by commuting the penalty from burning to beheading. After the others were beheaded on May 17, it was Anne's turn. Instead of risking a botched execution with a common ax, Henry had an expert swordsman brought from France to kill the woman he had once wanted so badly. The man was Jean Rombaud, executioner of Saint-Omer. According to one account, Henry sent observers to watch Rombaud in action before hiring him. He impressed Henry's men by executing two prisoners at the same time with one blow of his sword.

On May 19, 1536, Anne was taken to the place of execution inside the Tower of London. Execution within the Tower, hidden from gawping crowds of the general public, was a privilege granted to those of high rank in society. When the king's men finally came for her, she appeared relaxed and unconcerned about what she knew was about to happen. The lieutenant of the Tower had said she was the first condemned prisoner he'd ever known to be impatient for death. She addressed a small group of people who had gathered to witness her execution. In a voice that began weak but grew in strength as she spoke, she said:

Good Christian people, I am come hither to die, for according to the law, and by the law I am judged to die, and therefore I will speak nothing against it. I am come hither to accuse no man, nor to speak anything of that, whereof I am accused and condemned to die, but I pray God save the King and send him long to reign over you, for a gentler nor a more merciful prince was there never: and to me he was ever a good, a gentle and sovereign lord. And if any person will meddle of my cause, I require them to judge the best. And thus I take my leave of the world and of you all, and I heartily desire you all to pray for me. O Lord have mercy on me, to God I commend my soul.

Instead of crouching over a headsman's block, she knelt upright, which was the style of execution in France. As she repeated over and over again, "Jesu receive my soul; O Lord God have pity on my soul," the executioner decapitated the queen of England with a single sweeping stroke of his sword. As the executioner lifted her head, witnesses reported that her eyes and lips were still moving. Despite careful planning for the execution, no one seems to have remembered that a coffin would be needed. Anne's body had to be put into an arrow chest with her head tucked underneath her arm!

With Anne dead, Henry was free to marry Jane Seymour. And he lost no time in tying the knot. He married her less than two weeks after Anne's execution. And she finally gave him the son he wanted. The boy, named Edward, was born on October 12, 1537, but Jane fell ill and died twelve days later at the age of only twenty-eight. She was the only one of Henry's wives to be given a queen's burial. There are no records of any further mistresses after this, but Henry went on to wed three more times—to Anne of Cleves, Catherine Howard, and Catherine Parr.

THE HEADSMAN'S AX

Anne Boleyn was "fortunate" to have been executed by an expert swordsman. Beheadings in England at that time were usually carried out by means of the headsman's ax. It was a very unwieldy weapon that was difficult to use with any precision. Several blows of the ax were often needed to sever a head, even if the ax was sharp. There are many accounts of botched executions involving this weapon. On May 27, 1541, Margaret Pole was executed on the same spot where Anne Boleyn had died five years earlier, but Pole's execution went horribly wrong. She had been the governess to Catherine of Aragon's daughter, Mary. But as Henry VIII struggled to rid himself of Catherine, Margaret made the mistake of standing by the queen. She chose the wrong side. The king was furious and dismissed her. She retired to what she thought would be a quiet life in the country. However, her son publicly attacked the king from the safety of the Continent. Margaret begged him to stop, but it was too late. She was arrested and imprisoned in the Tower of London. After two years, and without any trial or even any charges having been laid against her, she was suddenly informed that she was to be executed within hours.

The execution was so rushed that there was no time to build a scaffold (a raised platform) or summon an experienced executioner. Instead, a novice was pressed into service. The *Calendar of State Papers* described him as "a wretched and blundering youth." It didn't help that Margaret is reported to have refused to lay her head on the block. The frail sixty-seven-year-old woman had to be forced down into the appropriate position while she struggled. In front of about a hundred witnesses, the inexperienced executioner swung his ax and missed Margaret's neck. He struck her on the shoulder. He swung the ax again and again—up to ten times, according to reports. He was said to have "hacked her head and shoulders to pieces" before the ghastly job was finally done. Margaret Pole's execution was an extreme case, but there are many other accounts of multiple blows of the ax being necessary. It took three blows to remove the head of Mary Queen of Scots when she was executed at Fotheringhay Castle in 1587. It was to avoid butchery like this that Henry decided to bring an expert in sword executions to England to dispatch Anne Boleyn.

THE MERRY MONARCH—CHARLES II

By 1660, the English people had been living under the austere rule of Puritan government for eleven years. But in that year, Charles Stuart, the son of the executed king, Charles I, returned from exile in Europe to claim the throne of England. The new king and his courtiers were determined to have fun— so much so that Charles II became known as "the Merry Monarch." He reopened the theaters, which had been closed by the Puritans. He also allowed women to appear onstage. Previously, all the parts in plays were taken by men and boys.

Even by the standards of the time, Charles was a particularly "active" monarch between the sheets. He had at least fifteen mistresses. Previous kings usually insisted on their mistresses being highborn titled women, preferably married, but Charles wasn't so fussy. If he liked the look of a woman, her social status was of no interest to him. And he had a particular penchant for actresses. The Puritans, although defeated in the civil war, hadn't gone away and they hated Charles. They described him as "that great enemy of chastity and marriage."

Just before he returned to England, he met the tall, voluptuous, and beautiful Barbara Palmer. Born Barbara Villiers, she had married Roger Palmer in 1659, when she was eighteen. Palmer's father disliked her and told his son she would make him miserable. He turned out to be a pretty good judge of character. Villiers had been a courtesan since the age of fifteen, when she became the Earl of Chesterfield's lover. She had been born into an aristocratic family, but her father, Viscount Grandison, blew his fortune on horses and his regiment, leaving his widow penniless when he died. Without any family wealth to speak of, Barbara's marriage prospects were ruined, and as a result, she sought lovers who could support her financially. She evidently enjoyed the fruits of her racy lifestyle, because she continued as Chesterfield's lover after her marriage to Palmer. She would go on to have six children, none of them by her husband. Five were fathered by King Charles, and the sixth is thought to have been fathered by another of her lovers, her second cousin John Churchill. Barbara traveled to the Continent shortly after her marriage to carry messages from royalists to the king in exile. As soon as Charles saw the tall, beautiful, auburn-haired Barbara, he wanted her. In no time at all, she was his mistress.

Charles spent his first night in London as king with her, and she fell pregnant very soon afterwards. Roger Palmer was compensated for his wife's service as the king's mistress by being made Earl of Castlemaine. Barbara thus became Lady Castlemaine. She felt so secure in her position as royal favorite that she had her second child at Hampton Court Palace while the king and his new wife, Catherine of Braganza, were away on their honeymoon. Theirs was a dynastic marriage, allying England with Portugal against their common enemy, Spain. Catherine brought with her a huge dowry in cash plus the territories of Tangier and Bombay, and trading privileges in Brazil and the East Indies. In return, Portugal got the promise of English military support. Catherine's job was to provide Charles with an heir, but while Charles had no difficulty in fathering children by his mistresses, Catherine suffered a series of miscarriages. She must have felt increasing pressure to deliver the goods for the king, but she was never able to have the desired child.

Most royal mistresses either avoided the queen or tried to get on with her, but Barbara constantly fought with Catherine. They loathed each other. The king's chief adviser hated Barbara, too. He was Edward Hyde, Earl of Clarendon and the king's chancellor, who also happened to be her cousin. He hated her because he felt her behavior shamed and embarrassed his family. Despite the queen's dislike of Barbara, Charles appointed her lady of the bedchamber, the queen's personal attendant. He made it clear that she, not the queen, was his favorite. He said, "whosoever I find to be my Lady Castlemaine's enemy in this matter, I do promise upon my word to be his enemy so long as I live." He ignored the queen's complaints about Barbara and disregarded her threats to go home to Portugal. Barbara, who clearly felt safe in her position as the king's favorite, eventually went too far. She ran up enormous debts by buying jewelry she couldn't afford. By then, her husband had left her and obtained a legal separation to protect himself from her debts. It was the king who paid up to cover what she owed. She was, in effect, helping herself to the king's privy purse, his own personal money. During the 1660s and 1670s, she applied herself to the serious business of amassing the biggest fortune she could get her hands on. Her avarice was legendary. Charles finally tired of her temper tantrums and demands. He moved her out of court, pensioned her off, and advised her to live quietly and cause no scandal. He gave her Berkshire House to get her out of court and gave her a handful of new titles—Baroness Nonsuch, Countess of Southampton, and Duchess of Cleveland—to keep her quiet.

In 1705, Barbara married Major General Robert "Beau" Fielding. But they had both lied to each other with disastrous results for Fielding. Fielding thought Barbara was a wealthy woman, but she'd spent her fortune. And she thought he was single, but he wasn't. His wife was still alive. Bizarrely, he had married her thinking she was a completely different woman! Then, just over two weeks later, he married Barbara. When his deception was discovered, his marriage to the duchess was annulled and he was charged with bigamy. Barbara Palmer, Duchess of Cleveland, died in 1709. She had been suffering from dropsy, swelling of the body's soft tissue due to the accumulation of fluid (known as edema today).

Meanwhile Charles, determined not to be dominated by any one woman again, embarked on a series of affairs. He didn't get it all his own way, however. One of the queen's ladies-in-waiting, Frances Teresa Stewart, was said by the diarist Samuel Pepys to be the greatest beauty he ever saw. Charles evidently liked the look of her, too, because he became infatuated with her.

However, she declined to be his mistress. She achieved a measure of immortality in another way when her face was used as the model for Britannia, the personification of Britain. Britannia has appeared on countless British banknotes and coins.

In May 1670, Charles's sister, Henrietta Anne, wife of Philippe I, Duke of Orléans, traveled from France to England for a short visit. She was accompanied by her lady-in-waiting, Louise de Kérouaille. When Henrietta Anne died after returning to France, Louis XIV sent Louise back to England to console Charles and also to spy on his royal court. After a brief resistance to his advances, she was soon consoling the king in his bedchamber and in due course gave birth to his son. She would remain his mistress for the rest of his life . . . along with his many other mistresses!

SCANDAL SHEETS

Coincidentally, at the time when England's most lascivious monarch for more than a hundred years took the reins of power, some of the first pamphlets and newssheets were being published for an increasingly literate population.

The forerunners of newspapers in the English-speaking world were small pamphlets called newsbooks and corantos. They were published irregularly, only when something newsworthy happened. They appeared first on the Continent, especially in Amsterdam, from where English and French translations were sent out to other countries. Regular weekly and, later, daily newspapers followed. At first, these newssheets and pamphlets dealt in factual reports of affairs of state, wars, trade, and business, but they increasingly covered local news and events, too. And their writers weren't afraid to ridicule or condemn the behavior of the aristocracy. Many of them weren't averse to publishing accounts that were little more than rumor.

Laws were already in place to enable people to defend their reputation against scurrilous gossip printed about them. In addition, a new law of seditious libel made it illegal to criticize public persons, the government, or the king. The maximum penalty was life imprisonment. In the seventeenth century, the courts were overwhelmed with libel cases brought by the government against printers in an attempt to restrict the freedom of the press to comment on royal and government activities.

The new libel law also marked the beginning of the end for the age-old pastime of English gentlemen—dueling. A gentleman whose character or reputation was insulted could take his case to the courts instead of risking life and limb (and a potential murder charge) with pistol or sword in a duel.

THE MISTRESS WHO MARRIED A KING . . . OR DID SHE?—LUCY WALTER

One of Charles II's mistresses made a claim that threatened to change the course of English history. Lucy Walter was born at Roch Castle in Wales in about 1630. When she was eight years old, her family moved to London. Soon afterwards, her father abandoned them. By then, the English Civil War had broken out. It was a war for the future of England, fought between Parliament and King Charles I. Lucy's family sided with the king. As a consequence, Roch Castle was captured and burned by Parliament's troops in 1644. Meanwhile, Lucy's parents spent years fighting each other over money and property.

At about this time, Lucy traveled to the Continent, where, in 1648, she met the eighteen-year-old Charles, then the Prince of Wales and heir to the English throne. The circumstances of their meeting are unknown. She may have been the mistress of Robert Sidney, one of Charles's personal servants. She became pregnant shortly after their meeting and gave birth to Charles's son in Rotterdam in April 1649. The boy was named James. By his fourth birthday he had been created Duke of Monmouth.

Meanwhile in England, Parliament's forces won the civil war and put the king, Charles I, on trial for treason. He was found guilty and sentenced to death. On January 30, 1649, he stepped onto a scaffold outside the Banqueting House on Whitehall in London and was executed. The identity of his executioner remains unknown to this day. The crowd that had gathered to watch the king die groaned loudly as his head was severed by a single blow of the ax. They had witnessed something previously unimaginable, the judicial killing of an English king who ruled as God's chosen sovereign on earth.

As soon as Lucy had given birth to her son, she left the baby behind in Rotterdam and rushed to Paris to be with the dead king's son, Charles, who was indulging in a string of affairs. In 1650, he traveled to Scotland, where he had been proclaimed King Charles II after his father's execution. His forces invaded England in an attempt to claim the throne. Meanwhile, Lucy gave birth to a second child, a daughter, in 1651. Charles could have been the father, but there were at least two other suspects.

LUCY'S "BLACK BOX"

Charles's invasion of England ended in defeat at the Battle of Worcester on September 3, 1651. He fled into exile on the Continent. On arrival, he made it clear to Lucy that she was no longer his mistress. She returned to London. Charles was rumored to have offered her money to stop her from publishing "certain papers" she kept in a "black box." Soon after her arrival in London, she was arrested and sent to the Tower of London as a suspected royalist spy. She didn't help her case by claiming to be Charles's wife. An investigation failed to prove her guilt, so she was deported back to the Continent.

She neglected her son's education and became an embarrassment to Charles, so much so that she was considered to be a threat to a possible restoration of the monarchy in England. But Lucy had the upper hand, because she had Charles's son and her mysterious black box of papers. Charles arranged for Lucy and her son to lodge with Sir Arthur Slingsby in Brussels, but this was no act of kindness. Charles had an ulterior motive. Slingsby had been instructed by Charles to get the boy away from Lucy. When Slingsby threatened to have her arrested for failing to pay her bills, she grabbed her son and ran out into the street with him, crying, shouting, and generally making as much noise as possible to attract attention. When a passerby tried to help her, Slingsby explained that he was under orders from Charles, causing Charles even more embarrassment. He now made it known that anyone helping or supporting Lucy in any way would earn his displeasure. She responded by threatening to publish all the letters he had written to her unless he paid her a pension. Threatening someone as powerful as Charles was a risky venture.

Another of Charles's agents, Edward Prodgers, tried once more to get the king's son away from Lucy, but he failed. By then, she was so worn out and ill that she finally gave in and handed the boy over to Charles, who threatened to disown him if she ever tried to get him back. He needn't have worried, because she was so ill that she lived for just a few months more.

She died before the end of 1658 of, according to one account, a disease "incident to her profession," or in other words, a sexually transmitted disease.

The question of whether Charles married Lucy Walter led to a rebellion that attempted to depose the next king, James II. The crown passed to James (Charles's brother), because Charles had no legitimate heirs. The matter of Charles's marriage to Lucy was important because if they had married, their son, the Duke of Monmouth, would have been the legitimate heir to the throne, not James. But if they were never married, Monmouth had no claim. The debate went on for years. Those who feared a Catholic successor to Charles supported Monmouth's claim. When Charles II died on February 6, 1685, Monmouth set sail for England to claim the throne. His army met the new king's army at the Battle of Sedgemoor. Monmouth lost and was arrested. He was taken to Tower Hill in London and executed on July 15, 1685.

The Orange-Seller, the Spy, and the Italian Temptress— Nell Gwyn, Louise de Kérouaille, and Hortense Mancini

The mistress most famously associated with Charles II is Nell Gwyn. She sold oranges, sixpence each, to theatergoers in the pit in front of the stage. Another of the orange-sellers was her sister, Rose. Nell was barely twelve years old and already a mistress, possibly kept by a man known as Captain Duncan. She had grown up in Coal Yard Alley in a poor slum of London. Her father was a soldier who had died in prison. Her mother sold beer in a brothel until she drowned in a ditch where she'd fallen down drunk. Nell probably worked in the brothel, too, serving customers beer. What she lacked in education and status, she made up for with wit and loud, earthy humor.

Actors began to notice the pretty young orange-seller working below their stage and thought she had the potential to be an actress herself. John

Lacy taught her to dance, and Charles Hart, thought by some to be the great-nephew of William Shakespeare, gave her acting lessons. She also became Hart's mistress. By the age of fifteen, she was a professional actress at the King's Playhouse on Bridges Street, London. Theaters have stood on this site since 1663, making it the oldest continuously occupied theater site in London. The current building is the Theatre Royal, Drury Lane.

Audiences loved Nell. She excelled in comedies and wasn't averse to ad-libbing to liven up a flagging production. But two major disasters interrupted the early years of her new career. A plague epidemic swept through London in 1665. It was the last major plague outbreak in England, and it caused widespread panic. Anyone who could leave the capital fled to escape the deadly disease. The lord mayor of London introduced orders to try to prevent the spread of infection. Every parish had to appoint examiners, watchmen, and searchers. Anyone who was appointed and refused to serve could be imprisoned. Examiners were tasked with recording which people in which houses had been infected with plague. Every infected house was to be assigned two watchmen, one for the day and one for the night, to stop anyone entering or leaving the house. If the watchman had to leave, he was instructed to lock the house and take the key with him. Searchers, invariably women, were instructed to search for bodies and summon a physician to ascertain whether the cause of death was plague. Cats and dogs were suspected of spreading the disease, so tens of thousands of them were killed.

Nell was one of the many citizens who fled from the capital. She made for Oxford. The king sought sanctuary in Oxford, too. It may have been more than coincidence. The King's Playhouse actors may have put on some private performances to keep the king and his court amused during their time away from London. By February 1666, the epidemic was in decline and the king returned to London. One sixth of the capital's population had died.

A GREAT FIRE

Just seven months later, as life was returning to normal and Nell resumed her work on the stage, a small fire started in Thomas Farriner's bakery on Pudding Lane. In the early hours of a Sunday morning, it grew and spread. When it was discovered, the lord mayor, Thomas Bloodworth, was roused from his sleep and summoned so that he could give his permission for buildings to be pulled down to create firebreaks. However, he was singularly unimpressed with the fire. He dismissed it as of no significance, saying, "A woman might piss it out!" before leaving to resume his night's sleep. His lack of action enabled the fire to spread further. It quickly developed into a conflagration that became known as the Great Fire of London. It destroyed more than thirteen thousand houses, dozens of churches, and Saint Paul's Cathedral. Tens of thousands of Londoners were made homeless. At the same time, England was fighting the second of four wars with the Dutch. The war ended in 1667 with a humiliating defeat for England.

Even so, it wasn't long before London's theaters were in business again. Despite plague, war, and fire on an epic scale, people wanted to be entertained. The King's Playhouse was often visited by Charles and his courtiers. Some of its actresses hoped to be whisked away to a life of luxury as the wife or mistress of an aristocrat. Nell had the misfortune to be chosen by an admirer who turned out to have no money. Fortunately, she had also been noticed by two noblemen close to the king, the Earl of Rochester and the Duke of Buckingham. They found her a better prospect as a lover—Lord Buckhurst. Buckhurst offered her one hundred pounds a year to become his mistress. She spent an idyllic summer with him and decided not to return to the theater. However, after a few months, their relationship was over and Nell was back at work onstage.

Buckingham and Rochester came to her aid again. They were looking for a new mistress for the king to replace Barbara Palmer. Another young actress, Moll Davis, snared the king first, but he showed no interest in retaining her services. There is a story that Nell tried to spoil Moll's chances by doctoring some of her tea cakes with laxative before she was due to spend a night with the king!

ODDSFISH!

A few months later, Nell went to the theater to see a play and found the king sitting in the next box. They got talking, and when the play was finished they had supper together in a nearby tavern. Charles had no money with him, so Nell had to pay! Mimicking the king, she said, "Oddsfish! But this is the poorest company I ever was in." He was delighted by her. Her honesty was a refreshing change from the sycophants at court. She continued working as an actress while also visiting the king as his mistress. When news of her relationship with the king became public knowledge, bigger audiences came to see her. But as the king's demands increased, she had less and less time to appear onstage.

On May 8, 1670, she gave birth to the king's son and, with the king's permission, called him Charles. Soon after baby Charles was born, Nell was pregnant again. The king now set her up in her own house in a fashionable part of London.

A FRENCH SPY AT COURT

Nell faced no competition for the king's affections until the arrival at court of Louise de Kérouaille, a French noblewoman. She had been trained as a courtesan by her own parents in the hope of becoming a mistress to Louis XIV. She failed, but was then sent to England to spy on Charles. When he saw her, he was immediately attracted to her. To keep her close, he appointed her lady-in-waiting to the queen. Meanwhile, Nell gave birth to a boy on Christmas Day 1671. She called him James after the king's brother. Soon afterwards, she retired from the theater. Now it was Louise's turn to fall pregnant by the king. She gave birth to a boy on July 29, 1672. She suggested to the king that a title would be a fitting gift for her. He acquiesced and created her Duchess of Portsmouth. She was now a serious rival to Nell for the king's affections. Nell mocked her mercilessly and nicknamed her Squintabella after her eye defect. Unlike Nell, Louise took the trouble to form alliances and friendships at court. However, the public never took to her because she was an aristocrat, foreign, Catholic, and, worst still, French. When an anti-Catholic mob stopped a carriage, thinking Louise was inside, Nell appeared at its window and calmed the angry crowd by shouting that she was the king's *Protestant* whore. Nell was never given a title, because of her slum-poor origins, but her royal-blooded sons were. Belatedly, she realized the importance of having friends in high places. She even befriended the queen. Ambassadors, even French ambassadors, soon learned that the best way to reach the king was to bypass the bureaucracy and intrigue at court and go straight to Nell.

Nell's position seemed assured when Louise caught the pox and blamed the king, risking his wrath by accusing him of consorting with common prostitutes. She was no longer the elegant woman who had turned the king's head when she arrived at court. She had put on a lot of weight, earning her the unflattering nickname "Fubbs." But just as Nell was feeling secure in her position, another rival for the king's affections appeared—Hortense Mancini.

Hortense was one of the Mazarinettes, the seven nieces of France's chief minister, Cardinal Mazarin. Two of her sisters, Marie and Olympia, had affairs with King Louis XIV. Hortense had moved from Italy to Paris with her mother, her sister Marie, and her brother Philippe in 1654, when she was only eight years old. She discovered that her uncle, Cardinal Mazarin, lived in astonishing luxury there, having amassed a huge fortune. When her mother died from a mysterious fever two years later, the cardinal took responsibility for Hortense and her siblings. His priority was to arrange advantageous marriages for them. The exiled heir to the English throne, Charles Stuart, had volunteered himself as a husband for Hortense, but the cardinal thought he was a poor marriage prospect with an uncertain future. However, just a few months later, England restored its monarchy and the poor marriage prospect became King Charles II . . . but he was no longer interested in marrying an obscure niece of a French government minister.

The fourteen-year-old Hortense was married to a man who had been obsessed with her for years—Armand-Charles de La Porte, duc de La Meilleraye. Just over a week after they were married, Cardinal Mazarin died. Hortense and her new husband, now the duc and duchesse de Mazarin, moved into the cardinal's palatial residence. Armand-Charles turned out to be an insanely jealous husband. He hated seeing Hortense having fun with anyone else, so he stopped her friends from calling on her and insisted that she accompany him everywhere he went. Not surprisingly, given their enforced closeness, she gave birth to four children in rapid succession. His behavior became increasingly bizarre and threatening until Hortense could stand it no longer. She fled from him to join her sister Marie, Princess Colonna, in Rome. After four years in Rome, she decided to return to France and deal with her husband once and for all.

When Armand-Charles learned that his wife had arrived back in France, he tried to have her arrested, but the king stepped in and stopped it. Armand-Charles was so angry that he burst into the Mazarin palace and attacked its priceless collection of paintings and statues with a hammer and black paint. Once again, the king intervened, but Hortense's well-being wasn't his main concern. He wanted the problem to go away, so he offered Hortense a handsome pension of her own if she would be reconciled with her husband and live with him again as the dutiful wife polite society expected her to be. But it was too much to ask. In February 1671, she fled Paris again for Rome. However, just as Hortense began to enjoy her freedom and independence, her sister Marie's marriage collapsed. The two sisters went on the run.

Too recognizable together, they split up. Hortense stayed in Chambéry in Savoy, an independent state where she would be beyond the reach of France and Italy, while Marie headed for Paris to appeal to the king for help. He agreed to let her live in a convent near Paris and to support her financially. However, she soon tired of convent life and left. She traveled around Europe, looking for a place where she could be free and happy, eventually settling in Madrid.

Meanwhile, Hortense began enjoying her new life in Savoy. She attended salons and hunting parties, and wrote her memoirs. However, trouble was brewing. The wife of the head of state, Charles-Emmanuel, thought her husband was paying far too much attention to the beautiful young Hortense. There was also tension between Hortense's French staff and the local people. When Charles-Emmanuel died in June 1675, his wife immediately told Hortense to leave. She decided to move to England.

UPSETTING THE APPLECART

The twenty-nine-year-old Italian beauty arrived in London at the end of 1675. When King Charles saw her, he was instantly infatuated. Louise de Kérouaille reacted with fury. The French government wasn't happy either, because Louise was an important informant, relaying information to France from within the English court. There were fears that Hortense could upset this useful arrangement. Nell Gwyn was less troubled. She thought the king would soon discard Hortense. But Hortense was no passing fancy. She quickly replaced Louise in the king's affections and moved into an apartment in Whitehall that had been occupied by a previous mistress, Barbara Palmer. The king spent his afternoons with Hortense, his evenings with Nell, and attended occasional parties with Louise. Sometimes, he played cards with all three of them. Hortense could have spent the rest of her days in this comfortable position, but she seemed to be incapable of acting in her own best interests. She began a liaison with a visiting nobleman, the Count of Monaco.

When the king found out, his affection for her ebbed away. She was able to continue living in London only because the king didn't cut off his financial support for her.

In 1678, Hortense's sister Marie had a meeting with her husband, Lorenzo, when he arrived in Spain, having managed to get himself appointed Viceroy of Aragon. When she discovered that he was plotting to have her locked up, she ran to the French ambassador and begged for asylum. However, on Louis XIV's instructions, she was denied help. A few days later, guards broke into her home, dragged her out, and took her to the Alcázar fortress in Segovia. Several months after that, she was taken to a convent in Madrid as a novitiate nun and told that she would remain there for the rest of her life. Lorenzo left Madrid and returned to Rome, where he died in 1689.

In the early 1680s, Charles II's health began to deteriorate. He had been a very sporty king, keen on riding and hunting, but by 1684, he felt able to do little more than go for short walks. On February 2, 1685, he suffered an apoplectic fit and died four days later. Any sudden death in the seventeenth century was liable to be described as apoplexy. The actual cause might be a heart attack, a stroke, or something similar. Charles's symptoms are thought to indicate kidney failure. As he lay dying, none of his mistresses were allowed to visit him. On his deathbed, he famously said of Nell Gwyn, "Let not poor Nelly starve." He is also reported to have said of Louise de Kérouaille (Duchess of Portsmouth), "Do well by Portsmouth." Just before he died, he was received into the Catholic Church.

The new king, James II, settled Nell Gwyn's debts and paid her a pension of £1,500 a year. Nell herself suffered a stroke just two years later and died on November 14, 1687, at the age of only thirty-seven. After Charles's death, Louise de Kérouaille left for France, where she lived until her death on November 14, 1734, at the age of eighty-five. Hortense was very well looked after by the new king because her cousin was James's queen, Mary of Modena.

In 1689, a French court ruled on a case brought against Hortense by her husband. The court found in his favor and ordered Hortense to return home. She said she would rather die than go back to her husband. During the 1690s, friends noticed that she was drinking excessively and neglecting her health. Her condition steadily worsened until she died on June 11, 1699. Her husband wanted her body returned to him, but her creditors refused to let it go until he settled her debts. Bizarrely, when he got it back, he took it with him on his travels around France for several months before reluctantly agreeing to allow her burial.

AN UNPOPULAR KING—JAMES II

James II proved to be an unpopular king because of his favorable treatment of English Catholics and conflict with Parliament. He believed in the divine right of kings, and so he treated Parliament's views as mere advice that he was entitled to ignore. When his relationship with Parliament became more troublesome, his response was to dismiss it altogether and rule on his own.

Despite James's conversion to Catholicism, he continued to pursue mistresses. He was just as much of a rake and a libertine as Charles had been. He had at least eleven mistresses, although few of them have left their mark on history. James preferred young, plain-looking girls in their teens. Perhaps he found them less threatening than the volatile and often demanding beauties pursued by his predecessors.

The first mistress of any note was Anne Hyde. She met James briefly in 1656. Three years later, they met again. This meeting quickly led to romance and a pregnancy. Unusually for an aristocrat, James married his pregnant mistress. He had rashly promised to marry her, and his brother Charles insisted that he keep his promise. By then, the monarchy had been restored in England and Charles was king. James's marriage wasn't officially announced, and when news leaked out, no one could quite believe that the king's brother had married a commoner—not only that, but a commoner who had worked as a servant at court (a maid of honor to Mary, the Princess Royal). Samuel Pepys, the famous diarist, recorded his thoughts on the matter in characteristically blunt terms: "that he doth get a wench with child and marries her afterward, it is as if a man should shit in his hat and then wear it."

James and Anne Hyde would go on to have eight children, although only two would survive, both girls. And they both became queens of England—Anne and Mary II. During her pregnancies, James reverted to type and took a series of mistresses. In rapid succession, he bedded Lady Anne Carnegie, Lady Elizabeth Chesterfield, Miss Goditha Price, and Lady Margaret Denham. Lady Denham's sudden and rather inconvenient death left a vacancy. To fill it, he discovered Arabella Churchill, sister of the great military commander, John Churchill, and an ancestor of Britain's greatest modern leader, Sir Winston Churchill.

Arabella wasn't a great beauty according to the prevailing tastes of the time, which favored voluptuous, curvaceous women. She was described by the Count de Grammont as tall, pale-faced, and nothing but skin and bone. According to one story, she came to James's attention when he saw her fall from her horse while hunting and land awkwardly, revealing her attractive legs. Their relationship lasted for nearly ten years and produced four illegitimate children. By then, James's wife, Anne Hyde, had died and James had converted to Catholicism. It took two years to find another wife for him. The "lucky" girl was the fifteen-year-old Mary of Modena, who saw James for the first time on the day they married. Mary, a Catholic, was described by James's opponents as "an agent of the pope."

In 1678, Arabella had the misfortune to reach the great age of thirty. James lost interest in her, abandoned her, and traded her in for a younger model, the twenty-year-old Catherine Sedley, who worked for his wife. Catherine's mother had been driven to insanity by her father's philandering and incarcerated in a convent for the rest of her life. Like Arabella, Catherine didn't conform to the prevailing idea of beauty. She was described as ugly, thin, flat-chested, and squint-eyed, but James saw something lovable in her. When he became king in 1685, he made her Countess of Dorchester, but he faced increasing opposition to her from the church and his wife.

Catherine's time at court ended in 1688 when James fled from Britain after the Protestant William, Prince of Orange, was invited by influential English Protestants to invade and seize the throne. The trigger for the invasion was the birth of a son to James and Mary, presenting the country with the deeply unpopular prospect of a Catholic succession. The invasion was successful, and William reigned as King William III jointly with his wife, Mary II (James's Protestant daughter with Anne Hyde). After the sexually indulgent James II and Charles II, William III took only one mistress during his reign. She was Elizabeth Villiers, a cousin of Barbara Villiers/Palmer, one of Charles II's many mistresses. Elizabeth had gone to Holland in 1677 as a servant of William's new wife, Mary. The newly married William was instantly attracted to Elizabeth. When his wife discovered the relationship, she was distraught, although, as James II's daughter and Charles II's niece, she surely must have known that such arrangements were commonplace in royal circles. She was eventually persuaded to accept William's mistress. But William had so few women as friends and so many close male friends that his sexuality was the subject of gossip, especially among his Catholic French and Jacobite enemies.

RIGGING THE SUCCESSION

William III was succeeded by James II's other daughter, Anne, in 1702. She was acceptable to Parliament because she had been brought up as a Protestant, but when she died without any surviving children in 1714, the strongest claimants to the throne were all Catholic. Parliament was determined that a Catholic monarch would never sit on the British throne again. Parliament had already anticipated the succession issue and dealt with it by passing the Act of Settlement in 1701. This extraordinary Act of Parliament stated that on Anne's death, more than fifty Catholic claimants to the British throne would be passed over in favor of the closest Protestant claimant, Sophia, Electress of Hanover. The electors belonged to an elite group of European leaders empowered to elect the Holy Roman Emperor. However, Sophia didn't live long enough to inherit the British throne. It was her son, George, who became king, the first of a line of Georges.

The Georgians treated mistresses as a necessary part of being king, but their hearts weren't really in it. They had a reputation for being grumpy or insane or both, but they oversaw dramatic changes in Britain. Between the reigns of George I and George III (from 1714 to 1820), Britain's population almost doubled, the American colonies declared their independence and successfully fought for it, the Industrial Revolution swept through Britain, and there was a mass movement of people from the countryside to the new factories in the towns and cities. The Georges also had to deal with endless wars in Europe, two Jacobite rebellions at home, and uprisings in Ireland. And there was a financial scandal, the South Sea Bubble, that discredited the monarchy and the government and almost bankrupted the country. With all of that on their plate, perhaps it isn't surprising that they had little time for mistresses!

THE KING AND THE MAYPOLE—
EHRENGARD MELUSINE

King George I already had a wife, a mistress, and an illegitimate child by the time he became king in 1714. The child was the product of a short affair with his sister's undergoverness in 1676, when he was only sixteen years old. However, it didn't interrupt the serious business of finding an appropriate wife for him. The woman who was selected, Sophia Dorothea of Celle (in Lower Saxony, Germany), was chosen to form an alliance between Hanover and Celle. She wasn't exactly a willing spouse. When she was told whom she was to marry, she shouted, "I will not marry the pig snout!" (George's unflattering nickname in Hanover), and she fainted when she met him for the first time. Nevertheless, the marriage took place on November 22, 1682. Dissatisfaction set in very quickly. George was always either away at war or dealing with affairs of state, leaving his wife on her own for long periods of time. Even when they were together, they constantly argued. Soon after their first daughter was born in 1687, George almost strangled his wife in public. It marked the end of their life together. From then on, they wanted nothing to do with each other. Then in 1690, Ehrengard Melusine von der Schulenburg arrived in Hanover. Somehow, the eternally busy George managed to find time for her.

Melusine was born in Emden, Germany, on December 25, 1667, to a minor aristocratic family. She failed to find a husband, so she was going to have to work for her living. Her family was delighted when in 1689, at the age of twenty-two, she found a position as maid of honor to George's mother, Sophia, Electress of Hanover.

It wasn't long before George noticed Melusine. He evidently lost no time in cultivating her friendship. They found that they shared interests in art, music, and architecture. George's mother disapproved of the relationship and was openly rude about Melusine, who was unfashionably thin, earning her the nicknames "scarecrow" and "maypole." Even so, George's friendship with her quickly turned into something more intimate, because she was pregnant barely a year later. She gave birth to Anna Luise Sophie von der Schulenburg in 1692. Another daughter followed the next year, and a third girl in 1701, but George never acknowledged the three girls as his children.

By the time their third illegitimate daughter arrived, George's marriage had been dissolved in dramatic circumstances.

A SCANDAL AT COURT

George's wife, Sophia Dorothea, had met a tall and handsome Swedish count, Philip Christoph von Königsmarck. Their friendship was to cost him his life. According to some accounts, they had met and flirted with each other when Sophia Dorothea was sixteen. When they met again in 1688, they were initially no more than friends. However, they grew closer over the next couple of years and embarked on a more intimate relationship. Somehow, their love letters to each other (or possibly forgeries) reached her father-in-law. George's extramarital affairs and illegitimate children, although disapproved of, had no constitutional significance, but any affair involving Sophia Dorothea was completely forbidden. If she were to give birth to a child whose parentage was in doubt, it could jeopardize the succession, so it was vital to end her affair one way or another.

On July 1, 1694, Philip visited the Leineschloss palace in Hanover to see Sophia Dorothea. He was never seen alive again. He is thought to have been murdered on the orders of George's father, Elector Ernst August. His body was never found. One report speculated that it may have been weighted down and thrown into the river Leine, which runs past the palace. Sophia Dorothea was arrested and sent back to Celle, where she was imprisoned in Ahlden Castle. Her marriage to George was dissolved on December 28, 1694, and she was held at the castle until her death more than thirty years later. She was never allowed to see her children, causing a rift between George and his eldest son, George Augustus (born in 1683). George became Elector in 1698 on the death of his father, and Melusine took her position beside him as his official mistress. He was a distant and formal father to his two legitimate children, George Augustus (who later became King George II) and Sophia Dorothea, but Melusine had a close and loving relationship with them.

On June 8, 1714, George's mother died suddenly and unexpectedly. She had been walking in the grounds of her summer palace at Herrenhausen when she was caught in a shower of rain. As she ran for shelter, she suffered a stroke and collapsed. She died moments later. Her claim to the British throne passed to George. Two months later, on August 1, the British queen suffered a stroke and died. George, Elector of Hanover, was now also King George I of Great Britain and Ireland. He was the first British king from the House of Hanover, the royal house that would rule Britain until Queen Victoria.

When George traveled to London as king, Melusine went with him. They set up home in St. James's Palace. Britain was rather different from Hanover in a number of ways. Tiny Hanover had a population of about six hundred thousand, whereas Britain's population numbered nine million, with the addition of a growing empire overseas. Trading with the empire and supplying weapons and materials to the armed forces had made Britain's cities and ports wealthy. George ruled with absolute power in Hanover, but in Britain he found a country where the power of the monarch was limited by Parliament. George had no choice but to work with the government.

In anticipation of a move to England, Melusine had learned to speak English, albeit with a heavy German accent. Over the next few years, George showered her with titles. In 1716, he made her Duchess of Munster, Countess of Dungannon, and Baroness of Dundalk. Then in 1719, he made her Duchess of Kendal, Countess of Faversham, and Baroness of Glastonbury. George's grasp of English was poor, so he surrounded himself with an inner circle of German advisers. This isolated him from his British ministers and courtiers. They quickly learned that if they wanted to reach the king, they had to go through one of his advisers or Melusine, causing further resentment.

Melusine usually had a calming influence on the king, but she failed in one respect—his relationship with his son, George Augustus. They could barely tolerate each other's presence. Their relationship reached a new low in 1716 when the king paid a visit to Hanover and left his son as regent in his place, but refused to grant him the full powers of a regent. He simply didn't trust his son. George Augustus was deeply offended. The following year, the king's interference in choosing godparents for George Augustus's son caused a blazing row. The king banished his son from the palace. His wife went with him, but their children were not allowed to leave. As they were part of the royal family, they were the property of the king. George Augustus took his father to court to try to get his children back, but he lost. The rift between them was complete. George Augustus created a rival court, which became a focus for political opposition to the king. The king responded by cutting off anyone who visited his son. The two courts competed with each other to attract supporters. The rift was dangerous politically as well as a curse on the royal family. There was a reconciliation of sorts in 1720, but it was overshadowed by a great scandal that severely damaged the royal family and the government—the South Sea Bubble.

THE BUBBLE BURSTS

The South Sea Company had been established in 1711. It was granted the sole right to trade with South America, which should have generated substantial profits. Shares in the company rose rapidly in value. Everyone who had some spare money, including members of Parliament, lords, and clergymen, bought shares. Many others who couldn't afford to buy shares from their own resources took out loans to buy them. The company had been set up on the assumption that the War of the Spanish Succession would end with Britain negotiating permission to trade with South America, but this didn't happen, so the company wasn't actually trading or making any money. Nevertheless, investors' confidence in it was boosted in 1718 when the king became its governor and again in 1720 when it took over responsibility for paying off Britain's national debt, which then stood at thirty million pounds.

Inevitably, the inflated share value eventually crashed, and thousands of people lost fortunes. An inquiry found that several government ministers had accepted bribes to push through legislation in favor of the company. Members of Parliament had also been investors in the company, creating a conflict of interest. King George and his mistress attracted personal blame for the mess. Melusine was accused of taking bribes to guarantee the king's support for the company. At the height of the crisis, it was feared that Britain might be overwhelmed by revolution. The mess was eventually sorted out by Robert Walpole, who became Britain's first prime minister. He would go on to dominate British politics for the next two decades.

Having survived the South Sea Bubble, Melusine was quickly plunged into another scandal. In 1722, the king granted her the right to produce Irish coinage. She sold the right to William Wood, as she was entitled to do. However, Wood produced poor-quality coins. The Irish were unhappy with the coins, the fact that they were minted in England, and the tax they were required to pay for them. Melusine got the blame. However, she weathered this storm, too, and King George came to depend increasingly on her, especially in matters of diplomacy with other heads of state.

When the king's estranged and imprisoned wife, Sophia Dorothea, died in 1726, there were rumors that the king married Melusine, who by then had been his mistress for thirty-six years. Contemporary accounts talk about him marrying her "by the left hand." This was a reference to a morganatic marriage, a marriage between two people of different social status or rank so that neither of the spouses nor their children could inherit property or titles from each other. Its name comes from the Latin phrase *matrimonium ad morganaticum,* which describes the ancient Germanic custom of a husband presenting a gift to his wife on the morning after their wedding. So, a morganatic marriage is one in which the wife is entitled to nothing from her husband beyond the morning gift. In the case of King George I and Melusine, historians have not been able to prove or disprove reports that they married.

The king left on one of his many excursions to his beloved Hanover in June 1727. After spending a night in Delden in the Netherlands, he set off on the next leg of his journey—but an hour later, he suddenly collapsed. The royal party continued to his brother's home in Osnabrück, where he died on June 11, at the age of sixty-seven. When Melusine, who was traveling behind him, reached Osnabrück, the king was already dead. When she returned to Britain, she was not allowed to live in any of the royal palaces or houses, so she bought a house in London and also built a country retreat, Kendal House at Isleworth.

There were reports that George had told her he would never leave her, not even in death, and said he would return and visit her after he died if it were possible. When a large raven flew in through her window at Kendal House, she thought it carried the soul of her dead royal lover. However, reports of the "possessed" raven can be traced back to a rather racy publication of the day called the *Good Fellows Calendar,* so there may be no truth in it. In 1728, Melusine's health took a sudden turn for the worse. She was plagued with poor health for the following fifteen years until her death on May 10, 1743, at the age of seventy-six.

The Duelist's Daughter—
Henrietta Howard

King George II, unlike his father, was devoted to his wife, Caroline of Ansbach. His father didn't want him to have a loveless marriage like his own, so in June 1705, he sent the young prince in disguise to check out Caroline before he married her, but she wasn't taken in by his disguise. He was favorably impressed with her, and they were married two months later. However, being happily married didn't stop him from taking mistresses. One of them, more of a dedicated courtesan than a hapless mistress, set out to be noticed by the king in a deliberate attempt to solve her own financial problems.

Henrietta Hobart was born on May 11, 1689. During her childhood she saw a lot of death. When she was just nine years old, her father was killed by a sword wound suffered during a duel. It was the last duel fought in Norfolk, a large rural county in the East of England. Sir Henry Hobart was a Whig politician. When he stood for election in 1698, he was soundly beaten. Then he discovered that a neighbor and political rival, Oliver Le Neve, had been spreading rumors that Sir Henry had displayed cowardice at the Battle of the Boyne in Ireland. Consequently, Hobart blamed Le Neve for his defeat. His response was to challenge Le Neve to a duel. Le Neve had no option but to accept the challenge.

Hobart expected to win because he was an accomplished swordsman. When the two men met, Hobart drew the first blood by slashing Le Neve across his arm. However, in the flash of blades that followed, Le Neve managed to thrust his sword into Hobart's stomach. Fearing that he'd killed Hobart and might be arrested for murder, he made for the east coast port of Yarmouth and escaped to the Continent. Despite the attentions of a surgeon, Sir Henry died the next day.

Soon afterwards, Henrietta's mother died of consumption. Then over the next four years, four of the eight Hobart children died—not unusual in the days before modern medicine, especially antibiotics. Henrietta, sixteen years old in 1705, was the oldest of the surviving children. She appealed to a distant relative, the Countess of Suffolk, for help. When the countess's first husband, Sir John Maynard, died, Henrietta had inherited part of his estate. And now the countess was entrusted with Henrietta's upbringing. The young girl's modest inheritance was enough to attract the interest of Charles Howard, the Earl of Suffolk's son from his first marriage. A few months later, on March 2, 1706, Henrietta and Charles Howard were married. She was now Henrietta Howard.

A few days before the marriage, Henrietta placed most of her inheritance in a trust, thus protecting it from being grabbed by her new husband and guaranteeing a small income for herself. It proved to be a wise move. Charles, a military man, needed money so badly that he sold his army commission. When he'd spent those profits, he took Henrietta's income from her trust and squandered it on drink and gambling. As the couple had little other income, they were soon in debt. Worse still, soon after the marriage, Henrietta discovered that her husband had a violent temper.

Nine months after her wedding, Henrietta gave birth to a son, Henry. The new addition to the family wasn't a source of joy and delight for Charles, who saw his son as yet another drain on the family's limited finances. His response was to go to court to try to get his hands on Henrietta's inheritance, although he would ultimately be unsuccessful. And the novelty of marriage had worn off. He sent Henrietta and her son away to live in lodgings in the country while he stayed in London and returned to his favorite diversions—gambling and whoring. Because of their debts, Charles and Henrietta were both evicted from their respective lodgings. They spent the next few years being evicted from one home after another. Relatives gave them a roof over their head for a while, but they soon tired of Charles's behavior and ordered them to leave. Charles preferred the company of London whores, so he spent little time with his family and was rarely able to pay his bills. He took out his frustration on Henrietta.

SEEKING A ROYAL RESCUE

Henrietta had had enough. She decided to leave Charles, and she had a plan. She sold everything she had to raise enough money to cross the English Channel and make her way to Hanover. Since the Act of Settlement in 1701, Britons had known that the next king or queen of England would come from Hanover. If Henrietta could ingratiate herself with the royal court there, it could pay significant dividends. However, when Charles learned how much money the sale had made, he took it and spent it. She started again, saving as much money as possible and even selling her hair to wig-makers. It took her a year to raise enough money. But she had a change of mind about leaving Charles. She calculated that she had a better chance of securing employment at the Hanoverian court if she and Charles presented themselves together, so, eight years after her wedding, she left her young son behind in England and set out for Hanover with Charles.

Luckily, the electress was keen to meet people from the country she ex-pected to rule in due course, so Henrietta was quickly received at court. And Sophia liked her. Henrietta became a regular visitor at the palace. She also became friends with Princess Caroline, wife of the electress's grandson, George. Sophia promised Henrietta a position at her court when she be-came queen of England. Amazingly, Henrietta's husband, Charles, also man-aged to impress the male members of the royal family enough to be offered a position, too.

When Sophia and Queen Anne died, George and Caroline (now the Prince and Princess of Wales) moved to London with the new king, George I. Charles and Henrietta Howard went with them. After an anxious wait of a few weeks, Henrietta was appointed woman of the bedchamber by Caroline, and Charles was appointed groom of the bedchamber by the king. They now had a regular income and rent-free accommodation at St. James's Palace. Henrietta's plan had actually worked. She proved to be very popular at court. She won the friendship and affection of one courtier after another. One of her admirers was George, Prince of Wales. By then, Henrietta and her husband were not only working apart in different house-holds, but they were also living apart. A liaison with the prince offered Henrietta the possibility of escaping poverty forever. George loved his wife, Caroline, but he saw it as his royal duty to take a mistress. The relationship was one of convenience for both of them. It probably began in 1718, when Princess Caroline, then aged thirty-five, was expecting her seventh baby. It may have been the princess's "unavailability" that prompted the affair.

The Princess of Wales knew about the affair and accepted it as any well-brought-up princess would. It helped that she liked Henrietta. The two women even worked together to persuade the prince to repair his terrible relations with his father. The attempt at a reconciliation failed. Henrietta found it increasingly difficult to serve both the prince, as his mistress, and the princess, as her servant. She was seeing less and less of her friends. The stress of the situation was affecting her health. This was the time Henrietta's husband chose to begin taunting her again. He had renewed his attempt to seize her inheritance.

When the prince learned of her predicament, he decided to help her to deal with her husband. He gave her a fortune in stock, silverware, gold, diamonds, the furniture from her royal apartments, and a shipload of valuable mahogany timber. In the document settling all this property on her, the prince stated explicitly that it was solely for Henrietta and if she chose to use it to buy a house, the house was not to be for the use or benefit of her husband. Henrietta did indeed have a new house built for her. It stood by the river Thames at Twickenham, then a village southwest of London, now part of the capital. The house was designed in the Palladian style that was very popular in Georgian London.

Charles continued to make trouble for his wife. He calculated that if he became enough of a nuisance, the prince might pay him off handsomely to get rid of him and keep him quiet. He took every opportunity to criticize his wife. When he obtained a warrant that enabled him to seize her by force and return her to his home, she was afraid to set foot outside.

THE KING'S MISTRESS

On June 11, 1727, King George I died and his son became King George II. Henrietta was now the king's mistress, which instantly made her a more powerful and influential figure. All manner of lords and ladies sought her assistance in the hope that she had the king's ear and could present their cases to him. Anyone who wanted an important job for himself or a member of his family went to her for help. Queen Caroline was wary of Henrietta's growing influence and treated her as an increasingly troublesome rival. She took every opportunity to undermine Henrietta and sow seeds of doubt about her in the king's mind. The king's desire for Henrietta cooled, and he became more ill-tempered and impatient toward her, although he was still seeing her every day.

Charles thought his wife was in an even better position to help him with his money problems now that she was the king's mistress. Everything else had failed in the past, so this time he made a direct and very noisy approach. He pushed his way into the queen's quarters, shouting loudly for his wife until his way was barred by the queen herself. The noise attracted palace guards, who dragged him out. It was the last straw for Henrietta, who asked a lawyer to begin proceedings for separation. Unfortunately, her lawyer died while preparing her case. She asked the queen if she would pay Charles off, but the queen refused. Perhaps it was too much to expect the queen to pay off the husband of her own husband's mistress. Reluctantly, Henrietta appealed to the king. Despite the cooling of their relationship, he agreed to increase her allowance by precisely the same amount of money that Charles was demanding, enabling her to pay him. Meanwhile, she'd found someone, the Duke of Argyll, to help her with her application for separation. On February 29, 1728, Charles finally accepted that his marriage and his claim on his wife's finances were over, and signed the legal papers agreeing to her separation from him.

Henrietta was delighted. She could finally complete her new home in Twickenham. However, she was unable to move in, because the queen ensured that she was kept busy at court, even when she was ill. She seemed to enjoy inconveniencing her husband's mistress. Life for Henrietta was becoming increasingly lonely. Life expectancy in the eighteenth century was such that at the age of forty, she had already lost many of her former friends and relatives. Even the king was spending less and less time with her, and he was also venting his famously short temper on her more often.

In 1731, her estranged husband became Earl of Suffolk on the death of his brother. Although she was separated from him, they were still married, and so Henrietta became the Countess of Suffolk. Her ennoblement entitled her to a more senior position in the royal household. The queen promoted her to mistress of the robes, the most senior position on the queen's staff. Her income increased and her duties were cut, finally giving her time away from court to enjoy her Twickenham home. It enabled her to make new friends, ending her long period of loneliness. In the early 1730s, she was introduced to George Berkeley, a son of the Earl of Berkeley, and the two became very close friends.

LEAVING COURT

On September 28, 1733, Charles Howard, the husband who had made Henrietta's life such a misery for so long, died. She was finally free of him. She could now enjoy her relationship with Berkeley without fearing an accusation of infidelity or adultery. Her happiness with Berkeley contrasted with her frustration with life at court and the king's temper. During a break from work to recover from a spell of poor health, she was accused of keeping company with the king's political enemies. By the time she returned to court, the identities of her acquaintances had reached the king, who, predictably, flew into a rage at her apparent disloyalty. He refused to see her ever again. She left the royal court for the last time on November 22, 1734. The departure of the king's mistress was the subject of gossip, speculation, and newspaper stories across the country. The queen, who was glad to see the back of her husband's mistress, soon regretted her absence, because she now had to entertain the king herself, listen to his tedious conversation, and endure his flashes of temper without relief. But this was of no concern to Henrietta, who was finally free of it all. In 1735, after a suitably respectable time since her husband's death, she married George Berkeley. They would go on to enjoy eleven happy years of marriage until George's death in 1746.

Meanwhile at court, the queen had tried to find a suitable replacement for Henrietta to amuse her husband—that is, a woman who would entertain him harmlessly and discreetly while presenting no challenge to the queen. She tried to interest him in Camilla, Countess of Tankerville, but George had other plans. He had already found someone. After a short dalliance with Mary Scott, Countess of Deloraine, he had become besotted with Amalie Sophie Marianne von Wallmoden during a visit to Hanover. This dark, voluptuous beauty was more than twenty years younger than he. Within a few months of their meeting, she was pregnant. Several men could have been the father, but she assured the king that the baby was his. The queen's patience was sorely tested when George hung a full-length portrait of his new mistress by his bed!

The king spent so much time in Hanover with his mistress instead of in Britain with his queen that public opinion turned against him. The queen suggested that George should bring his new mistress to London and move her into Henrietta's old royal apartments. It might seem to be a very strange thing to do, but she hoped that keeping Madam Wallmoden close would enable the queen to control her as she'd controlled Henrietta. However, the queen's health was failing. The king was oblivious until she collapsed in agony on November 9, 1737. Her physicians administered a series of gruesome treatments. She was bled and purged, but when these remedies proved ineffective, she endured a horrific exploratory surgical operation without anesthetic. This revealed large abscesses in her abdomen. Eighteenth-century medicine had no answer for this, and the queen never recovered. She died on November 20, 1737, at the age of fifty-four. Just before she died, she is said to have asked the king if he planned to marry again, but he said, "No, I shall have mistresses." The king mourned her passing, genuinely distressed, for several months.

Madam Wallmoden arrived in London in June 1738. Her husband was less accommodating than other cuckolds in similar circumstances. He divorced her the following year. In 1740, she became a British citizen and was made Countess of Yarmouth by the king.

Henrietta outlived the king, who met a rather undignified end. On October 25, 1760, he rose from bed and visited his water closet. Soon afterwards, a loud thud was heard from inside. An attendant ran in to find the king lying on the floor. Doctors were summoned, and the king was lifted from the floor to his bed, where he was found to be dead. An autopsy revealed that the right ventricle of his heart had ruptured. As he had outlived his son, he was succeeded by his grandson, George William Frederick. The new king, George III, cleared the royal court of every sign of his grandfather, including his mistress. The Countess of Yarmouth was evicted from her apartment and returned to Hanover, where she died from breast cancer five years later. The king also stopped paying Henrietta Howard's royal pension. By 1766, she was suffering from painful gout, but she managed to attend a friend's New Year party. However, she sat so close to the fire to keep warm that her clothes caught fire and she was badly burned. She recovered, but on July 27, 1767, she collapsed while preparing for bed and died half an hour later.

THE DANDY PRINCE

Like his grandfather and great-grandfather, George III wasn't much of a ladies' man. There were rumors that he secretly married a Quaker girl called Hannah Lightfoot, but there appears to be no evidence to support this. History records that he married Princess Charlotte of Mecklenburg-Strelitz on September 8, 1761. They met for the first time on the day they were married. Despite this, they enjoyed a happy marriage that produced fifteen children— nine sons and six daughters. Two of their sons became kings of the United Kingdom—George IV and William IV.

George IV was self-centered, flamboyant, and fashion conscious, something of a dandy. He had terrible relationships with both his father and his wife, Princess Caroline of Brunswick, who was also his first cousin. After the birth of their only child, Princess Charlotte, they lived apart for the next twenty-five years, leaving the field open to ambitious social climbers and gold diggers. Caroline left the country and lived abroad, but when George became king in 1820, she returned to Britain to claim her position as queen. George despised her and wanted rid of her. However, at that time, a married couple could divorce only if one of them was guilty of adultery. Neither George nor Caroline would admit to adultery, so George had a bill, called the Pains and Penalties Bill, presented to Parliament in an attempt to have the marriage dissolved. Its intention was to "deprive Her Majesty Queen Caroline Amelia Elizabeth of the Title, Prerogatives, Rights, Privileges, and Exemptions of Queen Consort of this Realm; and to dissolve the Marriage between His Majesty and the said Caroline Amelia Elizabeth." The stated reason for dissolving the marriage was Caroline's alleged adultery with "a foreigner of low station," namely Bartolomeo Pergami, a member of staff she had hired in Italy.

The House of Lords, Parliament's upper house, debated the bill, but this wasn't a polite discussion between a bunch of stuffy lords in ermine. It was nothing less than a public trial of the queen. Witnesses were called to give evidence against her and then they were cross-examined by the queen's legal team. Newspapers reveled in all the salacious details. When the vote was finally taken, the bill passed with a very narrow majority, but to become an Act of Parliament, it would also have to be passed by Parliament's lower house, the House of Commons. However, when the Commons saw how narrowly it had passed in the Lords and learned that the public were siding with the queen, they withdrew the bill, condemning the king to an unwished-for marriage.

George had thrown himself into a series of affairs from his teens onward. Events usually followed the same course: When he discovered a new love interest, he bombarded the poor woman, who was usually older than he, with letters and gifts. If he didn't receive the desired response, he feigned illness and even threatened suicide like a spoiled brat throwing a tantrum until he got what he wanted. Having conquered his prey, he quickly tired of her and soon discovered the next object of his passion. His many mistresses included Frances Villiers (Countess of Jersey), the Marchioness of Hertford, the Marchioness Conyngham, Elizabeth Armistead, Grace Dalrymple Elliott, Lady Augusta Campbell, Lady Melbourne, Elizabeth Billington, the Countess of Salisbury, and Countess von Hardenberg, but his most notorious mistresses were Mary Robinson, who blackmailed him, and Maria Fitzherbert, who married him (illegally).

THE MISTRESS WHO BLACKMAILED
A KING—MARY ROBINSON

Mary Darby learned from an early age that men take mistresses. Her father, a merchant in the port city of Bristol, lost all his money in a failed business venture and had to sell his home and its contents. Then he informed his wife that he was leaving the family to live with his mistress. A few years later, Mary's own husband would make no secret of his affairs with other women, so it's not surprising that she became a mistress herself.

The man who would marry her and then cheat on her was Thomas Robinson. He proposed to her when she was about sixteen years old. He'd given her the impression that he was in line to receive a large inheritance. When Mary's mother heard that Robinson was about to become a wealthy man, she was all for the marriage and pressured Mary to go ahead with it. They were married on April 12, 1773, at St. Martin-in-the-Fields, a famous church in a part of London that later became Trafalgar Square. However, Mary soon discovered that Robinson's inheritance story was a lie. It didn't stop him from spending as if he really were about to inherit a fortune. With his debts mounting and creditors demanding payment, he and Mary went on the run in Wales. Inevitably, the law caught up with him, and he was sent to cool his heels in a debtors' prison.

Before her marriage, Mary had planned to embark on a stage career, against her mother's wishes. She had even been auditioned in London and offered work by the famous actor-manager David Garrick, at the Theatre Royale in Drury Lane. Her plans were interrupted by Thomas Robinson's proposal. Now aware that Thomas was not going to be the reliable provider she'd expected him to be, she returned to Drury Lane and resumed her stage career.

FLORIZEL FINDS HIS PERDITA

King George III was an enthusiastic theatergoer. He was often accompanied on his visits to the theater by other members of the royal family, including the Prince of Wales. On a December evening in 1779, the royal party attended the theater at Drury Lane. They saw a performance of *Florizel and Perdita,* an adaptation of Shakespeare's *Winter's Tale* written by Garrick. The role of Perdita was played by Mary Robinson. As the actors bowed at the end of the play, the twenty-two-year-old Mrs. Robinson looked out into the audience and found herself gazing into the eyes of the seventeen-year-old Prince of Wales. The young prince was instantly smitten. The chase was on, but of course, the prince didn't personally run around after a woman. He had a man to do the job for him. The man in question was Lord Malden.

A few days later, Lord Malden called on Mrs. Robinson and delivered a note from the prince. It was addressed to Perdita and signed Florizel. And the letters kept coming. The prince's friends were appalled that he was pursuing a woman engaged in such a low, disreputable occupation as acting. To complicate matters, Lord Malden, the go-between selected by the prince to carry messages and gifts to Mrs. Robinson, confessed that he had fallen for her, too. One of the letters from the prince promised her twenty thousand pounds a year (an enormous sum) when he came of age. In the meantime, he sent her gifts including jewelry and a miniature portrait of himself.

They met secretly, probably with the knowledge of Mr. Robinson. The meetings took place near Kew Palace, a royal residence on the banks of the river Thames. The prince often crept out of bed at dead of night to meet Mrs. Robinson at a nearby inn. They had to meet like this because the teenage prince's days were strictly controlled and structured by his father, and the king or queen often checked on him after he had gone to bed. He had to wait until everyone was asleep before he could get away. His brother, the Duke of York, often helped him with his nocturnal adventures. Although the relationship was supposed to be secret, the king found out about it, and so did most of London. Wherever Mrs. Robinson appeared, crowds gathered to see the prince's mistress.

While Mrs. Robinson amused herself with the prince, her husband wasn't sitting at home twiddling his thumbs. He took lovers of his own. His wife discovered him in the company of a young woman at the Theatre Royal, Covent Garden. Worse still, his willing acceptance of his wife's liaison with the prince was widely known and ridiculed in the scandal sheets of the day. It was the last straw for his wife, who decided to leave him.

A Bolt from the Blue

Less than two years after their eyes had met across the footlights at Drury Lane, the prince sent Mrs. Robinson a note informing her that their affair was over and they would not meet again. He had replaced her with a seasoned courtesan, Elizabeth Armistead. The two women became bitter rivals. They tried to outdress each other, outjewel each other, and generally outdo each other to catch the attention of the prince at the theater.

When Mrs. Robinson finally accepted that she would not win back the prince's affection and had been permanently abandoned, Lord Malden stepped in and became her protector and financial backer. But she refused to accept her dismissal by the prince without proper compensation. She threatened to publish his love letters to her unless he provided for her. Negotiations for the return of the letters went on for months. Eventually, she was offered a single payment for them, but it wasn't enough. To compensate her for giving up her career and losing her reputation, she wanted her debts settled and the payment of an annuity for the rest of her life. Letters flew back and forth between the prince's officials and Mrs. Robinson's supporters, but in the end she gave in and handed over all the letters for just five thousand pounds. She insisted that it should be made clear in the settlement that the payment was for the return of the letters, not for her services as the prince's mistress. The rent on her town house was being paid by Lord Malden, who also paid her a small annuity. However, his days as her lover were numbered.

While Mrs. Robinson was sitting for a painting by Joshua Reynolds in 1782, she met another of his subjects, a soldier and politician from Liverpool with the magnificent name of Banastre Tarleton. The embodiment of eighteenth-century beefcake, Tarleton had distinguished himself as a cavalry officer in the American Revolutionary War. He was also a man of substance, having made his fortune from the slave trade and plantations in the West Indies. When Lord Malden found out about his lover's relationship with Tarleton, he left her and stopped paying the rent on her home. Within a few weeks, she had moved on to yet another new lover, Charles James Fox. Fox was a prominent politician with a notorious private life. He was famous for opposing the king and supporting America during the American Revolutionary War. Even at a time when drinking and womanizing were accepted as the norm, Fox's behavior was thought to be excessive. And he couldn't have been more different from Tarleton. Fox had been a fashion-conscious dandy in his youth, but as he aged, he became overweight, hairy, unwashed, and disheveled. Whatever his appeal to Mrs. Robinson had been, it didn't last long. Within a few months, she was back with Tarleton again.

Meanwhile, she still had her note from the prince promising her twenty thousand pounds when he came of age. He never paid the twenty thousand, but instead agreed to pay her an allowance. It was supposed to be paid quarterly, but the payments were irregular and she often had to remind him that she had not received the latest installment. She fell ill during 1783, leaving her partially paralyzed, and her debts increased. When she appealed to the prince for help, he declined to rescue her. She had to auction off some of her belongings. She spent the next few years traveling around the spas and health resorts of Europe, looking for a cure for her illness. She also spent a great deal of time writing poems, novels, and plays. Her search for a cure was in vain. Toward the end of 1800, her condition steadily worsened until her death on December 26, at the age of forty-three. She had requested that two locks of hair should be cut from her head and sent to former lovers. Tarleton received one. The other was sent to the Prince of Wales. He is said to have been buried with it.

An Illegal Royal Marriage—
Maria Fitzherbert

The twenty-four-year-old Mary Smythe was already twice married by the day of her marriage in 1785. This wedding was remarkable because of the identity of the bridegroom—the Prince of Wales (later King George IV). It was highly unusual for someone of the social status and royal rank as the Prince of Wales to marry a commoner. Moreover, the marriage was illegal.

Mary Anne Smythe was born on July 26, 1756, in a small rural village in Shropshire. She was the first of eight children. Her family had acquired its wealth and property through a series of fortunate inheritances and dowries. As was usual at that time, Mary was educated at an English convent in France. It gave the unpolished country girl a veneer of poise and genteel behavior.

At the age of about twenty, she married Edward Weld, who was fifteen years older than she. They had hardly begun settling into married life when, after only three months together, Edward died. According to one account, he had suffered a fall from his horse. According to another, he simply contracted an illness and died a few days later. As was normal practice, his land and grand houses remained within the Weld family, to be handed down through the male line. Mary was able to inherit only Edward's personal cash and property, or at least the part of it that she had been promised in their marriage contract. So, Mary inherited none of Edward's thousands of acres of land or his family home of Lulworth Castle in Dorset. She was now in urgent need of a new husband to provide her with a home and respectability. In the meantime, she stayed with friends and relatives, who introduced her to a string of prospective partners.

The search for a husband took three years. The "lucky" man was Thomas Fitzherbert, who was ten years her senior. He was already known to the Smythe family and was godfather to one of Mary's sisters. Mary and Thomas married on June 24, 1778. Later that year, Thomas's father died and he inherited Swynnerton Hall in Staffordshire. Eager to make the estate his own, he hired the famous landscape gardener Capability Brown to revitalize the hall's grounds. Mary fell pregnant, but her son died at birth or soon afterwards. At about this time, she changed her name by Latinizing it to Maria, a common custom in the eighteenth century.

The Fitzherberts divided their time between Swynnerton Hall and Thomas's town house near Hyde Park in London. In the capital, they would have seen the young Prince of Wales riding through the park. On occasions, Maria thought the prince had noticed her.

Thomas was not a well man. He appears to have been suffering from tuberculosis, which was a common ailment of the time. Despite his visit to the warmer climate of Nice, France, Thomas's condition worsened relentlessly, and he died on May 7, 1781. He had recently revised his will, so Maria was left with an annuity of one thousand pounds and a house in London's prestigious Mayfair district. She also had eight hundred pounds a year from her first husband's estate and possibly another few hundred pounds a year from her father. She was now twice widowed and, as a result, quite a wealthy woman. She adopted the fashionable habit of taking the air in Brighton, a resort on England's south coast. Visitors to the town bathed in the sea and drank the seawater, which was said to have health-giving properties—although, given the state of eighteenth century sewage disposal at the coast, the sea was probably far from healthy to bathe in or to drink.

BATHING BY MACHINE

Of course, in Georgian Britain, even bathing in the sea had to be done in a particular way to preserve the bathers' modesty. The procedure was particularly onerous for women. They needed a piece of equipment called a bathing machine. It looked like a garden shed on wheels. Women entered a bathing machine, closed the door and changed into their top-to-toe bathing costume. Bathers who didn't own a costume could hire one. The machine was dragged down into the sea by a horse or winched down at the end of a rope. The demurely dressed bather could then open the door and climb down the steps into the water. The first bathing machines had a tent called a modesty hood that was lowered onto the water so that bathers could enjoy the curative effects of the seawater completely hidden from view. For safety's sake, if the sea was rough, the bathers were sometimes tethered to the machine by a rope. Men and women bathers were strictly segregated . . . of course.

Members of the royal family started visiting Brighton. The Prince of Wales rented a house there. Over several years, the house was enlarged and extended to form an elaborate Royal Pavilion with onion-shaped domes reminiscent of an Indian temple. As usual, wherever the royal family went, others followed.

By 1783, Maria had recovered her joie de vivre. She was attracting male attention again and was enjoying her life as an independent woman. By then, fun-loving courtiers and royals had abandoned the dull and stuffy entourage of the mentally fragile King George III and formed a new and altogether livelier court around the more rakish Prince of Wales. When the prince turned twenty-one in August 1783, he was granted more money and a new home, Carlton House, by the king. It gave the prince more independence and, as a consequence, more opportunity for romantic adventures.

In March 1784, Maria Fitzherbert had reluctantly agreed to accompany her cousin and her uncle, Lord Sefton and Henry Errington, to the opera.

After the performance, they were waiting outside for a carriage when a man approached Errington and asked who his pretty companion was. Errington introduced Maria to the inquisitive man. He was the Prince of Wales. For the prince, the chase was on. He treated Maria to his customary campaign of letters and gifts. Gossip about the prince's latest infatuation spread through the lords and ladies of high society, the so-called bon ton. Newspapers began reporting where Maria went and which events she attended. Maria proved to be much more resistant to the prince's approaches than his other prey. He persuaded the Duchess of Devonshire to appeal to her on his behalf.

By then, he was telling friends that if she wouldn't be his mistress, he would marry her. There were two difficulties with this: First, she was Roman Catholic. The law not only excluded Catholics from the monarchy, it also prohibited the monarch or the heir to the throne from marrying them. Second, the Royal Marriages Act prohibited a descendant of King George II from marrying without the prior consent of the monarch. And if an heir ignored the law and married anyway, the king could have the marriage annulled. The prince must have known that if he had asked for permission to marry Maria, the king would certainly have refused it. Despite the force of law and Acts of Parliament, illegal royal marriages were not unknown. The Royal Marriages Act was passed after one of the king's own brothers, Prince Henry, Duke of Cumberland and Strathearn, married a commoner, Anne Horton, against the king's wishes. Then when the act passed into law, the king was shocked to discover that another of his brothers, Prince William Henry, Duke of Gloucester and Edinburgh, had been married secretly for six years! While his relatives were marrying for love, the king himself had been condemned to an unwanted marriage for purely dynastic reasons.

A PETULANT PRINCE

Maria was beginning to realize the constitutional significance and potential dangers of marrying the prince. She would be setting herself against the law and the king. She kept her distance from the prince until, on July 8, 1784, she was told that he had stabbed himself and his life was in danger. She rushed to him, but she had the foresight to take the Duchess of Devonshire with her as a chaperone . . . just in case! They found the prince lying in bed swathed in bloody bandages. He claimed that his life could be saved only if she agreed to marry him. She agreed, and even signed a document saying as much, but she didn't regard it as a promise she could be held to because of the circumstances. She left immediately for the Continent in the hope that the petulant and manipulative prince might come to his senses, or better still, he might be married off to a European princess in a dynastic marriage like the king's. However, his letters pursued her—lots of them! He threatened to kill himself if she didn't marry him. He even offered to give up his claim to the throne.

In addition to his desire to marry Maria, he was anxious to escape from massive debts he had incurred by his extravagant spending. When the king discovered the scale of the debts his son and heir had accumulated, he was furious. The king and the government could see that this had the making of a serious constitutional crisis—a bankrupt heir marrying a Catholic lover in anti-Catholic England. It could destabilize the monarchy or even destroy it. If this seems rather melodramatic, remember that the French executed their royal family less than ten years later.

Maria finally returned to London at the beginning of December 1785. By then, she had surrendered to the idea of marrying the prince. Perhaps his constant letter-writing had worn her down. Perhaps she simply couldn't see any way to escape his intentions. And there were obvious social and financial advantages to marrying the heir to the throne. On December 15, Maria and the Prince of Wales were married at her home, witnessed by a few close friends. The ceremony was conducted by Reverend John Burt, the only clergyman they could find to risk the displeasure of God and the king. He'd had to be sprung from the Fleet debtors' prison and paid a fortune to settle his debts and calm his troubled conscience. News of the marriage quickly spread through London. Newspapers reported the gossip. The prince's friends publicly denied that any marriage had taken place while knowing that it had. Public virtue concealed private vice, not for the first time (nor the last) in the upper echelons of British society.

The prince continued to rack up considerable debts. In desperation, he appealed to the king and government for help. They offered him a lifeline, but he refused to accept the conditions attached to it. Eventually the prime minister, William Pitt the Younger, managed to negotiate a settlement between the king and his son. The alternative would have been a debate in Parliament about the prince's financial situation, which would likely have involved discussion of his "marriage." Meanwhile, Maria and the prince were kept busy with an endless round of dinners, balls, and visits to the opera. When not in London, they retired to Brighton.

In 1788, the king fell ill with a bout of mental instability. In recent years, there have been several attempts to diagnose the cause of his illness. It may have been entirely psychiatric or it could have been caused by a physical illness such as porphyria, a blood disorder that can cause physical or mental problems, or it might have involved both psychiatric and physical elements. Whatever the cause, the king's condition worsened to such an extent that Parliament debated whether the prince should be declared regent and rule in his place. The prime minister delayed the discussion of a regency in Parliament for as long as possible, because if the prince became regent, he would very likely dismiss Pitt and ask the opposition party, led by his friend Charles James Fox, to form a new government. The issue of whether the prince was married or not was coming to a head. The gossip was that he would have to clarify his marital status if he were to become regent, so an announcement was expected.

The Regency Bill was debated by the House of Commons in January 1789. It didn't simply hand over all the king's powers to the prince. There were conditions, the most important of which was that the prince had to keep the king's government—in other words, he couldn't dismiss the existing government and ask someone else to form a new government. The bill was passed in the Commons and was then sent to the upper house, the Lords. However, it was never debated there, because the king recovered. The crisis was over. Maria and the prince returned to the serious business of attending balls and dinners. The prince also started pursuing other women. Maria responded by flirting with young men. During 1793, their relationship grew increasingly rocky. By June 1794, it was over. Maria claimed that the prince ended it, but the prince's friends claimed that the relationship foundered because of Maria's temper tantrums.

By now, the prince was keen to get on with marrying the bride selected for him—Princess Caroline of Brunswick. The king encouraged him by agreeing to settle his considerable debts when he married. The marriage treaty was negotiated as quickly as possible. Any suspicions that the prince might already be married to Mrs. Fitzherbert were cast aside. Even if the gossip was true, he had been under the age of twenty-five and hadn't received the king's approval, so the king, the courts, and Parliament would all have ruled the marriage invalid.

When the prince and Caroline met for the first time, neither of them was particularly pleased with the other, but both were resigned to their fate. The prince was more interested in Caroline's lady-in-waiting, Frances Villiers, the Countess of Jersey, with whom he was already conducting an affair. He and Caroline married on April 8, 1795, at the Chapel Royal in St. James's Palace. Just before the ceremony, Maria left London for her house in the country. George, perhaps suffering from a bout of premarriage cold feet, chased after her on horseback. When she refused to see him, he rode up and down outside her house until he accepted the inevitable and returned to London. By coincidence, the house Maria fled to was Marble Hill, the same house that was built by another mistress (Henrietta Howard) to a previous Prince of Wales, George's great-grandfather.

ROME DECIDES

George, Prince of Wales, and Princess Caroline of Brunswick loathed each other. After only two nights of married life together, they'd had enough of each other. It was just long enough for the prince to do his royal duty. Almost exactly nine months later, Caroline gave birth to a daughter, Princess Charlotte. The prince hoped for a reconciliation with Maria, but it was not to be. He tried a reconciliation with his wife, but she wasn't interested either. He kept up relentless pressure on Maria, but she felt unable to return to him unless the pope ruled that her marriage to him was valid. Her confessor, Father Paul Nassau, was dispatched to Rome in 1799 or 1800 to plead her case. He returned to England in October of that year with the answer—in the eyes of the church, she *was* the prince's wife. Soon afterwards, they were together again. And they seemed genuinely happy, which must have been a novel experience for the normally surly prince. But by 1806, he had reverted to type and found a new love—Isabella, Lady Hertford. The amply proportioned Lady Hertford was happy to be pursued by the heir to the throne. He had flings with other women, too, including a notorious courtesan, Harriette Wilson. Maria became increasingly unhappy with this behavior. On December 18, 1809, she wrote him a letter explaining why she was, for the first time, not prepared to accept his latest invitation to join him. She spelled out the insults and indignities she had suffered at his hands and said she was not prepared to endure them anymore.

THE REGENCY PERIOD

In November 1810, the king's favorite daughter, Princess Amelia, died. The king was so distressed that his mental problems returned. This time, there was no recovery. As a result, the Prince of Wales took his place and ruled as Prince Regent. In June 1811, he held a grand celebration of the beginning of his regency. Maria was invited, but when she discovered that she was not to be seated at his table—and, worse still, that Lady Hertford *would* be at the top table—she refused to attend. She saw him for the last time soon afterwards at a gathering held at Devonshire House. The last straw appears to have been her discovery of the prince enjoying a private encounter with Lady Hertford. From then on, Maria spent most of her time in Brighton, where she was feted as a queen in all but name. The prince continued to visit Brighton, but rarely left his Royal Pavilion. They encountered each other occasionally at society gatherings in London, but they didn't acknowledge each other.

The king, diminished by dementia, no longer aware that he was king, slipped from this world at Windsor Castle on January 29, 1820. The prince regent was now King George IV. He had made promises to Maria about what he would do for her when he ascended the throne, but they came to nothing. Maria faded from the public's mind as the war between the king and his wife intensified. The king failed to win the divorce from Caroline he demanded, but he needn't have worried, because she wouldn't trouble him for much longer. She ignored instructions to stay away from his coronation at Westminster Abbey. When she turned up, she had to be barred at bayonet point from entering the abbey. Within hours of being persuaded to leave, she fell ill, and three weeks later she died. The cause of her illness and death has never been established. When her funeral cortege attempted to sneak out of the capital unseen, her supporters stopped the procession and tried to force it through the center of the city. Soldiers on horseback rode through the unruly crowd with sabers drawn. Others opened fire. Two persons were killed. Eventually, soldiers managed to get the queen's body out of London to the coast and on its way to a burial in Brunswick. King George, now without a wife or a mistress, sought solace in the arms of the Marchioness Conyngham.

In his later years, he lived as a virtual recluse in Windsor Castle. His weight, and his waistline, grew enormously. When Maria heard rumors of his ill health, she took them with a pinch of salt. He had feigned illness many times in the past. But on June 26, 1830, his latest bout of illness was real and so serious that he died in the early hours of the morning. The new king, William IV, one of George's brothers, accepted Maria as the late king's wife and granted her a pension for life. Finally free of her disputes with the late king over money and now accepted by the royal family, Maria was at last a happy and contented woman. In March 1837, at the age of eighty, she caught a cold. It quickly developed into a more serious fever. Less than a week later, she was dead.

REGENCY DANDIES

Royal mistresses and courtesans, especially the demimondaines in France, dressed extravagantly to draw attention to themselves and advertise their success, excess, and availability, but men also took inordinate care of their own appearance and fashion from time to time. The Regency was one of these times. Regency dandies were known for their sharp dressing and fastidious toilette. The epitome of the Regency dandy was George Bryan Brummell, better known as Beau Brummell.

Brummell has had a bad press. He has acquired a reputation as a powdered and pampered fop, but actually he believed that if his clothes attracted attention, he had failed. He certainly dressed well and dressed fashionably, but he wasn't flamboyant or showy. His regular attire was a tightly buttoned blue coat, buff-colored pantaloons, black boots, and a smart cravat. He was also rather self-deprecating. He said, "I have no talents other than to dress. My genius is in the wearing of clothes." There were certainly other dandies who dressed to turn heads, but Brummell wasn't one of them.

He was a junior officer in the 10th Royal Hussars, the Prince of Wales's own regiment. He served as long as the regiment was based in London, but when it was sent north, leaving the capital was unacceptable to Brummell, who resigned his commission. His elegance and his friendship with the Prince of Wales admitted him to the prince's royal circle. He was a flirtatious man, but had few serious relationships. He never married. His attention to cleanliness, not universal at that time, began to influence his high-society friends. However, he wasn't as wealthy as many of his friends and soon ran up large debts. He fled from Britain to the Continent in 1816 to escape being incarcerated in a debtors' prison. He continued overspending in France and was eventually imprisoned in Calais for nonpayment of debts. Friends in Britain had to club together to pay for his release. He died penniless and insane because of syphilis in 1840.

Spurned and Betrayed—
Dora Jordan

In the early hours of July 5, 1816, a fifty-four-year-old woman died alone in a modest rooming house in Saint-Cloud, near Paris. She was probably the most grievously mistreated British royal mistress. She was betrayed at every turn by everyone she trusted. Her name was Dora Jordan.

Although she was known as Mrs. Jordan, Jordan was an invented name. Her marital status was invented, too. There was never a Mr. Jordan. She was born on November 22, 1761, and named Dorothy. Her parents, Francis Bland and Grace Phillips, had married when they were underage, so the marriage was invalid. Francis's father had the marriage declared void shortly before Dorothy was born, rendering her illegitimate. However, Francis and Grace continued to live as man and wife until Dorothy was thirteen years old, when Francis suddenly left. The family immediately faced severe financial difficulties. To help out, Dora joined the workforce when she was fourteen and soon followed her mother onto the stage. Her career began in Dublin. Her best feature was said to be her legs, which she showed off to great advantage in "breeches roles"—theatrical roles in which women played men wearing tight-fitting breeches.

In July 1782, she left Ireland for Leeds to escape the clutches of a disreputable theater manager called Richard Daly who had gotten her pregnant. In Leeds, she auditioned for actor-manager Tate Wilkinson. He was so impressed with her that he employed her immediately. It was Wilkinson who came up with her stage name, Jordan. It came to him when he likened Dora's escape from Ireland across the Irish Sea to the Israelites' escape from Egypt across the River Jordan. To add a measure of respectability, she called herself "Mrs." Jordan. Dora was probably very grateful to Wilkinson for his offer of employment, but she was less than flattering in her comments about his theater. She said, "It was miserable and cold, half the upper part of it admitting the wind and the rain."

In November 1782, she gave birth to Daly's daughter, a baby girl. She named the girl Frances but always called her Fanny. A few weeks later, Dora was back onstage. After three years touring theaters around Yorkshire, she was spotted by a talent scout from London and accepted an offer to work in the capital. She arrived in London toward the end of 1785. Success in Yorkshire didn't guarantee success in London, so she was taking a risk. She went to work at the Theatre Royal in Drury Lane, then under the management of the playwright Richard Brinsley Sheridan. Her first appearances attracted modest audiences, but word of mouth and favorable press reviews soon filled more seats. As her fame grew, it became impossible for her to go out on foot without attracting a small crowd of fans. The theater rewarded her with a contract, probably to prevent another theater from snapping her up.

Noblemen and their ladies began to notice Dora. And so did the son of one of the Drury Lane theater's co-owners, Dr. James Ford. Richard Ford was an up-and-coming lawyer with his eye on a parliamentary seat. He also had an eye for the attractive new actress at Drury Lane. They lived together as man and wife for five years, and had three children together, although the second, a son, died soon after birth. Dora eventually realized that Ford was never going to deliver on his promise to marry her, so she was ready for someone new in her life. In about 1790, William, Duke of Clarence, the third son of King George III, saw her onstage and began pursuing her. When newspapers got wind of the duke's latest infatuation, they printed a running commentary of the developing relationship. Some of it was even true! She took her time weighing up whether to stick with Ford or take her chances with William. By the end of 1791, the twenty-six-year-old Dora had decided to throw in her lot with the thirty-year-old duke. When newspapers discovered that she had accepted his advances and had become his mistress, they turned on her and savaged her. In their eyes, she had deserted the man widely thought to be her husband for a philandering duke for reasons of social climbing and financial advantage. Audiences began to boo and hiss her onstage.

As was normal at that time, the duke made financial provision for her, namely an allowance of £840 a year. It was a significant sum. Dora spent it all on her family. She paid school fees for her three daughters and put away dowries for their marriages. Meanwhile, Ford left her and married some-one else.

In 1792, Dora became pregnant but suffered the first of three miscar-riages. Then in January 1794, she had the first of ten children by the duke. Miraculously for this time, all of them survived birth and infancy. They were all given the surname FitzClarence, an Anglo-Norman name meaning "son of Clarence" (William was the Duke of Clarence). A few months later, Dora committed herself to working at Drury Lane for another five years, but the theater's owners grew increasingly frustrated at the amount of time she had to take off because of one pregnancy after another. Her home life with the duke was happy and settled. At the beginning of 1797, when they had been together for four years, they received an unexpected offer from the king. He proposed to give them Bushy House, a grand house standing in more than a thousand of acres of parkland to the southwest of London. It had pre-viously been the home of the prime minister, Lord North, until his death in 1797. It was an ideal home for the couple and their ever-growing family.

As the third son of the king, William had to live on a small (in royal terms) allowance from the king. He was constantly in debt, especially after he embarked on a program of alterations to Bushy House. Through all of this, Dora carried on working as an actress. She divided her time between Drury Lane and summer seasons at provincial theaters. William missed her so much when she was away that, in 1805, he asked her to stop working. She managed to give up for about eighteen months before money trouble drove her back to work.

A ROYAL COMMAND

Disaster struck in 1809 when the Drury Lane theater burned down. Dora threw herself into benefit performances to help the backstage staff who'd lost their jobs. Then, without warning, William exercised his royal preroga-tive to prohibit her from appearing on the London stage. However, his debts were such that she had to continue touring. Now approaching the age of fifty, she had lost the youthful figure that won her such admiration in her breeches roles, but she gained a new generation of admirers who praised her for her acting ability and comic powers.

She was away from home touring for long periods, months at a time, and while she was away, William's ardor finally began to cool. Dora had noticed that the duke was spending less time at Bushy House. He was beginning to think about marriage and realized that a common actress wasn't a fitting wife for the future king's brother. Dora knew that her time as a royal mistress was up and it was confirmed in a meeting between her and William on October 5, 1811. From then on, he avoided her. He proposed to a young woman called Catherine Tylney-Long, the daughter of a baronet who had recently inherited a large fortune, but she had no interest in marrying him.

The customary negotiations that accompanied the end of a royal relationship began. The duke's negotiators assured Dora that she would be well looked after, so she accepted the situation and went without a fuss. She was evicted from Bushy House without any other accommodation to go to. Worse still, when her children reached the age of thirteen, she lost custody of them to the duke. She was also told that she wouldn't even be able to see her children if she continued to work as an actress. The financial settlement provided her with 4,400 pounds a year, but it would be halved if she did anything that William disapproved of, including performing onstage. She asked the duke and other members of the royal family for help in finding a new home, but none of them responded. Despite her many years of loyalty to the duke, she was treated as an embarrassment who had to be got rid of. Not only that, but the duke's advisers seemed determined to deprive her of not only her home but also her children and her livelihood. It's hard to understand why Dora was treated in such an extraordinarily vindictive way. It's probably simply that a weak, spineless duke was in the hands of very traditional and conservative advisers.

A DREADFUL DISCOVERY

When gossip suggested that Dora was about to publish the duke's love letters to her, she immediately handed them over to him as evidence that this was entirely false. When his payments under their financial settlement began, she could finally afford a new home. She decided that she would have to return to the stage, even though she risked losing half of her income from the duke. In 1812, she packed her bags and took to the road, resuming her old life as a jobbing actress touring the provinces. After working hard for three years, the money she had earned and her allowance from the duke enabled her to retire at the age of fifty-three. However, no sooner had she hung up her stage costumes for the last time than she made a dreadful discovery. She was horrified to find that Frederick March, the husband of her daughter Dodee, had been taking money from her bank account and running up enormous debts in her name. She turned to Sir John Barton, one of the duke's advisers, for help. She then fled to the Continent, fearful of arrest and detention in a debtors' prison, while Barton tried to sort out her affairs. She thought she would be away for a few days, but she would never return to England.

Under the name Mrs. James, she took a small cottage near Boulogne. When it became clear that she wouldn't be able to return to England in the near future, she moved on, finally settling in Saint-Cloud, near Paris. Meanwhile, Barton had done nothing to help her. Everyone she trusted had let her down. Her health gradually deteriorated until she died on July 5, 1816, at the age of fifty-four. The local authorities at first refused her a burial in the Saint-Cloud cemetery because she was Protestant and, worse still, an actress. But they eventually relented under pressure from unnamed English supporters.

On January 29, 1820, George III died and his son became King George IV. Ten years later, on June 26, 1830, George IV died without issue and Dora's former lover, William, became king. One of his first acts as King William IV was to commission a sculptor called Francis Chantrey to create a statue of Dora. Chantrey worked from portraits because Dora had been dead for fourteen years. He created a life-size statue of her with two of her children. William intended it to stand in Westminster Abbey, but the dean, John Ireland, refused to allow it. Saint Paul's Cathedral declined to give it a home, too. When William died in 1837, it still stood in Chantrey's studio. It was eventually claimed by members of Dora's family, who ultimately bequeathed it to Queen Elizabeth II. The queen had it brought to Buckingham Palace, where it still stands—in a building that Dora herself was never allowed to set foot in.

"PUBLISH AND BE DAMNED!"—
HARRIETTE WILSON

Very few courtesans managed to snare royal clients. Most circulated in the lower echelons of the aristocracy. They usually tried to avoid becoming an embarrassment to their clients, but Harriette Wilson was an exception. After serving as a lover to a series of rich and powerful men, she informed them that she would name them in her forthcoming memoirs unless they paid up.

Harriette was born in 1786, the sixth of fifteen children born to Swiss clock-maker John Dubouchet and his wife, Amelia. She tried several respectable jobs, including working as a teacher in a girls' boarding school, but she couldn't put up with the rules and regulations for more than a few months before she returned home. Her father had no sympathy for her abandonment of a perfectly good teaching post. He wanted her out of the house and earning her own living. She tried the stage next and seems to have been quite successful as a comedy actress . . . until her father discovered what she was doing. He was furious with her new job, because actresses were seen as no better than prostitutes, and theaters were little better than brothels. No daughter of John Dubouchet was going to shame the family in that way. He forbade her from having anything to do with stage work. After a blazing row, she left home. She ran to a neighbor, who introduced her to a friend, Lord Craven. She became his mistress, but she found him boring and deeply unfashionable. By then she had lost her good name, so there was only one direction for her after that. Without intending to, she had become a courtesan.

Because of the well-to-do part of London where she grew up and her father's wealthy customers, Harriette started at the top of her profession. Her name doesn't appear in the lists of London courtesans that were published at the time. One of these, *Harris's List of Covent-Garden Ladies,* was published annually from 1757 to 1795. It gave details of more than a hundred women who worked in and around Covent Garden, London. About eight thousand copies were sold with a cover price of half a crown (two shillings and sixpence). Being included in *Harris's List* could increase a woman's earning potential and bring her to the notice of more privileged clients. Harriette Wilson didn't have to advertise her services in this and similar directories, because she already moved in the social circles that would provide her living. Details of her services spread by word of mouth. At some point early in her career as a courtesan, she changed her name to Wilson, probably to protect her family.

The etiquette of introductions to a courtesan was very strict. Men were not permitted to approach a woman they didn't know unless they had been introduced by a mutual friend or the woman had expressly requested a meeting. Another option was to use the services of a procuress as a go-between. When Harriette saw or heard of a man she was interested in, she wrote to him inviting him to visit her. One of the men Harriette contacted was reputed to be the Prince of Wales (later King George IV).

Although Harriette was keen to be rid of Lord Craven for someone more exciting, it was actually Craven who ended their relationship. He had been told that she was spending rather a lot of time with another man, Frederick Lamb. Craven instantly ended their affair and packed her off to Lamb, who was by then serving with his regiment in Hull. The fifteen-year-old Harriette is rumored to have taken not only Lamb as a lover, but also his brother and his father, Lord Melbourne. The Lamb family was accustomed to controversy, scandal, and intrigue. Frederick Lamb's father had an affair with the courtesan Sophia Baddeley. His mother, Elizabeth, was known for her affairs with a series of men, including the Prince of Wales (later King George IV) and Lord Byron. His brother William's wife was the notorious Lady Caroline Lamb, who, like her mother-in-law, had an affair with Lord Byron.

Frederick took it upon himself to educate his young charge to make her more acceptable in high society. It wasn't long before other men were taking an interest in Harriette and seeking introductions to her. Her smart, confident, and saucy nature was very successful in attracting men. She had also written to several prominent men and introduced herself, suggesting that they should meet. One of the men who responded was the Marquess of Lorne, heir to the dukedom of Argyll. He was handsome, rich, and aristocratic, and she was instantly attracted to him. They carried on an affair under Lamb's nose until Lorne moved Harriette into his London home. Only then did she tell Lamb that she was leaving him. The betrayal he felt was almost unbearable. But Harriette didn't enjoy a perfect life with her new lover. He refused to give up his existing mistress for her. Harriette consoled herself by spending his money and using her position as his lover to put herself on show to prospective clients.

One of her main rivals on the society scene was one of her own sisters,

Amy. The two sisters had fought with each other since childhood, and now, as courtesans, they lost no opportunity to outdo each other. A third sister, Fanny, also a courtesan, often had to act as peacemaker between the two. Later, a fourth sister, Sophia, joined them. Harriette and Amy's rivalry came to a head when Lorne abandoned Harriette for Amy. Harriette never forgave Amy for stealing her patron and lover.

In about 1805, an Irish soldier called Arthur Wellesley sought an introduction to Harriette. She met him and he was soon her lover, although she found him less than impressive in conversation and in bed. She described him as looking like a rat catcher. He would later become one of the most famous and revered figures in England. By the time he was better known as the Duke of Wellington, the victor of the Battle of Waterloo, and, later, prime minister, his affair with Harriette was a distant memory. She had spotted her next prey—a devilishly handsome rake, Lord Ponsonby. She adored him from the first moment she saw him, but she gave up any hope of snaring him when she discovered that he was married to Frances Elizabeth Villiers, who was so beautiful that she was described as "the loveliest creature on earth." Then one day Harriette was amazed to receive a letter from Ponsonby saying that he would like to meet her. When they got together, they hit it off straightaway. Although Ponsonby was married, they managed to meet daily. Harriette educated herself in history, literature, and the politics of the day so that she could talk to him about the things that interested him.

When Ponsonby had been with the twenty-three-year-old Harriette for about three years, he suddenly left her because his wife had found out about his infidelity. He felt so guilty about dumping Harriette that he offered to provide for her for the rest of her life, but amazingly she refused his generous offer. She quickly realized that she had confused a business arrangement with a love affair and vowed never to make the same mistake again. The pain of her break from Ponsonby was made all the worse when she learned that he had taken up with one of her own sisters, the fourteen-year-old Sophia.

SAVING WORCESTER

Having turned down an income from Ponsonby, she had to find another protector and provider quickly. She considered several candidates and "auditioned" at least one of them. However, none of them took her fancy. But when the nineteen-year-old Marquess of Worcester was introduced to her, he was instantly besotted with her. He followed her around like a lovesick puppy. His parents were so alarmed by his infatuation with Harriette that they had him posted to the Iberian Peninsula to serve in the Duke of Wellington's staff in the hope that he would forget her. They agreed to pay Harriette an allowance while Worcester was away if she refrained from following him abroad for a year. They were sure she would move on to another lover. But she didn't. When the year was up, Worcester's family told Harriette to get lost, but she had no intention of going quietly. She claimed to have letters from Worcester promising marriage, and she would publish them unless they paid her an annuity of several hundred pounds. They agreed to an annuity of two hundred pounds on condition that she never contacted Worcester again. Soon afterwards, they discovered that she had written to him, so they stopped the payments. She'd lost a regular income for the second time.

In 1817, Harriette went to see a lawyer called Henry Brougham for advice about recovering the annuity she'd lost. Brougham was a remarkable man. He would later become a Member of Parliament, adviser to royalty, and lord chancellor. He also published several scientific papers and as a result was elected a Fellow of the Royal Society. Before long, Harriette and Brougham were lovers. He advised her to sue Worcester's father, whom he expected to be keen to avoid the shame of the story being aired in public. He was right. On the day the case was due to be heard, Worcester's father offered an out-of-court settlement of £1,200. Harriette accepted it, but she'd spent it within a year.

She moved on to many other clients, including Viscount Palmerston, Lord Francis Conyngham, Lord Charles Stewart, and the Earl of Clanricarde. But as she grew older, she had less and less appeal to her clients. Lovers who were prepared to pay for her upkeep were harder to find. She decided to make some money for her old age by writing a revealing and sensational account of her life. Courtesans often wrote their memoirs, but they usually disguised the identities of their clients. Harriette intended to name names. She may have gotten the idea from the story of Mary Ann Clarke, a mistress of the Duke of York, who had tried the same thing and was paid seven thousand pounds plus an annuity in exchange for the suppression of her memoirs, or Mary Robinson, who blackmailed the Prince of Wales (later King George IV) when he ended their affair. Harriette and her publisher, John Joseph Stockdale, contacted about two hundred of her former lovers with a note saying that embarrassing parts of her forthcoming memoirs could be omitted on payment of a suitable sum of money—say, a lump sum of two hundred pounds, or at least twenty pounds a year for the rest of her life. It was blatant blackmail. The Duke of Wellington's response is reputed to have been, "Publish and be damned," although there is no evidence that he actually said it. King George IV is said to have paid Harriette to keep his own dalliance with her years earlier quiet.

Inconvenient Facts

Wilson's memoirs were published in installments between February and August 1825. Stockdale managed their publication expertly. He leaked details of which men would be featured in the first installment. Then each installment teased readers with details of who would appear in the next installment. Each issue was illustrated with lurid drawings of incidents described in the text. Harriette didn't let inconvenient facts spoil a good story. She said, "Dates make ladies nervous and stories dry." The memoirs caused a sensation. They were read avidly by the nobility, especially those who had known Harriette. Some men paid up to protect their reputation. Others brazened it out. Stockdale was hard-pushed to meet the demand for copies. There were also pirate editions produced by other publishers, sold at a lower price to undercut Stockdale.

Despite the popularity of Harriette's memoirs, or perhaps because of it, she was increasingly treated as a pariah, vilified by the upper class and also by the newspapers of the day. She moved to Paris to escape the furor. Stockdale had rashly agreed to bear the cost of any court cases resulting from the memoirs, and he was indeed taken to court. Charged with libel, he defended himself, but he failed to convince the court that all he was doing was exposing bad behavior in high places. He was ordered to pay three hundred pounds. A second trial resulted in an order to pay seven hundred pounds plus costs. The sale of all his possessions failed to raise enough money, so he was jailed in a debtors' prison.

Harriette had enjoyed her taste of writing, so she tried her hand at fiction. She wrote a book called *Paris Lions and London Tigers,* published in 1825, about an English family visiting Paris, but it failed to attract much interest. Despite the money she received for her memoirs, she was penniless again by 1829. She wrote another book, a novel called *Clara Gazul,* and published it herself in 1830. But it was no more successful than *Paris Lions*. By 1832, she was desperate, writing to old flames like Ponsonby, begging for money. She returned to her old profession, working as a procuress this time and calling herself Mrs. Du Bouchet. Then in 1840, she made an apparently odd decision. She renounced her previous life and converted to Catholicism under the name Mary Magdalen. She did it for the same reason that old, ailing kings usually sent their mistresses packing and confessed their sins shortly before their death. Harriette was preparing for the next life. She died on March 10, 1845, at the age of fifty-nine. A few of her old lovers paid a few pounds each to cover the cost of her burial.

6

PRINCES OF PLEASURE

The son of the British monarch traditionally takes the title Prince of Wales. As the heir to the throne, he has often found it difficult to carve out a meaningful role for himself while waiting for the current monarch to die. With few official duties to occupy his time, the Prince of Wales has had ample time for self-indulgence at the gaming tables and in the bedroom, none more so than Queen Victoria's eldest son, who became King Edward VII. One of his conquests proudly claimed to be the greatest whore in the world. The many others included the famous actress Lillie Langtry; Daisy, Countess of Warwick; and Alice Keppel. By a strange quirk of history, Alice Keppel's great-granddaughter, Camilla Parker Bowles, was the mistress of Edward's great-great-grandson, Charles, Prince of Wales.

FLIRTY BERTIE —

PRINCE ALBERT EDWARD

Queen Victoria's eldest son, Prince Albert Edward, known to the royal family as Bertie, was a notorious pleasure seeker. He pursued women, usually other men's wives, with such enthusiasm that he became known as Edward the Caresser and the Prince of Pleasure. The prince and his coterie of fellow partygoers were known as the "Marlborough House Set" after his London residence.

Bertie had a very difficult relationship with his parents. He was a disappointment to them in many respects. Even his appearance was disappointing. The queen said of him, "Handsome I cannot think him, with that painfully small and narrow head, those immense features, and total want of a chin."

He was deliberately excluded from state business by a mother who thought him incapable of dealing with it, so he sought his diversions elsewhere. He had a series of mistresses who were tolerated by his wife, Alexandra of Denmark. Not content with bedding any attractive woman who took his fancy, he was also a frequent visitor to French brothels, known more delicately as *maisons de tolerance*. In one, Le Chabanais, he was such a frequent and valued visitor that he had his own room. It was even decorated with his royal coat of arms! A special chair called a *siege d'amour* (love seat) was built specially for him by the furniture-makers Soubrier. It enabled the grossly overweight prince to "entertain" women more comfortably. In the same establishment, he is also reputed to have bathed with a companion or two in an extravagant swan-necked copper bath filled with champagne.

He frequently tried the patience of the French police officers whose job it was to protect him. He constantly tried to lose them so that he could meet yet another woman without being observed. He sometimes made a show of ordering his car for a particular time and then quietly summoned the driver an hour earlier. If he spotted an officer spying on him during an assignation, he was furious.

Ironically, his introduction to the pleasures of the flesh was brought about inadvertently by his straitlaced father, Prince Albert. In 1861, Albert, despairing of Bertie's lack of application to any serious or academic study, thought a spell of military service might toughen him up, focus his mind, and instill a measure of self-discipline, but the plan backfired. Bertie was sent to the Curragh Camp in County Kildare, Ireland, to serve with the elite Grenadier Guards regiment. It was just a few years since the end of the Great Irish Famine, when, out of a population of about eight million, one million people died and another million emigrated. In 1861, times were still very hard for the Irish people. Women sometimes turned to prostitution simply to survive, and the twelve thousand troops stationed at the Curragh were an attractive source of "trade."

A local prostitute called Nellie Clifden was instructed by two officers to go to a particular room at the camp and wait. When its tenant arrived, she set about her business. The soldier who was the object of her attention was the Prince of Wales, and he enjoyed the experience so much that Nellie was invited back a few days later, and again the following night. News of the events in Bertie's quarters spread among the officers and reached one of Prince Albert's advisers. When the very prim and proper Albert was informed about what his son had been up to, he described Bertie's behavior as "depraved." He was terrified that Nellie might accuse Bertie of fathering a child and destroy his chances of attracting a suitable wife, not to mention the embarrassment he might cause to the entire royal family. When Prince Albert died a few months later, in December 1861, the grieving queen blamed his death on the worry that Edward's dalliance with Nellie Clifden had caused and a chill he caught after a walk in the cold with Bertie to discuss his behavior. From then on, the queen treated her wayward son with contempt.

MARRYING BERTIE

A decision was made to marry Bertie off as soon as possible before he could disgrace the family any further. He married Alexandra of Denmark in 1863, but that didn't curtail his pursuit of other women. He is thought to have had dozens of liaisons. One of them, with the wife of Sir Charles Mordaunt, resulted in Bertie having to give evidence in court.

In the summer of 1868, while Sir Charles was away indulging in his main interests of hunting, shooting, and fishing, his bored and lonely wife entertained a number of male visitors and lovers, including the Prince of Wales. Sir Charles arrived home unexpectedly and found the prince admiring Lady Mordaunt's carriage driving skills. The carriage was being pulled by two white ponies. When the prince left, Sir Charles dragged his wife outside and made her watch the two ponies being shot. One of her affairs resulted in the birth of an illegitimate daughter. Lady Mordaunt eventually confessed everything to her husband, who was so outraged that he began divorce proceedings. When the case came to court, the prince was called as a witness—the first time in history that any Prince of Wales had given evidence in open court. He admitted to visiting Lady Mordaunt but nothing more. The jury decided that Lady Mordaunt wasn't of sound mind and dismissed Sir

Charles's divorce petition. He appealed and eventually won a decision that a wife's state of mind did not prevent her husband from divorcing her, so he finally divorced her in 1875. The case was catastrophic for Lady Mordaunt. Her family disowned her and had her declared clinically insane. She was detained in various asylums for the rest of her life.

A year later, Bertie was involved in another scandal. When the Marquess of Blandford ran off with Lord Aylesford's wife, the cuckolded Aylesford threatened to publish incriminating letters between the Prince of Wales and Lady Aylesford as part of his divorce proceedings. In the end, the letters were never published, but they were the subject of widespread gossip, causing embarrassment and humiliation to the prince's wife, Princess Alexandra.

The Mordaunt and Aylesford cases were close calls, but they didn't deter Bertie from the serious business of pleasure seeking. His many mistresses included the actress Lillie Langtry, Jenny Churchill (the American-born mother of Sir Winston Churchill), Alice Keppel, and the woman said to be the love of his life—Daisy Warwick.

THE VERY DISCREET "SKITTLES"— CATHERINE WALTERS

The name Catherine Walters doesn't stand out prominently in the long list of Bertie's conquests, because she avoided scandal, she was discreet, she didn't publish her life story, and she didn't keep any diaries or records. The woman who would become the courtesan called Skittles was born to a customs official in Liverpool in 1839. She earned her nickname after a short spell of work in a bowling alley in London where a game called skittles was played. By the time she was sixteen, she was the mistress of Lord Fitzwilliam, who took her to London and set her up in her own home. When Fitzwilliam dispensed with her services two years later, he gave her a payment of two thousand pounds and a pension of three hundred pounds a year. She moved on to Lord Hartington, who set her up in a new home with a stable of Thoroughbred horses and a tutor to give her the education she'd missed out on as a child. When he left her after four years, because his family thought she would damage his future political career, he gave her a pension of five hundred pounds a year.

Catherine enjoyed horse-riding and turned out to be a very good horse-woman. She could outride most men. The tailor she bought her riding clothes from, Henry Poole & Co. in London, still exists. Its records include forty pages of orders from "Miss Walters" for new riding habits and also for frequent repairs and essential maintenance to her riding clothes. Her rides on Rotten Row wearing a skintight riding habit drew huge crowds. Aristocratic ladies copied her clothes, although few of them could match her eighteen-inch waist.

Rotten Row still exists. It's a sand track running through Hyde Park in London where high-society men and women rode their horses and drove their carriages to be seen. It was originally called the *route de roi* (the king's road), because it was established by King William III as a route kept free of highwaymen between Kensington Palace and St. James's Palace. In time, the name was corrupted and mispronounced as Rotten Row. Today, the Household Cavalry, part of the queen's personal bodyguard, use it to exercise their horses.

In 1863, Skittles traveled to New York with Aubrey de Vere Beauclerk, but a year or so later, their relationship was over and she moved on to Paris to try her luck in the demimonde. She made sure she was noticed by driving her own carriage through the Bois de Boulogne accompanied by two mounted, uniformed grooms. She is said to have been Emperor Napoléon III's lover during this time. She also had a relationship with the poet Wilfrid Blunt, who fell head over heels in love with her. Unfortunately for Blunt, his fiancée's father, the British ambassador to France, found out about his new love and sent him back to England in disgrace. He continued writing to Skittles for the rest of her life. She returned to London in 1870 and started holding regular tea parties that were attended by important men. It was at about this time that her relationship with the Prince of Wales, the future King Edward VII, began.

Two of Skittles's most valuable assets were her discretion and loyalty. When she returned three hundred love letters written to her by Edward, the grateful and relieved prince rewarded her with a pension. In the 1870s, she started calling herself Mrs. Baillie, although she never married. She "borrowed" the name from one of her lovers, Alexander Horatio Baillie. When she was forty, she met her final lover, Gerald de Saumarez—he was only sixteen years old. When she died, after suffering a brain hemorrhage in 1920, she left her estate to Saumarez.

THE JERSEY LILY—LILLIE LANGTRY

The famous socialite and actress Lillie Langtry had a three-year affair with Bertie, the Prince of Wales, in the 1870s. It transformed her life, but ruined her husband's.

Langtry was born on October 13, 1853, on the island of Jersey and named Emilie Charlotte Le Breton. Her father was a prominent churchman, the dean of Jersey. Despite being a cleric, he had a reputation as a ladies' man and adulterer. Lillie, as she was known in the family, led a tomboy childhood with her six brothers. She was also taught by their tutors, giving her a better education than most girls at that time. She was clearly a very attractive girl, because she started receiving marriage proposals when she was just fourteen years old. When she was twenty, a wealthy landowner called Edward Langtry took her sailing in his eighty-foot yacht, *The Red Gauntlet,* with her father, the dean, going along as chaperone. She wanted to see more of the world, and Langtry was her best chance of getting off the island, so she married him. Her father presided over the ceremony on March 9, 1874. Then as she'd hoped, Edward took her away, first to Southampton and then to London.

Their first year in London was rather lonely, because they knew no one. Then a chance encounter with Lord Ranelagh, whom Lillie had known on Jersey, resulted in their first invitations to swanky parties. Lillie's beauty and the simple way she dressed quickly attracted attention. She wore a plain black dress with no jewelry—quite a contrast to the fine gowns and gems worn by society belles. She was in black because she was in mourning after the death of her young brother Reggie and also because she didn't yet have any fine dresses or jewelry of her own. An artist called Frank Miles painted her portrait. He sold one of his sketches of her to a printer, and soon her face was staring out from scores of shop windows. She sat for other well-known artists of the day, including John Everett Milais, Edward Poynter, James McNeill Whistler, and Sir Edward Burne-Jones. Milais called one painting of her *A Jersey Lily,* and the name stuck. She arrived in London just as a craze for collecting photographs of beautiful women was taking off. Photographs of Lillie were very popular. Between photographs and paintings, Lillie's face was everywhere.

She became a regular guest at high-society gatherings and soon counted Oscar Wilde and Sir Arthur Conan Doyle, the creator of Sherlock Holmes, among her friends. It was a social circle that didn't tolerate airheads, so Lillie Langtry must have been more than just a pretty face. Conan Doyle is said to have based the character of Irene Adler on her—Adler, born in New Jersey, was an intellectual match for Sherlock Holmes. Langtry's husband was delighted with her success on the social scene, but he was a reluctant socialite himself. He preferred to go fishing or drinking with his friends when he wasn't compelled to don formal evening dress for a night out with his vivacious wife.

It wasn't long before the heir to the throne heard about her. Queen Victoria had all but retired from public life following the death of her husband, so it was the Prince of Wales who was the visible embodiment of the royal family. And he threw himself into it, attending an endless round of parties, dinners, and balls. He arranged to sit next to Lillie at a dinner party in 1877. Although they were both married, it wasn't long before she was his mistress. He encouraged his friends to invite Edward Langtry to outings, leaving Lillie at home alone and thus available to meet him. He built a house for her in Bournemouth, Dorset, where they could meet secretly. Lillie designed the house herself. This royal love nest is now a hotel.

Very soon, the prince acknowledged Lillie as his official mistress and appeared in public with her. They were seen riding together in Hyde Park and attending horse races, which sparked Lillie's lifelong interest in horses. They enjoyed yachting regattas and weekends in the country. She was finally able to wear the finest dresses, given free of charge by designers who wanted the famous Lillie Langtry to be seen wearing their creations. Aristocrats and foreign royalty wanted to meet her, too. And everyone wanted to know about the events she attended, what she wore, how her hair was styled, what she said, and what she did. She was as famous as a film star today. In 1878, she was even presented to Queen Victoria. "Presentation" was an essential requirement for a woman to be acceptable in the loftiest echelon of society. That done, Lillie was now courted by continental princes and invited everywhere, including Buckingham Palace.

The Final Straw

Lillie's relationship with Bertie began to cool in 1879. She found herself increasingly having to compete with other women for his attention. The final straw was a fancy dress dinner when she wore the same costume as Bertie. When he objected, she put ice cubes down his back. He took great offense, but she refused to apologize, triggering the beginning of her exit from high society. Lillie herself always denied that this incident ever happened. At about the same time, rumors suggested that Langtry's husband was preparing to divorce her and cite the Prince of Wales as co-respondent. He also accused the prince of having an affair with another woman, Patsy Cornwallis-West. Her husband sued a journalist, Adolphus Rosenberg, for defamation after he'd written stories about the allegations. Rosenberg's accusations regarding Lillie Langtry and the prince were aired in the case, too. Rosenberg pleaded guilty and was sentenced to two years in prison.

Meanwhile, Lillie had begun an affair with the young Prince Louis of Battenberg. Before long, she discovered that she was expecting his child. A financial settlement was quickly arranged, and the prince, a naval officer, was suddenly posted to a warship, HMS *Inconstant,* which set sail for the other side of the world. Bertie took pity on her and arranged for her to go to Paris in the company of another lover, Arthur Jones. In March 1881, she gave birth to a girl, Jeanne Marie. The girl was handed over to Lillie's mother, while Lillie returned to London. Jeanne Marie grew up believing that Lillie was her aunt.

Lillie and her husband had run up substantial debts. While she was the prince's mistress, creditors kept their distance, but once it became known that she and the prince were no longer together, the creditors pounced. Edward was declared bankrupt, and Lillie had to sell many of her possessions to clear their debts.

Oscar Wilde suggested that she should capitalize on her fame by taking to the stage. She got her first taste of performing onstage at an amateur dramatic production in Twickenham, southwest London. That led to an appearance in a charity performance at the Haymarket Theatre in London. Her name on the bill and the attendance of the Prince of Wales ensured a full house. The critics praised her performance. As a result, she was offered a contract to appear professionally at the Haymarket. The prince continued to take his place in the royal box to support her. Even though they were no longer lovers, they remained friends.

A CONTROVERSIAL DIVORCE

In 1882, after success in Britain, Lillie founded her own theater company and took it on a tour of the United States. She found that her reputation had preceded her, so she played to full houses wherever she went. She made repeated tours of the States that were equally successful. And she collected male admirers along the way. One of them, wealthy horse breeder Freddie Gebhard, spent a fortune on her. Her earnings from the theater and Freddie's expensive gifts enabled her to start a winery and, like Freddie, breed horses. She became an American citizen in 1887, which enabled her finally to have her marriage to her first husband, Edward, dissolved. The marriage was ended by a California court, but legal opinion at the time suggested that the divorce was invalid in Britain and indeed anywhere outside California.

After she returned to Britain in 1889, her career took a turn for the worse. She needed money and she soon found a likely provider. George Baird was a bachelor who had inherited millions of pounds from his family in Scotland. He and Lillie shared a passion for horses and racing. He rode under the pseudonym Squire Abingdon. Lillie had her eyes firmly on his money. Unfortunately, as well as money, he also had a violent temper. He attacked Lillie on more than one occasion and then felt such remorse that he tried to buy back her affection with expensive gifts, including a steam yacht called *White Ladye*. Their turbulent affair ended in 1893 when Baird died of pneumonia during a visit to the United States. He left her some of his horses, which encouraged her to take up racing more seriously. And she made a success of it. Under the name Mr. Jersey, she bought a racehorse named Merman, which won a famous race called the Cesarewitch in 1897. Bertie was there and escorted her into the winner's enclosure. Merman and her other horses won the Ascot Gold Cup, the Lanark Silver Bell, the Jockey Club Cup, and the Goodwood Cup. Bertie had his own racing stables near Lillie's, so they often met.

In 1899, when she was forty-five, she married Hugo de Bathe. He was an odd choice for her. He was nineteen years younger than she, and he had no money to speak of. His main attraction seems to have been his father's title. When the old man died, Hugo would inherit his title and Lillie would become Lady de Bathe. She was able to go ahead with the marriage with a clear conscience, because her troublesome first husband, Edward, had died of a brain hemorrhage in an insane asylum just over a year earlier, ending the speculation over the validity of her California divorce.

Hugo persuaded Lillie to sell her riding stable and horses, because he didn't think it was proper for a woman to own racehorses. The couple lived on Jersey for a time, but when Hugo volunteered for army service in the Boer War and left for South Africa, she returned to London and resurrected her stage career. Initially, she was just as successful as before, but her appeal was slowly waning. She tried vaudeville in New York and she made a film. In 1907, her marriage to Hugo finally paid off. Hugo's father died and she became Lady de Bathe.

Lillie often holidayed in Monte Carlo and finally retired alone to a cliff-top villa there, called Le Lys. She died there on February 12, 1929, after a long illness. Her body was taken back to Jersey and buried at her father's old church. Her husband, Hugo, did not attend the funeral, and she left him nothing in her will.

In 2013, a photograph album full of Lillie Langtry's publicity photographs, signed by her, was discovered in America. It was compiled for a wealthy friend, Freddie Gebhard. In April 2014, it was sold at auction in New York for US$22,500.

THE BABBLING BROOKE—DAISY GREVILLE, COUNTESS OF WARWICK

When Lillie Langtry caught sight of her former lover, the Prince of Wales, at horse races, he was often in the company of his new love, Daisy Greville, Countess of Warwick.

Daisy was born as Francis Evelyn Maynard on December 10, 1861, to an aristocratic family. Her father was the son of the third Viscount Maynard and her mother was a descendant of King Charles II. Her grandfather, Viscount Maynard, was so besotted with the young Daisy that he left her most of his fortune. He died when she was only three years old, making her one of the richest people in Britain, almost certainly the wealthiest three-year-old!

In a bizarre coincidence, when the young Daisy was taken to the studio of artist Frank Miles so that he could make sketches of her, she met Lillie Langtry. They would both later become mistresses of the Prince of Wales. Daisy said she thought Lillie was the most beautiful woman she'd ever seen.

When she was nineteen years old, Daisy married. The British prime minister, Benjamin Disraeli, had spotted her and thought she would make a suitable wife for Queen Victoria's son Prince Leopold. The queen summoned Daisy and her parents to Windsor Castle to give the prospective royal bride the once-over. Daisy's father had died just before her grandfather, so it was her mother and stepfather, Lord Rosslyn, who accompanied her to the castle. The queen approved of Daisy, but before the marriage arrangements could be finalized, Francis Greville, Lord Brooke, proposed to her. At the same time, Prince Leopold confessed that he was in love with someone else. That suited Daisy, because she preferred Lord Brooke to the frail, sickly, hemophiliac Leopold. Daisy and Lord Brooke married on April 30, 1881, in Westminster Abbey, London.

As she settled into married life at Easton Lodge, she particularly enjoyed hunting on horseback. She was known for her figure-hugging riding costumes. She quickly learned that it was accepted in her elevated social class for married women to have a string of admirers and affairs, a custom Daisy took to enthusiastically.

One of her most intense affairs was with Lord Charles Beresford. She was so smitten with Beresford that she hoped to elope with him. But her ambition to be more than a "bit on the side" scared him off. Daisy was outraged when he abandoned her and went back to his wife. She wrote to him claiming that he was the father of one of her children. Unfortunately, the letter was opened by Lady Beresford, who lost no time in handing it to her solicitor. Fearing public scandal and disgrace, Daisy appealed for help from Beresford's friend, the Prince of Wales. The prince tried in vain to persuade Lady Beresford or her solicitor to destroy the letter, so he cut them out of his social circle.

During his meetings with Daisy, the Prince of Wales fell for her and they began an affair. He became so close to her that he started calling her his wife. They were inseparable. Wherever he appeared, Daisy would invariably be there, too. He even took her with him on his frequent visits to Paris. Her husband, known as Brookie, gave tacit approval to his wife's affair with the prince.

BLABBERMOUTH

In 1891, Daisy and the prince were caught up in a scandal—no longer a novel experience for the prince by then. Bertie was a keen gambler and cardplayer. His game of choice was baccarat. While he was playing baccarat with Sir William Gordon-Cumming, he realized that Sir William was cheating. When challenged about it, Sir William confessed and agreed to sign a statement saying that he would never play cards again on condition that no one breathed a word about it. Inevitably, the story got out. The blabbermouth could have been any of the dozen or so guests at the house party where the incident occurred, or any relatives or friends they'd told, but Sir William blamed Bertie and Daisy. It earned her the soubriquet, "the Babbling Brook." Sir William sued. Although he lost, the court case revealed the prince's dissolute life of parties, gambling, and affairs with married women. People made their opinion on his behavior clear by booing him when he appeared in public. The queen was furious with him . . . again.

Encouraged by Bertie's humiliation in the Gordon-Cummings case, Lord Beresford threatened to damage him further by bringing his own accusations against the prince and his mistress into the public domain. Lady Beresford added that she wanted nothing less than a public apology from the prince. Then Lady Beresford's sister circulated a pamphlet detailing Daisy's affair with the prince. The prime minister, Lord Salisbury, managed to persuade Lord Beresford to refrain from releasing further damaging details of the prince's private life, while Daisy agreed to withdraw from court for a while.

Then she did something almost unheard of for such a well-connected member of the nobility. She stood for election! And she won. She was elected as a workhouse trustee and used her position to inform the Prince of Wales about workhouses and their inmates.

In 1893, Lord Brooke became the 5th Earl of Warwick on his father's death, so Daisy became the Countess of Warwick. They also inherited Warwick Castle. After mourning the loss of the fourth earl, they celebrated their arrival at the castle by holding an extravagant costume ball. The castle had never witnessed anything like it in its eight-hundred-year history. Hundreds of guests wore Louis XVI fancy dress. Daisy was dressed as Marie Antoinette. Trains were hired to transport guests to the castle, and hairdressers were brought from Paris to tend to their coiffure.

Newspaper reports of the ball were generally complimentary, but one vilified the Brookes for their monumental waste of money. Daisy went to the paper and burst into the editor's office to vent her fury. But the editor managed to argue his case that such excess was unacceptable in a country where many people still lived in grinding poverty. Daisy thought about what he'd said and ended up agreeing with him. With customary zeal, she threw herself into good works. She started several charitable organizations, including a needlework school and an agricultural college for women. The Prince of Wales had little sympathy for her good causes, and by 1897, he was beginning to lose interest in her. But it was Daisy who ended the relationship. She was eager to retain this friendship, because she expected him to be king before long. Trying his patience by prolonging the relationship beyond its natural end would likely ensure her exclusion from high society once he became king.

Then later in 1898, she discovered that she was pregnant with her third child. By the end of the year, she had given birth to a boy, Maynard, and also acquired a new lover. At thirty-one, the army captain Joe Laycock was five years younger than Daisy. When Laycock left for service in the Boer War, Daisy worried every moment he was away, but that was nothing to how desperate she would feel soon after he returned. He suffered a riding accident while hunting and was tended to by the young, attractive Marchioness of Devonshire. Inevitably, he fell for her, and the two embarked on an affair. Daisy's alarm rose to fever pitch when she heard that the marquess intended to divorce his wife because of her adultery with Laycock. Her worst fears were realized when Laycock married Kitty Devonshire as soon as she was free of her husband. She dealt with it by throwing herself into her charitable causes and a scheme to forge closer relations between Britain and America. Bertie continued to write to Daisy and send gifts on her birthday, but otherwise, he kept his distance. She kept all his letters. Later, she would try to use them to her advantage.

It was at this time, in the early 1900s, that Daisy's life took a surprising turn. She had never shown any interest in party politics before, but now she joined the Socialist Democratic Federation. With her furs, jewelry, aristocratic title, and grand houses, she wasn't a typical socialist. By 1907, she was in financial trouble. Creditors were pursuing her. She was approached by publishers who tempted her with large sums of money to write her life story, but she resisted and instead sold property to settle debts and closed some of her charities to save money.

A FINAL FAREWELL

Daisy met Bertie, now King Edward VII, for the last time in 1910. She was shocked by how ill he looked. He thought he was suffering from the after-effects of influenza injections, but in fact his health was far worse than he imagined. He was dead a few weeks later.

Daisy's financial problems continued, and by 1914 she was desperate. The only thing of any value that she still had was her story. Bertie and some of the others she had bedded were dead by then and couldn't be hurt by her revelations . . . or sue her. The letters she had received from Bertie had become all the more valuable because he had ordered all his own private correspondence to be destroyed when he died. However, instead of publishing her letters, she tried to blackmail the new king (George V) into paying her for her silence.

She let it be known that she was planning to publish the letters. As intended, the news reached the ears of George V's private secretary, Lord Stamfordham, who relayed it to the king. Keen to avoid a scandal, the king's representatives asked how much she wanted for the letters to stop publication. The price tag was one hundred thousand pounds. The Palace tried to negotiate with Daisy, but it soon became apparent that this was just a delaying tactic to give them time to take out a temporary injunction preventing her from publishing. Unfortunately for Daisy, Britain declared war on Germany on August 4, 1914. It was unfortunate because four days later, the British Parliament passed the Defense of the Realm Act. This gave the government sweeping new wartime powers. Among its many measures, it made spreading "false reports or reports likely to cause disaffection to His Majesty" illegal. The Palace contended that this applied to Daisy's letters, so if she published them in Britain, she could face prosecution and imprisonment. Undeterred, Daisy threatened to sell them to an American publisher. Finally, she reluctantly handed them over to a wealthy industrialist and politician, Arthur Du Cros, in return for his offer to settle sixty-four thousand pounds of her debts. Du Cros was rewarded for his loyalty to the king with the award of a baronetcy. Several years later, she did publish two volumes of autobiography, but they glossed over much of the more lurid details of her relationship with the late king.

Daisy continued to embrace socialism. After the war, she joined the Labor Party. In 1923, she even stood for election as a Labor Party MP

(Member of Parliament), but she lost. The following year, her long-suffering husband died. Perennially in debt, she offered one of her homes, a country house called Easton Lodge, to the Labor Party and then to the Trades Union Congress, but they declined to buy it, mainly because the home of a countess didn't suit their working-class image. She became disillusioned with socialism and retreated into an old age dominated by her many animals. The increasingly eccentric Daisy died on July 26, 1938, at the age of seventy-six.

THE QUEEN OF PLEASURE HOUSE— ALICE KEPPEL

After his relationship with Daisy Warwick ended, the Prince of Wales lost no time in finding a replacement. Alice Keppel was a well-known society hostess and wife of the Honorable George Keppel. She would be the prince's greatest love.

The Prince of Wales met Alice Keppel in 1898. At twenty-nine, she was twenty-six years younger than he. She was beautiful and elegant—the two do not always go hand in hand. She also had the spirited nature of a tomboy. It was a quality, shared by Lillie Langtry and Daisy Warwick, that the prince found attractive. But, unlike Daisy, the Babbling Brooke, Alice was known for her discretion. The prince and Mrs. Keppel often got together at her home, known appropriately as Pleasure House. Her husband obligingly left when the prince arrived. When he left the army, one of the prince's friends helpfully employed him and sent him to the United States, leaving Alice at home and available to the prince.

On January 22, 1901, Queen Victoria died at Osborne House on the Isle of Wight. Bertie was now King Edward VII. Alice continued as his mistress. He was devoted to her. It was said that when they were in the company of others, he never took his eyes off her. She was no shrinking violet. On the contrary, her ability to stand up to Bertie's famously short temper was appreciated by other members of the court. She was also known for her sweet nature. She didn't repeat malicious gossip. But she certainly had an eye for the main chance. She kept close to Sir Ernest Cassel, a self-made multimillionaire who advised the king on financial matters. She knew her time as a royal mistress was probably limited. She could fall out of favor at any time and be replaced at any moment, as her predecessors had been. Sir Ernest understood how important Alice was to the king, and so he was more than willing to provide whatever advice and assistance she needed.

The queen and Mrs. Keppel were sometimes invited to the same social gatherings. It was a tricky problem for hosts—invite the queen and upset the king, who preferred the company of his mistress, or invite Mrs. Keppel and offend the queen, or invite both of them and risk an embarrassing confrontation. Hosts feared making the wrong decision and possibly suffering a fate worse than death—exclusion from high society. In fact, the queen and Alice managed to coexist perfectly well. If they were both invited to the same occasion, they would respectfully avoid each other.

Every Easter, the king spent a month with Alice in Biarritz. There, he could avoid the royalty, politicians, diplomats, and others who invariably expected audiences with him during visits to the Continent's capital cities. In Biarritz, he could give his undivided attention to Alice. Even though their relationship was well known, the social standards of the day required them to be accommodated separately, so Alice stayed in a villa a respectable distance from the king's hotel. Then the king and his mistress would make their way, separately, back to Britain and their respective spouses.

Alice was often thanked by politicians and diplomats for her help in informing the king on some matter or changing his mind when they felt he was wrong. Even when the king was in his sixties, he most definitely still had an eye for the ladies. However indispensable Alice was to him and however devoted he was to her, she wasn't his only mistress. Alice never tried to monopolize him and never complained about his other liaisons. He took his pleasure with countless women during his frequent visits to Paris and his favorite spa town, Marienbad.

ALICE'S RIVAL

One of Alice's rivals for the king's affection was Agnes Keyser. He had met Agnes in the same year that he met Alice, but the two women couldn't have been more different. Unlike Alice, Agnes wasn't interested in being seen in society, enriching herself, or benefiting from her association with the prince. She was as much a friend and nanny to the prince as she was his lover.

The Keyser family had come to Britain with Prince William of Orange during the Glorious Revolution of 1688. They'd done well, having made their fortune on the stock market. Agnes, born on July 27, 1852, was happy to be unmarried. She disliked the restrictions women were subjected to, especially in marriage, so she enjoyed the independence of spinsterhood. She also liked the attention of men, but she didn't intend to marry one. She was said to be rather bossy and tended to intimidate others, a stark contrast to the welcoming, charming, and friendly nature projected by Alice Keppel.

During the Boer War, Agnes and her sister Fanny used their London home in Grosvenor Crescent, Belgravia, to help sick and wounded army officers. The eminent doctors who worked there gave their services free of charge. The Prince of Wales suggested that the house should become a hospital, which it did in 1899. The prince was its first patron. In 1904, it was named the King Edward VII Hospital for Officers. The king was often seen at the hospital, apparently visiting army officers being treated there, but also secretly meeting with Agnes, now known as Sister Agnes because of her good works. More recently, it has become known as the hospital of choice for members of the British royal family. Queen Elizabeth, the queen mother, Prince Philip, Princess Margaret, the Countess of Wessex, Prince Charles, the Duchess of Cornwall, and the Duchess of Cambridge have all been treated there. In 2000, its name was changed to King Edward's Hospital Sister Agnes to recognize that it is no longer solely for army officers and royalty.

FINAL DAYS

A bout of illness at the beginning of 1910 didn't stop the king from setting off on his annual visit to Biarritz. As usual, Alice traveled there separately. But the king was so ill that he was confined to his room. He slowly recovered, but fell ill again on his return to England. Despite worsening bronchitis, he carried out his duties as usual. By the beginning of May, he was so ill that doctors called the queen back from a Mediterranean cruise. On May 6, he insisted on getting up and following his planned schedule. In the afternoon, he suffered a series of heart attacks. At his request, the queen sent for Alice. The two women sat with him, but when he lost consciousness, the queen ordered Alice out of the room. She was distraught and had to compose herself in another room before leaving the palace. A few hours later, just before midnight, the king died.

The Keppels left Britain for the Far East to avoid publicity and stayed away for two years. Unlike Daisy Warwick, Alice never published her story. Bertie had ensured that she was looked after financially. She entertained lavishly. Her dinner parties were famous. In 1927, the Keppels moved to Italy. They returned to London in the 1930s and stayed there during World War II. When King Edward VIII abdicated to marry Wallis Simpson, Alice was overheard saying, "Things were done much better in my day." Her health began to fail in 1946. After a long illness, she died in Italy on September 11, 1947. She was buried in the Cimitero degli Allori in Florence. Her husband, George, followed her to the grave two months later.

THE COURTESAN VERSUS THE ESTABLISHMENT—MARGUERITE ALIBERT

The last member of the British royal family known to have availed himself of the services of the demimonde was Bertie's grandson, the Prince of Wales, who would later become the ill-fated King Edward VIII. Edward, known as David within the royal family, was a rather shy and timid man, and a late starter sexually. While he was serving with the army in France during World War I, the twenty-two-year-old prince finally scored in 1916, thanks to the efforts of two members of his staff. They engineered a meeting between the prince and a French prostitute—reminiscent of his grandfather's initiation in the pleasures of the flesh with Nellie Clifden at the Curragh army camp fifty-five years earlier. David clearly enjoyed the experience, because he set out to find a courtesan to make his own. The woman who fitted the bill was known as Maggie Meller. She was actually Marguerite Alibert, a prostitute who had been schooled in the skills of the courtesan while working in a high-class brothel in Paris. She plied her trade among the British army officers who spent their leave from the front line in the French capital. Fate brought the prince and Marguerite together in April 1917, at the Hôtel de Crillon in Paris, where they had gone for lunch. The moment he saw her, he was instantly smitten with her. When he had to return to England to perform royal duties, he couldn't wait to get back to France to see her. Unwisely, he wrote scores of very frank letters to her. As the war drew to a close, his military and royal duties took him elsewhere for long periods and his feelings for Marguerite cooled.

A chance meeting during an air raid in London introduced the prince to his next love interest, Winifred Dudley-Ward. However, Marguerite was not one to go quietly. The prince now regretted the candor of his many letters to her. He expected to receive a demand for money accompanied by a threat to make the contents of the letters public, but none came. Meanwhile, a failed marriage and a series of affairs with wealthy men had made Marguerite a rich woman. Then, at the beginning of 1923, the thirty-two-year-old Marguerite married an Egyptian playboy, Prince Ali Kamel Fahmy Bey, who was ten years her junior. Within days, she was bored stiff with life as a traditional Egyptian wife who was expected to obey her husband without question. The newlyweds fought and argued constantly, often coming to blows. In the summer of 1923, they were in London, staying at the swanky Savoy Hotel. In the early hours of July 10, after arguing for most of the evening, a hotel porter heard the sound of three gunshots from their suite. Inside, he found Fahmy slumped against the wall with a gunshot wound to the head. Marguerite was standing nearby holding a gun. Fahmy, still alive, was rushed to the hospital, but nothing could be done for him. He died just over an hour later. Marguerite was arrested and charged with murder. Two months later, she stood in the dock at London's Central Criminal Court, better known as the Old Bailey. If she had been found guilty of murder, as seemed inevitable, she would have been taken from the court to a place of execution and hanged.

The case was soon making lurid headlines in the British papers. When the Prince of Wales and his closest aides learned of Marguerite's predicament, they feared that his relationship with her might be made public during the trial and cause the royal family great embarrassment. They made it their business to find out everything they could about the trial and to do whatever was necessary to keep the prince's name out of it. This was essential, because British royalty no longer had any real power or independence. Their position, now as then, depended on popular support. Behind the scenes, negotiators succeeded in securing the return of the letters and an agreement that the prince's name would not be mentioned in the trial. But what was she offered in return?

Marguerite was defended by one of the most famous British lawyers of the day—Edward Marshall Hall. Her defense was that she had fired the gun in the air to stop Fahmy from attacking her. When he continued toward her, she had pointed the gun at him and pulled the trigger, thinking the gun was empty by then. Marshall Hall portrayed Fahmy as a brutal and depraved husband and argued that Marguerite had fired at him because she feared for her life. Andrew Rose proposed in his book *The Woman Before Wallis: The Prince, the Parisian Courtesan, and the Perfect Murder* that there was an establishment conspiracy to ensure an acquittal in return for Marguerite's surrendering the prince's letters and a guarantee that his name would not be mentioned in court. The trial was certainly unusual in several respects. Important forensic evidence that would have supported the prosecution case was not presented, Marguerite's shady past was not revealed, several relevant witnesses were not called, and the judge's summing up was decidedly partial in favor of Marguerite. It's little wonder that the jury took just an hour to reach a verdict—not guilty. Marguerite then sued the Fahmy family for her late husband's considerable fortune. However, an Egyptian court disregarded the British court's verdict, declared his death to have been due to murder, and dismissed her claim.

King George V died on January 20, 1936, and "David," the naïve and immature Prince of Wales with the film star looks, became King Edward VIII, but he would never be crowned. He was intent on marrying his latest partner, Wallis Simpson. She had been married twice before. At that time, the Church of England did not allow a divorced person to marry if his or her previous partner was still alive. Both of Wallis Simpson's husbands were still alive. The Church of England's regulations did not apply to her first marriage in the United States nor her second marriage in a London register office. However, when the king declared his intention to marry her, church regulations could not be ignored, because he was the head of the church. It was made clear to the king that he could not remain on the throne if he carried out his wish to marry Simpson. The king's solution was the nuclear option. He decided to give up the throne. He abdicated on December 11,

1936, and lived with Simpson as the Duke and Duchess of Windsor until his death in 1972. Meanwhile, Marguerite faded from public attention. She died on January 2, 1971, at the age of 80. A few of the prince's letters to her were found among her personal effects, but they were destroyed by her lover.

A CROWDED MARRIAGE—
CAMILLA PARKER BOWLES

After King Edward VIII, the next Prince of Wales, Prince Charles, was encouraged by his dashing great-uncle, Lord Louis Mountbatten, to sow his wild oats while he could, before he had to find a suitable wife and settle down to his royal destiny. He followed Mountbatten's advice enthusiastically. One of the many young women he met in the early 1970s was Camilla Shand. She reputedly said to him, "My great-great-grandmother [Alice Keppel] was your great-great-grandfather's [King Edward VII's] mistress, so how about it?" Her bold approach worked. They had a brief affair, but after Charles left for several years' military service, Camilla married cavalry officer Colonel Andrew Parker Bowles. Then in 1981, Charles married Lady Diana Spencer. By then, Charles had lost his mentor, Mountbatten, who had been murdered by a terrorist group, the Irish Republican Army, in 1979. Diana was rated highly as a suitable wife for the heir to the throne because she had royal ancestry (she was a direct descendant of King Charles II), she wasn't Catholic, she had not been married before, and, because of her youth (thirteen years younger than Charles), she had no "past" that could embarrass the royal family. Their marriage ceremony, described as the wedding of the century, was watched by a global television audience of 750 million people in seventy-four countries—still the biggest television audience for any wedding.

However, their marriage began to fall apart after only five years. Charles, who often appeared withdrawn and melancholy, was unable to cope with Diana's fragile personality. She found life under the constant gaze of the world's press particularly difficult and later complained that she received no help or training from the royal family for her official role as Princess of Wales. She felt as if she had become a "product" that other people were making money out of. Her problems were compounded by postpartum depression after the birth of her boys, the princes William and Harry, and she also suffered from the eating disorder bulimia. Although she was desperately unhappy, she felt enormous pressure to make her fairy-tale marriage work, but it was to no avail. Charles resumed his relationship with Camilla in 1986. Diana would famously say in a television interview in 1995, "There were three of us in this marriage, so it was a bit crowded." Diana looked for happiness outside the marriage, too, embarking on a five-year affair with former household cavalry officer and tank commander Major James Hewitt, who had been her riding instructor. The inevitable happened. The prime minister announced the Prince and Princess of Wales's separation in December 1992. They led independent lives although they remained married until the queen intervened to resolve this messy arrangement. In 1995, she wrote to both of them, advising them to divorce. Direct "advice" from the queen is code for "Do it!" They complied, and the divorce was finalized in August 1996. As the mother of two royal princes, Diana remained a member of the royal family and retained her residence at Kensington Palace until her death in a controversial car crash in Paris on August 31, 1997.

Meanwhile, Charles continued his relationship with Camilla, who had divorced in 1995. Their image was carefully managed by public relations advisers. They were not photographed together until 1999. In February 2005, they announced their engagement and married in July of the same year. There were two last-minute hitches to the wedding. Initially, the ceremony was to be held at Windsor Castle. However, it was discovered that to comply with the law, the castle would have to be licensed as a wedding venue for everyone, not just Charles and Camilla, so the venue was switched to Windsor Guildhall. Then, the ceremony had to be delayed by a day so that Charles could represent the queen at the funeral of Pope John Paul II.

As soon as their engagement was announced, there was great speculation as to what titles Camilla would take after their marriage and when Charles becomes king. Clarence House, Prince Charles's private office, clarified the situation in a press statement. After their marriage, Camilla would be known as Her Royal Highness, the Duchess of Cornwall. (Charles is the Duke of Cornwall as well as the Prince of Wales.) She is entitled to be known as the Princess of Wales, but she has never used this title, probably because of its association with Diana. The statement went on to say that when Charles becomes king, it is intended that Camilla will not be known as queen, but will take the title princess consort.

7

THE AMERICAS

There are very few examples of American courtesans, probably because the United States is a relatively young country whose leadership shunned the royal and imperial excesses that were common elsewhere. However, there have been some notable cases. Clara Ward was an American who went hunting for European royalty to marry, but having snared a prince, she ran away with a gypsy violinist. Klondike Kate was famous for her trademark Flame Dance in the Yukon during the gold rush. Fanny White was a New York madam whose death in mysterious circumstances was the subject of rumors alleging foul play and a forged will. Eliza Lynch aspired to be a South American Joséphine to her Paraguayan Napoléon, but her ambition turned to dust in one of the world's most destructive wars.

THE AMERICAN PRINCESS—
CLARA WARD

Clara Ward went to Europe to hunt for a European aristocrat who could give her a title. The story that unfolded was followed avidly across two continents.

Clara had every advantage in life. She was born in Detroit in 1873 into an extremely wealthy family. Her father, Eber Brock Ward, was the richest man in Michigan. He was said to be the state's first millionaire. He'd started with nothing as a cabin boy working on Great Lakes ships. By saving every cent he could and making clever investments, he started to make money. In a few years, he was the part-owner of a ship. Then he got involved in building ships. From there, he branched out into all sorts of industries, including mining, logging, railroads, and steelmaking. The former penniless cabin boy was eventually worth well over $100 million in today's money. He was known as the "King of the Lakes."

Clara barely knew her father, because he died before her second birthday. Her mother, Catherine, took Clara and her brother to New York, where she met and married a Canadian lawyer called Alexander Cameron. He settled his new family in Toronto. When Clara was fifteen years old, she was sent away to finish her education in London. Two years later, her mother took her on a tour of Europe to search for a suitable husband, especially one with an aristocratic title.

When they reached Nice, France, they found what they were looking for. They met Prince Marie Joseph Anatole Élie de Riquet de Caraman, nineteenth prince de Chimay. He was in his thirties, nearly twice as old as young Clara, and unmarried. He would compete in the 1900 Olympic Games as a fencer. Despite the difference in their ages, they evidently hit it off, because they were married in May 1890. The papal nuncio in Paris presided over the ceremony. On her marriage, Clara became the princesse de Caraman-Chimay. Their first child, Marie Elizabeth, arrived in May of the following year, and a son, Joseph Anatole, was born in 1894. Clara spent some of her considerable inheritance from her wealthy father paying off the prince's debts and repairing his château.

She appeared to have settled into her new life in Belgium, but trouble lay ahead. The voluptuous American princess attracted the attention of the Belgian king, Leopold II, provoking the displeasure of the queen. Gossip about the king's roving eye and the woman who was the object of his desire spread. Clara was ostracized by polite Belgian society, who saw her as the guilty party leading their king astray. Her husband's response was to move his family to Paris. He couldn't know it, but the move would make matters even worse.

THE GYPSY VIOLINIST

While the prince and Clara were dining at the Café Faillard, a Hungarian gypsy called Rigó Jancsi was playing the violin to entertain the customers. Clara was instantly attracted to him. In December 1896, she disappeared from home. The prince eventually discovered that she had run away with Rigó. To the annoyance and embarrassment of her family, the press found out what had happened and reported it. And they carried on reporting sightings of the couple as they traveled across Europe to Hungary. The prince divorced Clara, and her mother disinherited her. When her mother died in 1915, she left the bulk of her estate to various relatives, but left only one thousand dollars to Clara. The prince won custody of their children, and Clara had to pay alimony amounting to half the income from her father's inheritance.

Clara married her gypsy lover just over a year after her divorce. Rigó carried on working as a violinist while Clara started performing a curious "act" onstage. She adopted a theatrical pose and stood absolutely still, wearing a skintight flesh-colored costume. Strange as it may seem, she was able to earn several thousand dollars a month performing her *poses plastiques,* as she called them, at venues including the Folies Bergère and Moulin Rouge. Her stage costume inspired the outfit worn by Parisian café owner and dancer Simone Pistache, played by Shirley MacLaine in the 1960 film *Can-Can.*

Clara's marriage to Rigó proved to be a stormy relationship. They were often heard shouting and screaming at each other in their hotel rooms. They divorced in 1904, and Clara immediately married Guiseppe "Peppino" Ricciardi, variously described as a waiter or a travel agency worker. This marriage failed, too. On December 18, 1916, Clara Ward, onetime princesse de Caraman-Chimay, died of pneumonia at her home in Italy. She left nearly all her estate, worth more than a million dollars, to Ricciardi and her two children.

THE QUEEN OF THE YUKON—
KLONDIKE KATE

Klondike Kate Rockwell is sometimes described as an American courtesan and she appears in lists of courtesans, but she doesn't fit the traditional definition of a courtesan. She didn't romance kings or dukes. She didn't pursue wealthy or powerful men for their money. But she did attract men in large numbers and occasionally used them to her advantage. She is said to have received more than a hundred marriage proposals.

Kathleen Eloise Rockwell acquired her nickname while she was working as an entertainer in the Yukon during the Klondike Gold Rush, but her story began in Kansas, where she was born in 1876. She seems to have inherited a rebellious streak from her parents, who had defied accepted social standards by divorcing their partners to marry each other. Sadly, the marriage didn't last. Kate's mother, Martha, remarried before Kate's fifth birthday and moved to Spokane, Washington, but this marriage failed, too. She then moved to Chile, where her grown-up son from a previous marriage was living.

During the sea voyage to Chile, the teenage Kate struck up a friendship with one of the ship's officers. She wanted to marry him, but her mother put a stop to the relationship and sent her to a convent school. The intention was clearly to keep men at a safe distance until Kate was older and a suitable husband could be selected for her, but even in the convent school, she received a marriage proposal. Her suitor this time was a young diplomatic attaché from Spain. An attractive young American girl in Chile had considerable novelty value, so she received more and more proposals, and she said yes to all of them. Before long she was engaged to seven different men at the same time. When her school found out, she was ordered to give the rings back.

A STAGE CAREER BEGINS

When Kate finished her education, she returned to the United States. She worked briefly as a chorus girl and found that she enjoyed performing onstage. In 1896, while she was working at a theater in Spokane, large gold deposits were discovered along the Klondike River in the Yukon. As news of the find spread across North America, tens of thousands of prospectors flocked to the area, hoping to make their fortune. They were followed by thousands of traders, entertainers, and prostitutes keen to get a slice of the action. New towns sprang up along the rivers where the prospectors panned for gold. One of them, Dawson City, grew from a population of five hundred in 1896 to more than thirty thousand only two years later. Its saloons grew rich on the prospectors.

Kate headed north toward the goldfields, stopping at towns along the way to work in vaudeville shows. However, the Mounties stopped her. They told her it was too dangerous for a woman to travel farther north to the Yukon. Undeterred, she simply dressed as a boy and carried on. She worked for a while as a tap dancer in Whitehorse and then joined the Savoy Theatrical Company in Dawson City. She wore daring costumes that were more revealing than most. Her beauty, red hair, violet eyes, husky voice, and sex appeal made her an instant favorite with audiences, earning her the nickname "Klondike Kate." She was so successful that a showman called Arizona Charlie Meadows tempted her away from the Savoy to work for him at the Palace Grande Theater. Meadows was named Abraham Henson Meadows at birth, but his Southern-leaning parents were so angered by Abraham Lincoln's policies that they renamed their little boy Charlie. His father was killed in an Apache raid at the family's Arizona ranch in 1881. Charlie's expertise with a rifle and skill on horseback led to his working in Wild West shows. It was Buffalo Bill Cody who named him Arizona Charlie. When the gold rush began, he headed north to sell all sorts of supplies to the prospectors, but instead he ended up opening a theater to entertain them.

Kate was a big hit for Meadows. She developed her trademark "Flame Dance" at the Palace Grande. She wore a red sequined dress trailing two hundred feet of chiffon that looked like flickering flames as she danced. It made her a star. She was paid a weekly wage, but this was dwarfed by the commission she earned on dances and drinks bought by the customers. On just one good night, she could earn several times her weekly wage in commissions. And some of the prospectors are said to have shown their appreciation by throwing gold nuggets onto the stage. There are stories of the management sweeping the theater floors at the end of each day and sieving the sweepings for gold dust. Kate acquired another nickname at the Palace Grande—"Queen of the Yukon." There is a story about her being crowned Queen of the Yukon on Christmas Eve 1900, with a crown surmounted by lit candles. The candles dripped hot wax onto her hair. When she found that she couldn't brush the wax out, she had her lovely long red hair cut down to a short bob, which was as daring as her costumes.

A STORMY RELATIONSHIP

At about this time, a Scandinavian miner called Johnny Matson saw Kate and instantly fell in love with her. Matson was out of luck—but only for a time. Kate was more interested in a Greek waiter, entertainer, and prize-fighter called Alexander Pantages. The two were soon living together. He borrowed a lot of money from her to launch a new career as a theater manager. When he opened his first theater, she was his headline act. By 1902, cracks were beginning to appear in their relationship. Pantages, a teetotaler, was unhappy with the amount of alcohol Kate drank. He was also coping with financial trouble in his theater chain. They grew further apart, literally—she went on a tour of the United States. She accused him of going back on a promise to marry her and of trying to cheat her out of her money. The Klondike Gold Rush was in decline by then. Many of the miners and prospectors had already moved on to the next gold rush in Alaska. Kate and Pantages headed south. Pantages set up a new chain of theaters in Seattle. Kate held out the hope of getting back together with him and eventually marrying him, so she was devastated when he suddenly abandoned her and married a violin player half her age from one of his theaters.

Kate's response to the news was to take Pantages to court. She wanted him to pay back all the money she had given him plus another twenty-five thousand dollars for breach of promise (to marry her). More than a year later, she settled out of court for a mere five thousand. She used the money to move to Fairbanks, Alaska, where she invested in a hotel. In 1907, after the hotel burned down, she left Alaska. She was penniless. She toured in vaudeville for a while, but in 1914 a leg injury ended her stage career.

She had been suffering from depression, which led to a nervous breakdown. On medical advice, she moved out to a homestead near a tiny town called Brothers in the Oregon countryside, well away from the hustle, bustle, and stress of her former life. Instead of starring onstage and playing to full houses, she did everything from washing dishes to running a convalescent home. A few years later, she moved to California, but it didn't work out. Unable to find employment apart from a bit of waitressing, she was soon penniless again. She had to borrow the few dollars she needed to get back to Oregon. There, she married a young cowboy called Floyd Warner. But she cheated on him and was single again by the early 1920s and living in Bend, Oregon, where she built a lodging house and could often be seen serving coffee to firefighters from the nearby fire station. She was known, rather unkindly, by some of the locals as "Our Destitute Prostitute." Kinder residents simply called her "Aunt Kate."

Her path would cross Pantages's once more. In 1929, he was charged with raping a seventeen-year-old girl. Kate was called as a witness by the prosecution. As it turned out, she didn't have to give evidence. Pantages was found guilty and sentenced to fifty years in prison. He was acquitted after a retrial two years later, but he suffered a heart attack and died soon afterwards. Meanwhile, Kate threw herself into fund-raising for good causes. And when the United States was overwhelmed by the Great Depression, she made soup for the homeless.

FROZEN TO DEATH

In 1933, Kate heard from someone from her past—Johnny Matson, the Scandinavian gold prospector who had fallen for her in Dawson City but lost out to Pantages. He proposed to her and she said yes. They were married on July 14, 1933, in Vancouver. At the age of seventy, Matson was still looking for gold. They decided that it was too dangerous for Kate to live with him at a remote camp during the winter. She would stay with him in the summer, but return to the United States before winter closed in. The danger at his remote Alaskan claim became evident in 1946, when he was found frozen to death in his shack.

Soon after Matson's death, Kate heard from someone else from her past. She was contacted by an accountant called William Van Duren, a man she had known nearly twenty years earlier in Oregon. Within two years, they were married and living in the delightfully named Sweet Home, Oregon. Kate died peacefully in her sleep there in 1957. She left instructions that her body was to be cremated and her ashes were to be scattered in the high desert of central Oregon. However, her husband died before he could carry out her wishes, and no one else came forward to take his place. A year later, when an undertaker told the story, Kate's friends offered to collect her ashes and scatter them as she wished.

NEW YORK MADAM—FANNY WHITE

Fanny White was one of the most successful courtesans of nineteenth-century New York. Her death was as controversial as her life. Did she die of natural causes, or was she murdered? And was her will a forgery?

Fanny White's real name was Jane Augusta Funk. She was born on March 23, 1823, to a German immigrant farmer, Jacob Funk, and his wife, Jane. She was a pretty girl, described as "unusually handsome, both in form and features." She was also an able pianist and enjoyed writing poetry. At the age of about eighteen, she fell prey to a "seducer"—an older man who seduced her with the promise of marriage, but then abandoned her. With her reputation ruined, her options were limited. She was unlikely to be able to find a respectable husband. Women in this position often ended up in prostitution. Jane left home and headed for her brother, John H. Funk, in New York City. However, John declined to help her. She would have to make her own way. After a short time working in a hotel, she went to work in a brothel on Church Street. To hide her real identity and save her family from shame, she changed her name to Fanny White. A few months later, she moved to another brothel on Leonard Street, near West Broadway. She prospered to such an extent that four years later she was managing her own brothel.

IMMORAL EARNINGS

In 1851, Fanny bought a house on Mercer Street and ran it as a high-class brothel for politicians, diplomats, and other influential clients. It was on the itinerary of many visiting dignitaries. She made sure to keep the police happy so that they overlooked her activities. By then, she had met lawyer and politician Daniel Sickles. When Sickles was elected to the New York State Assembly in 1847, he took her back to his hotel and introduced her to the guests, who were less than happy to be faced with the notorious Fanny White. When they went on a tour of the State Assembly chamber, they had to beat a hasty retreat before Fanny was ejected by the sergeant-at-arms. On another occasion, they went out together in costume. Fanny was dressed in men's clothes, which was illegal. They were spotted by police and spent a night in the cells.

Sickles's reputation was permanently damaged by his association with Fanny. There were persistent rumors that her immoral earnings had helped to fund his election campaign, and he was suspected of arranging the mortgage on Fanny's Mercer Street brothel. The mortgage was in the name of a friend of Sickles's, Antonio Bagioli. When Fanny suspected that Sickles was seeing someone else, she followed him one night and saw him meeting Bagioli's sixteen-year-old daughter, Teresa. She was so angry that she attacked Sickles with a riding whip. In September 1852, Sickles married Teresa.

The following year, Fanny traveled to England, where she managed to get herself presented to Queen Victoria. In the spring of 1854, she left England for the Continent. In France, she had to be removed from the Paris Opera by the police for being loud and disorderly because of an overindulgence in the best French wines.

When she returned to New York, she opened a new brothel behind the St. Nicholas Hotel. It was a great success, bringing her increased wealth. She also benefited from money and gifts lavished on her by her lovers. Some of them spent so much money on her that they bankrupted themselves. One unfortunate widower is said to have had second thoughts after giving her a house and annuity and went to court to recover it all. The court canceled the annuity, but Fanny was allowed to keep the house. She invested her wealth in property all over the city.

A Sudden Death

In 1859, Fanny married defense lawyer Edmon Blankman and so became Jane Augusta Blankman. She is said to have left her previous life behind her and regularly attended church. She was very generous to her family and paid her niece's school fees. She also bought a lease on a house and gave it to her widowed sister. Her husband wanted her to sign over their home to him, but she refused after she allegedly discovered that he'd tried to seduce her niece.

Fanny died suddenly at home on October 12, 1860, at the age of only thirty-seven. The day before her death, she had watched a procession in honor of the Prince of Wales (later King Edward VII) from a window in Bixby's Hotel. She got up on the morning of the twelfth and had breakfast with her husband, niece, and a Mr. Richardson, who was staying with them. She complained of feeling dizzy. After she'd seen her husband off to work, she went upstairs to her bedroom to make her bed, as was her custom. Sometime later, a servant found her kneeling beside her bed. Thinking Mrs. Blankman had suffered a seizure, the servant called for help to lift her onto her bed. It was then that they began to suspect that Fanny had died. A doctor who lived across the street was called to examine her. He confirmed that she was dead.

There were rumors that her husband had poisoned her to get his hands on her money and property. An autopsy requested by one of her brothers found the cause of death to be cerebral apoplexy (bleeding in the brain). Fanny's brother was satisfied, so she was buried in the Blankman family plot in Brooklyn's Green-Wood Cemetery. However, rumors of foul play persisted. An anonymous note was pushed under the coroner's door claiming that Mrs. Blankman's death was not natural. When the coroner questioned the doctors who had performed the autopsy, he discovered that they had not performed a full autopsy. They had examined only her head and neck. When they found bleeding in the brain serious enough to account for her death, they looked no further. As the possibility of poisoning remained, on the district attorney's advice, the coroner ordered Fanny's body to be exhumed for a second autopsy.

The result of the autopsy was given at the coroner's investigation. Evidence of tuberculosis, syphilis, cardiovascular disease, cancer, and bleeding in the brain were found, but there was no sign of poisoning. Edmon Blankman revealed the possible cause of the brain injury in his evidence. He testified that his wife had suffered an accident the day before her death. While she was at Bixby's Hotel watching the Prince of Wales's procession, a window roller and shade had fallen on her head. He hadn't seen it happen himself, but was told about it by his niece. The twelve-year-old niece confirmed this. After everyone who had witnessed events at the Blankman home and all the doctors present at the two autopsies had given their evidence, the jury retired. It took them only fifteen minutes to come to the conclusion that the cause of death was cerebral apoplexy and there had been no foul play.

Fanny left most of her estate to her husband. Her relatives contested the will, suggesting that it had been forged, presumably by Fanny's husband, Edmon Blankman. The court proceedings were reported in *The New York Times,* which published verbatim accounts of some of the evidence and cross-examination. Witnesses disagreed on the authenticity of signatures on the will. The case was lost, and the will was confirmed as genuine. An appeal to the Supreme Court failed, too, enabling the will finally to proceed to probate. A month later, in October 1861, Edmon Blankman sold Fanny's possessions at auction. They were advertised in *The New York Times* on October 28, 1861, as an executor's sale of "magnificent household furniture, rich French plate pier and mantel mirrors, superbly carved rosewood pianoforte, sterling silver plate &c." Thus ended the story of the New York madam Fanny White.

THE EMPRESS OF PARAGUAY— ELIZA LYNCH

An Irish immigrant courtesan is blamed by some for devastating a South American nation and starting one of the most destructive wars of modern times.

Between 1845 and 1852, a quarter of the population of Ireland either died or emigrated as a result of the Great Famine. One of the many Irish emigrants was a ten-year-old girl called Eliza Lynch, a native of Charleville in County Cork. The Lynch family left Ireland for France, but the situation there was little better. There had been crop failures in France, too. Food shortages and rising unemployment led to riots in the streets. The king, Louis-Philippe, abdicated and was replaced by Louis-Napoléon, the nephew of Napoléon Bonaparte.

On her fifteenth birthday, Eliza married a French army officer, Xavier Quatrefages, who was more than twice her age. The marriage would have been illegal in France because of Eliza's age, so the couple crossed the Channel to England and married there. When her new husband was posted to Algeria, she went with him. She quickly tired of army life in remote Algerian outposts and returned to France with a Russian cavalry officer she'd met in Algeria. While she was away, her father had died and her mother had moved to England. She lived in Paris with her Russian soldier until 1853, when the Crimean War broke out and he was summoned back to active service.

She now found herself alone in Paris with no one to support her. The only avenue open to Eliza to pay her way was to become one of *les grandes horizontales,* the courtesans who flourished in France at this time. She had the necessary assets—she was young, tall, beautiful, blue-eyed, and red-haired. And she moved in the same elevated social circles as the men she needed to attract. One of her friends was Princess Mathilde, Napoléon Bonaparte's niece, so she was invited to all the best dinners, parties, opera performances, and soirees. She soon had an impressive stable of lovers. And she had a head for business, too. She installed gaming tables at her home to encourage lovers to spend money even while they were waiting to see her. But no matter how much money she made, she spent it as quickly as she earned it. She decided that she'd rather have just one lover who was wealthy enough to take care of her.

AN EMPEROR IN WAITING

The man of her dreams arrived in Paris in the shape of a visiting South American soldier, Francisco Solano López, but he was no ordinary soldier. The main attraction for Eliza was that he was also the billionaire son of the Paraguayan president, Carlos Antonio López. One day he would be his country's president, but he had much bigger ambitions. He wanted his own South American empire in the style of Napoléon's French empire. And once he had been "entertained" by Eliza, he vowed to make her his empress if she would return to Paraguay with him. She knew when she was onto a good thing. They set sail for South America in November 1854 and arrived in the Paraguayan capital, Asunción, two months later. Asunción wasn't the grand city that Eliza had expected. It was tiny compared to Paris. The streets were unpaved and made of clay. And it was unbearably hot. Few of the people wore shoes, and everyone smoked, even the children.

The crowds of people who had gathered to greet Francisco were stunned when they saw the red-haired Eliza arriving with him. They hadn't known that she was coming, and they'd never seen anyone with red hair before. To them, she looked like a creature from another world. And by then, she was unmistakably pregnant. Francisco's family snubbed her, making it clear that she was not welcome. However, Francisco refused to give her up. She gave birth to a boy, Juan Francisco, who was known as Panchito. Just over a year later, a second child arrived, a girl called Corina Adelaida. Sadly, the little girl died from a fever at six months. Toward the end of 1858, Eliza gave birth to her third child, a boy called Enrique Venancio Lynch López.

Paraguay was sandwiched between two hostile neighbors—Brazil to the north and Argentina to the south, both vastly bigger than Paraguay. But as long as European merchants were based in Paraguay and it was well armed, the government felt safe. If European interests in Paraguay were threatened, the European powers would be sure to come to its aid. But Francisco had grander ambitions than simply keeping his enemies outside Paraguay's borders. He trained more and more soldiers until he had the biggest army in South America.

When the president died in 1862, Francisco assumed the presidency and immediately imposed his iron grip on the country. He jailed or executed anyone he thought might be opposed to his grand plans, even members of his own family. Many others fled from the country. Francisco's word was law, and, by association, so was Eliza's. And she controlled access to the president. Apart from the president, she was now the most important and powerful person in Paraguay. But they both feared dissent and revolution from the many enemies they'd made. They became so paranoid that, like many dictators before and since, they established a network of spies and informers who reported every bit of gossip back to them.

AN EXCUSE FOR WAR

In 1864, Brazil invaded Uruguay, which appealed to Paraguay for help, giving Francisco the excuse he needed to go to war. Eliza urged him to take this opportunity to strike against Brazil. In December, five thousand Paraguayan troops invaded the Matto Grosso, the Brazilian state to the north of Paraguay, and quickly took it. Then Paraguayan troops invaded Argentina and took the city of Corrientes. When Paraguay's territorial ambitions became clear, Argentina, Brazil, and Uruguay signed a Triple Alliance treaty to overthrow the government of Paraguay.

While Paraguay had more men under arms than all its neighbors added together, they were badly trained and poorly armed. They were kept in line by draconian punishment. Dissent and insubordination were punished by execution. Prisoners of war were routinely tortured and executed, too.

Eliza accompanied Francisco throughout the war. She was said to be more courageous than he under fire. Eventually, the war began to turn against Paraguay. Francisco and Eliza finally realized that they could be on the losing side, and they started shipping large sums of money abroad. In January 1869, Asunción fell to the Triple Alliance forces. The war seemed to be over, but Francisco was still free and trying to gather enough soldiers together to stage a counterattack. On March 1, 1870, Brazilian troops finally caught up with him. Francisco tried to escape on horseback but was caught and killed. Eliza was captured. Her oldest son, Panchito, a fifteen-year-old army colonel, tried to protect her and was killed. Eliza dug a grave and buried her husband and son. The war was finally over. Up to about a million Paraguayans, 80 percent of the population, were dead. Only about 220,000 survived, and only 28,000 of those were adult males. Paraguay lost large areas of land to Argentina and Brazil and had to pay hundreds of millions of dollars in reparations until the 1930s.

When Eliza was released, having had most of her property seized by the new government, she sailed for England. She was still only thirty-five. Five years later, she went back to Paraguay and tried to reclaim her property. However, the new president, Juan Batista Gill, banished her from the country. She died from stomach cancer in Paris on July 25, 1886, and was buried in Père Lachaise Cemetery. A hundred years later, the Paraguayan dictator General Alfredo Stroessner had her remains brought back to Paraguay, where she was reburied as a national heroine.

ASIA

Asian countries, especially India, China, and Japan, have a long history of courtesans, mistresses, and concubines. In most cases, they lived very tightly controlled lives, with little or no personal freedom. India had a particularly lively history of dancing girls, entertainers, and professional companions, but just as in the rest of the world, the courtesan culture in Asia went into decline at the end of the nineteenth century.

FROM MUGHAL EMPERORS TO BOLLYWOOD

Entertainers called *tawaifs* became popular in the seventeenth century during India's Mughal period. *Tawaifs* were similar to Japan's geisha girls—artistic entertainers and companions. As British rule spread, *tawaifs* and dancers called nautch girls entertained the British, too. Their popularity came to an end in the nineteenth century, when their Mughal-emperor patrons were disempowered by the British, and traditional Indian entertainment fell out of favor. The British branded *tawaifs* as prostitutes, forced them to register with the authorities, and subjected them to medical inspections to control sexually transmitted diseases. During the Indian Mutiny of 1857, the British suspected the *tawaifs* of supporting the enemy by helping to finance the rebellion and using their *kothas* (houses where they entertained clients) as meeting places for the rebels. They closed down the *kothas* and evicted the *tawaifs*. Despite those setbacks, India's courtesans, entertainers, and dancing girls were able to preserve traditional music and dance, which are still seen today in a refined and stylized form in Bollywood movies.

THE COURTESAN WHO RULED
A PRINCIPALITY—BEGUM SAMRU

Begum Samru was a courtesan who rose to become a ruler in her own right. Born in about 1753 and named Farzana Zeb un-Nissa, she was said to be the daughter of an Arab nobleman, Latif Ali Khan. When he died, she was taken from her birthplace in Kotana, Uttar Pradesh, to live in Delhi, where she became a dancer. She entertained troops, including a mercenary soldier called Walter Reinhardt Sombre. He was also known as Samru or Sumru, thought to be a mispronunciation of his surname. She lived with him and may even have married him. He was forty-five and she was in her early teens. She traveled with him on his military campaigns. Despite being a tiny girl just over four feet tall, she gathered her own force of troops and rode into battle with them. Samru was appointed Governor of Agra, and shortly before his death in 1778, he was appointed ruler of the principality of Sardhana by Shah Alam II. On Samru's death, Farzana took command of his army and inherited his position as ruler of Sardhana. She even managed to retain control of the region under British rule. In 1781, this extraordinary Muslim woman adopted Roman Catholicism, thus becoming the only Catholic ruler in India. She was baptized as Joanna Nobilis. In 1806, she built a palace at Chandni Chowk, which still stands today. When she died in 1836, she was denied permission to be buried at Sardhana Church, because she had once been Muslim. Instead, she was cremated on land donated by a friend.

VISAGE OF THE MOON — MAH LAQA

Mah Laqa was the courtesan of the second nizam of Hyderabad, a former state in central India. She was born as Chanda Bibi in 1768, and brought up by her stepsister. She was educated in Persian, Urdu, classical music, poetry, horse-riding, archery, and dance. Her Urdu poetry was admired by influential people, including the prime minister, who encouraged her to publish her work, making her the first woman to publish a divan (a collection of Urdu poetry). She gave poetry readings and dance performances, which brought her to the attention of the nizam. She became his close companion, even accompanying him to war in male battle dress. After one victory, he gave her the official title Mah Laqa Bai (meaning "Visage of the Moon") and granted her land. She was also given the right to be carried in a palanquin (a covered chair) with a bodyguard of one hundred soldiers. As she was carried around, her way was cleared by the beating of drums. Her procession must have been quite a spectacle.

When the second nizam died in 1803, she continued as court singer, dancer, and poet for the third nizam. She enjoyed power, wealth, and independence denied even to royal women in her time. She used her income to fund charities, festivals, and building work. Her popularity rejuvenated the almost extinct courtesan culture in Hyderabad. When she died in 1824, she was buried in a tomb she'd had built for her mother in Moula-Ali in Hyderabad. Its design is a blend of Mughal and Rajasthani styles. The tomb fell into disrepair and lay derelict for nearly two hundred years. Then in 2009, a two-year program of work began to renovate it, financed with help from the American Ambassadors Fund for Cultural Preservation. The renovated tomb was then opened to the public.

THE PEACOCK DANCER—
MORAN SARKAR

Another dancer caught the eye of a famous Sikh warrior called Maharaja Ranjit Singh. Born in 1780 in Gujranwala and battle-hardened since the age of ten, Ranjit Singh met a dancing girl called Moran at the festivities to celebrate his son's engagement in 1802. Before the end of the year, Ranjit Singh married Moran and she became the Maharani Sahiba. She was also known as Moran Sarkar. The Sikh community was outraged by their marriage, because Moran was a Muslim and had been a nautch girl (dancer) and *tawaif* who did not observe purdah (female seclusion). An alternative story holds that Ranjit Singh incurred the wrath of the community by visiting Moran on his arrival in Amritsar before paying his respects at the gurdwara (place of worship). Whichever story is true, it resulted in Singh being condemned to a public flogging by the Akal Takht, the highest Sikh authority. Because he readily accepted his punishment without dissent or complaint, the penalty was reduced to a fine. To end the intrigue and controversy, the maharaja sent Moran away to Pathankot. He continued to love her and considered her to be among the most beautiful of his queens (he had more than forty!). He had coins struck bearing her name and a peacock feather, because her dancing is said to have reminded him of a peacock.

A REBELLIOUS COURTESAN—
AZIZUN NISA

In 1857, sepoys (Indian troops serving in the British East India Company's army), unhappy because of worsening conditions of service, mutinied over new ammunition they were supplied with. The sepoys had been issued with a new type of rifle, the Pattern 1853 or P53 Enfield rifle-musket. It fired cartridges wrapped with greased paper. To load the weapon, a rifleman had to bite the end of the cartridge to tear it open and pour the gunpowder inside it down the barrel. Then the paper-wrapped bullet was rammed down the barrel on top of the powder charge. Rumors spread through the sepoys that the paper was greased with beef fat or lard (pig fat) or a mixture of the two. The first was offensive to Hindus, and the second was offensive to Muslims. Attempts to resolve the problem failed, and the troops mutinied. The mutineers fought against troops who remained loyal to the British.

The most famous courtesan of the Indian Rebellion of 1857 was Azizun Nisa. She was born in 1832 and worked as a dancing girl and courtesan in a *kotha* in Cawnpore (Kanpur today). She is said to have moved there from Lucknow, where she would have had to work under a more senior courtesan. In Cawnpore, she could enjoy a more independent life. She danced for British soldiers and knew a number of sepoys. She was particularly close to a sepoy called Shamsuddin Khan, who served with the British 2nd Cavalry. When Shamsuddin and other sepoys told her about atrocities committed by the British against Indians, she joined the mutiny. She helped to look after wounded fighters and assisted with the distribution of arms and ammunition. She transformed herself from a dancing girl into a warrior. She dressed as a man in full combat armor and armed herself with pistols and a sword. She was the only woman present when the Indian flag was raised at Cawnpore, the epicenter of the rebellion, and she rode into battle on horseback. Her fate is not recorded.

By the time British forces regained control, more than two thousand British troops and at least one hundred thousand Indians were dead—although some estimates of the Indian death toll are as high as ten million. The mutiny was so serious that it effectively ended a hundred years of East India Company domination of India. The company was dissolved, and the British government took direct control, marking the beginning of the British Raj.

Japan's Pleasure Quarters

Japan was largely a closed book to the rest of the world between the 1630s and 1850s, because of a policy called *sakoku* (meaning "chained country") introduced by the Tokugawa shogunate, the last feudal military government of Japan. It sealed off Japan from the rest of the world to stop foreign missionaries from converting Japanese citizens to Christianity and also to limit the power of Japan's warlords by preventing them from forming alliances with foreign countries and challenging the shogunate. At about the same time, the shogunate also decreed that prostitution would be restricted to specific districts. These were to be walled brothel areas or pleasure quarters—the Yoshiwara in Edo (Tokyo today), Shinmachi in Osaka, and Shimabara in Kyoto. Weapons were not allowed inside them in case a disgruntled customer drew his sword or dagger to settle a dispute. Arms had to be surrendered to guards at the entrance gates.

Inside the walls, thousands of courtesans and hundreds of geisha plied their trade in the brothels, bathhouses, and tearooms. Many of the girls began their careers in the pleasure quarters because they were sold to brothel-keepers by their parents. Others were high-class women who were sent to brothels by their families as punishment for some sort of transgression. They were then under contract to their brothel-keeper for up to ten years. They sat behind grilles so that passing customers could see them, rather like the caged crickets many of them kept.

Japan's courtesan class, called *oiran,* wore elaborate hairstyles and outfits to attract attention. They trained as *yujo* (women of pleasure). The best of the *yujo* might become *oiran,* and the cream of the *oiran* might become *tayu.* Rules dictated how each rank of courtesan should dress. Both geisha and courtesans were famed for their elaborate white-face makeup and black wigs. In time, the various ranks of courtesans died out, and they all became known as *oiran.* They were educated and trained in the same skills as geisha, but the courtesans offered sexual services, too.

Only the wealthiest and most powerful men could hope to engage an *oiran,* who might charge nearly three hundred times more for her services than a common prostitute. Unlike the lower ranks of pleasure women, who had little say in their choice of clients, an *oiran* actively selected the most promising clients from those who requested her services.

There were three stages in the selection process. First, the *oiran* would observe a potential client. Next, if she liked what she saw, she would sit with him for a while. If she was still not deterred by his appearance or behavior, the client progressed to the third stage. He presented her with a pair of chopsticks bearing his name and a payment. If she accepted them, he had formally engaged her services, and he could not visit any other *oiran* or prostitute from then on. To do so would cause a grave insult.

DECLINE OF THE PLEASURE QUARTERS

The *oiran* were so isolated behind the walls of the pleasure quarters that the rest of society moved on and left them behind. *Oiran* culture, language, and practices became more and more detached from the rest of society, and this eventually caused their demise. The Yoshiwara and other pleasure quarters began to decline at the beginning of the twentieth century as Japan opened up to the rest of the world. The process had begun in 1853 with the arrival of a small fleet of four American warships under the command of Commodore Matthew C. Perry. The United States was determined to trade with Japan—by force if necessary!

Perry ignored Japanese instructions telling him where he was allowed to dock and steamed straight to Edo. He presented Japanese representatives with a letter from the U.S. president, Millard Fillmore. Then he left immediately for China, saying he would return soon for a response. The next year, Perry returned with a bigger fleet, ready for a fight, but he was surprised to find a treaty waiting for him to sign.

As Japan's long period of isolation came to an end, it began to trade with more countries. As it modernized, fewer families were prepared to sell their daughters into bondage. Aging courtesans were replaced by more Westernized prostitutes who had little time for the tea ceremony or traditional music or poetry. And attitudes in the wider community were changing, too. Japanese wives were less tolerant of their husbands' infidelity. In the 1950s, the government finally closed down the Yoshiwara and the other pleasure quarters, bringing three hundred years of Japan's distinctive courtesan culture to an end.

One tradition associated with the *oiran* has survived to the present day. *Oiran* wearing their most elaborate costumes, and followed by a retinue of uniformed attendants and servants, would process to meet their clients and escort them back to their rooms. This tradition, called *oiran dochu,* is preserved today, if only as a tourist attraction. Women dressed as *oiran,* wearing six-inch high wooden shoes called geta, tower over everyone else as they and their uniformed attendants walk the streets. These impressive parades, held in Tsubame and Nagoya, attract thousands of spectators.

GEISHA: ARTISTIC ENTERTAINERS

There is a lot of confusion about the role of the geisha in Japan. In the West, they are often mistakenly thought of as prostitutes. In fact, sex was not part of their work—at least, not officially. *Geisha* comes from two Japanese words—*gei,* meaning "art," and *sha,* meaning "person." The geisha were artistic entertainers, skilled in music, poetry, games, and the tea ceremony. Geisha were originally forbidden from engaging in sex. Their job was to entertain guests waiting to see *oiran* in the pleasure quarters, so to have sex with clients would have deprived the *oiran* of lucrative work. When the *oiran* fell out of favor, the geisha rose in importance and popularity. Some were prepared to offer sex, especially to wealthy patrons. In the aftermath of World War II, when Japan was occupied by American troops, some prostitutes attracted clients by dressing as all-American girls with ponytails and bobby socks, but others emphasized their exotic oriental origin by dressing as traditional geisha. Hence, the geisha became linked with prostitution in the Western mind. Traditional geisha still exist in Japan, although in far fewer numbers than in past centuries. Today, they are mainly tourist attractions and picturesque hostesses at parties and large social events.

IMPERIAL CHINA

From the fifteenth century, the Chinese emperor's concubines were housed in the Forbidden City, the awesome walled imperial compound in Beijing that still stands today. "Awesome" is a grossly overused term, but the Forbidden City is truly awesome in scale, in style, and in its historical significance. It was called the Forbidden City because no one could enter it or leave it without the permission of the emperor. It was a vast complex of 980 buildings with 9,999½ rooms. The odd number of rooms was chosen because heaven was believed to have ten thousand rooms, and a mere earthly palace could not possibly be as perfect as heaven. The complex was born out of one of the most violent incidents in China's history. On just one night in 1402, tens of thousands of people were slaughtered, including 2,800 imperial concubines.

When the first Ming dynasty emperor, Zhu Yuanzhang (the Hongwu Emperor), died in 1398, his son Zhu Di expected to become emperor, but he was passed over. The emperor had outlived his successor, his eldest son, Zhu Biao, so he named Zhu Biao's son, Zhu Yunwen, as the new emperor, the Jianwen Emperor. However, Zhu Di was older than Jianwen and thought he had a greater claim to the throne. When he saw the new emperor flex his muscles and begin to restrain the power of his uncles, Zhu Di was spurred into action. Jianwen learned that his uncle was making preparations to attack him. To foil him, he bizarrely ordered his own palace in Nanjing to be burned to the ground. His wife and six-year-old son were found dead in the charred ruins together with the body of a man. No one has ever been able to establish whether this man was Jianwen or a hapless servant sacrificed to let Jianwen escape. Zhu Di declared himself emperor, the Yongle Emperor.

However, Yongle learned of rumors that Jianwen had escaped from the fire. Fearing that he might return with an army to reclaim the throne, Yongle tried to increase his power base by getting the support of society's elite. When he failed, he ordered the execution of anyone he thought might be a political opponent. Tens of thousands were murdered. Imperial concubines and eunuchs who hadn't died in the palace fire were executed, too. To demonstrate his power, Yongle moved his capital from Nanjing to Peking (Beijing) and built the Forbidden City as his impregnable base. Twenty-four emperors would rule China from behind its walls for the next five hundred years until the last emperor, Puyi, abdicated in 1912.

THE CONCUBINE WHO RULED
CHINA—CIXI

Imperial concubines could transform their fortunes and achieve great power by producing a male heir who had the potential to become the emperor. This is how a lowly concubine called Cixi (pronounced *Tsoo Shee*) became the most powerful woman in China for nearly half a century. She was largely responsible for creating modern China.

In 1852, a sixteen-year-old girl was brought to the Forbidden City in Peking (Beijing today). Her name was not recorded. She was to become one of the emperor's many concubines. It was seen as a great honor to be selected to serve the emperor in this way. The Xianfeng (Universal Prosperity) Emperor had occupied the Dragon Throne for just a year. He is said to have noticed the girl when he heard her singing. According to another story, she came to the emperor's attention only when a fellow concubine became pregnant and, according to custom, could not have sex with the emperor. Her unavailability gave the girl her chance. When the emperor summoned her, she was taken to his bedroom by eunuchs and left there naked to ensure that she hadn't brought any weapons with her. Three years after her arrival, she bore him a son. Giving the emperor a male heir immediately promoted her to the first rank of concubines.

Chinese emperors often died young. The Xianfeng Emperor died in 1861 at the age of only thirty. On his death, the concubine's five-year-old son was his only male heir. The young boy became the Tongzhi (Order and Prosperity) Emperor, and his mother became the dowager empress. She took a new name, Cixi (Kindly and Joyous). Because of the emperor's young age, a regent would have to rule until he was old enough to take the reins of power. Cixi and the dowager empress Zheng, the previous empress, served as co-regents, but Cixi was very much in the driver's seat. She had risen from obscurity to become the de facto ruler of China. She used her power and influence to begin opening up China to the rest of the world by encouraging the growth of overseas trade. She also began building up the navy. However, she rejected other changes, including the construction of railways and the introduction of the telegraph. Cixi's grip on power ended when her son reached his seventeenth birthday and began ruling on his own. He proved to be a lazy emperor who spent more time visiting houses of ill repute than attending to state duties. He died from syphilis or smallpox in 1875, less than two years after taking over from his co-regents. He had not produced an heir and had not even nominated a successor. Cixi's three-year-old nephew, Zaitian, was selected to become the new emperor, the Guangxu (Glorious Succession) Emperor.

Cixi once again found herself serving as regent, this time in partnership with Guangxu's mother. When the Guangxu Emperor was old enough to rule on his own, Cixi retired for a second time. But because of her age, seniority, and experience, she was still a powerful figure in the imperial family.

RESISTING REFORM

There was a growing feeling within China that the country needed to be modernized and Westernized, especially when China was decisively defeated in the Sino-Japanese War of 1894–95 by a country a tiny fraction of its size. The emperor was increasingly regarded as incompetent. Cixi was persuaded to return from retirement to take control again. With her help and guidance, the emperor embarked on a belated reform program to update the country's education, legal system, farming methods, and military forces. However, when Cixi learned of the emperor's involvement in a plot to kill her, she acted swiftly to have him imprisoned on a tiny island in the middle of an artificial lake next to the Forbidden City. He continued to rule, but only under Cixi's firm control. He was powerless. Cixi was the effective ruler of China once again. She had the plotters rounded up and executed.

In 1900, thousands of fighters, convinced that they were possessed by spirits and therefore invulnerable, arrived in Peking. They had come to expel or kill foreigners who were thought to have far too much power and influence in China. The fighters were members of the Yi Ho Tuan (Fists of Righteous Harmony), known as Boxers, and so the uprising became known as the Boxer Rebellion. Foreign civilians, soldiers, and diplomats in Peking found themselves under siege. Dozens of foreigners were killed by the Boxers. The siege lasted for fifty-five days until it was broken by a force of twenty thousand foreign troops sent by an alliance of eight nations. Cixi and the emperor fled the capital for Western China and didn't return for more than a year, after the foreign troops had left. Initially, Cixi had supported the Boxers, but when the rebellion was over and China had suffered yet another invasion and defeat by foreign forces, she realized what a mistake it had been. She also recognized the need for more reform to make China as wealthy and powerful as the nations that had defeated it. She outlawed torture by the state, which had been routine, and execution by the "death of a thousand cuts" method. She also ended the production, use, and trade in opium. And, most radical of all, she began to transform China from an autocracy to a constitutional monarchy with an elected parliament on the British model. She even allowed a free press.

She remained in power until her death in 1908 at the age of seventy-three, shortly after suffering a stroke. On the day before she died, the Guangxu Emperor died, too. Analysis of his remains in 2008 showed a very high level of arsenic, two thousand times higher than normal. He may have been poisoned on Cixi's orders so that he could not reverse the reforms she had instigated. Before she died, she nominated her three-year-old great-nephew, Puyi, as the new emperor. He was to be China's last emperor.

Cixi has been blamed for the demise of Imperial China, because her acceptance of the need for reform and modernization came too late. Puyi was removed from power and forced to abdicate by a revolution in 1912, ending two thousand years of imperial rule in China.

Cixi did not rest in peace. She was buried in a lavishly decorated stone tomb. However, in 1928, a warlord called Sun Dianying looted the emperors' tombs. He blew Cixi's tomb apart to get into it. Her coffin was opened and her body was stripped of its jewelry. The tomb was later restored by the People's Republic.

THE RETURN OF THE CONCUBINE

Concubinage among successful men in China was swept away by Mao's cultural revolution in the 1960s and '70s, but it has made a comeback since China embraced capitalism. The modern concubines and mistresses are known as *er nai* (second wife) or *xiao san* (little third). Sometimes, a man's official wife knows about his mistress and tolerates her, but not always. Wives have gone to court to recover property and money given by their husbands to their second wives.

In 2005, after a Mr. Wang gave his mistress, Miss Liu, a house, his wife demanded that the house should be returned. When the mistress refused, the wife sued her. The court upheld the wife's claim because in Chinese law property bought during a marriage is owned jointly by husband and wife. By giving the house away, the husband had infringed his wife's property rights. It seems that the wife was lucky to win this case, because legal opinion afterwards was that the person who had infringed her rights was the husband, not the mistress, and so the case should have been brought against the husband. This interpretation was borne out by a similar case in Jiangsu Province, where a wife sued her husband's mistress for the return of 210,000 yuan (about US$26,000) he had given her. In that case, the wife lost and her claim was ruled as invalid.

The wealthier and more powerful a man is, the more mistresses he can afford to support. The number of mistresses he has is a measure of his success and importance. In July 2013, a Chinese newspaper reported that an official in Jiangsu Province had kept 140 mistresses. However, a clampdown on corruption by the new Chinese leader, Xi Jinping, may bring about a fresh demise of concubines and mistresses. Many of the officials charged with corruption in recent years used their power and wealth to favor and enrich their mistresses. If "morally degenerate" appears on the charge sheet, this often refers to the keeping of mistresses. "Morally degenerate" officials are learning that the fury of a scorned mistress can be very expensive. Jilted mistresses sometimes turn in corrupt officials. When twenty-six-year-old Ji Yingnan discovered that her fiancé, a Communist Party official in Beijing, was already married, she posted hundreds of photographs online showing their life together, revealing a level of spending far beyond the official's modest salary. In another case, an energy official was sacked and prosecuted after a former mistress claimed that he had helped to defraud banks out of $200 million.

9

AND THE REST . . .

European courtesans and royal mistresses weren't confined to the British and French royal courts and the demimonde of nineteenth-century France. King Ludwig I of Bavaria had an eye for the ladies. One of them, Lola Montez, caused a revolution that ended his reign. Mata Hari consorted unwisely with senior military officers during World War I, leading to an accusation of spying. And then there was Jane Digby, the admiral's daughter who married a sheikh.

THE ADMIRAL'S DAUGHTER AND THE BEDOUIN SHEIKH—JANE DIGBY

Jane Digby was a remarkable and scandalous woman, although she is almost unknown today. She had four husbands, including an Arab sheikh, and also found time to romance at least a dozen aristocratic lovers. Two of them even fought a duel over her. She chose her men badly, and most of them betrayed her.

The Digby family's fortune came from a Spanish treasure galleon. Jane's father, Captain (later Admiral) Henry Digby, made a point of inconveniencing Britain's enemies on the high seas. He captured fifty-seven enemy ships in less than two years. In 1799, he captured a Spanish ship called the *Santa Brigida* and relieved it of its cargo of treasure.

It was standard practice in the Royal Navy at that time for a captain who captured an enemy ship to receive "prize money" based on the value of the ship and its cargo. The captain then distributed the money to his crew. The prize money was divided into eight equal parts. According to the rules in force in 1799, the captain received three eighths, one of which was passed on to the flag officer, usually an admiral, responsible for the ship. Three eighths were divided among the various officers and ranks down to midshipman. The remaining two eighths were distributed among the rest of the crew. The prize-money system gave sailors of all ranks an incentive to seek out enemy ships and seize their cargoes. The prize money Digby earned from his huge seizure made him incredibly wealthy.

His daughter, Jane, was born on April 3, 1807, at the family home, Forston House, in Dorset. Admiral Digby was often away at sea for long periods. When he was away, his wife often took Jane and her brothers to their grandparents' imposing country house, Holkham Hall in Norfolk. When Jane was older, she also spent some time at the family's town house in London. Once the sixteen-year-old Jane had been presented to King George IV, she became officially marriageable. Admirers lost no time in wooing her. And she liked the attention. Now living in London full-time, she was a regular guest at parties and dances. Foremost among her admirers was Edward Law, Lord Ellenborough. He was more than twice her age, rich, and very well connected. He was impatient to marry her and produce an heir, because his first wife had died childless. Jane, probably flattered by the attention of an older man, accepted his proposal of marriage. They were married at Admiral Digby's home on September 15, 1824. However, wedded bliss lasted for only a few hours. There were rumors that Ellenborough paid more attention to a young servant girl at the Brighton hotel where they honeymooned than to his wife. Ellenborough, known for his arrogance and acid tongue, was a cold fish of a man who spent a lot of time away from home. Like many young women of her time, Jane saw her new marriage as a romance, while Ellenborough treated it as a financial arrangement successfully accomplished. Jane soon started feeling lonely. When she discovered that her husband had a mistress, her response seems to have been, *Two can play at that game.*

Within a year or so, she was having an affair with a handsome young soldier-turned-politician called George Anson. Anson was well known as a womanizer. He was also Jane's cousin. He eventually realized that Jane was taking their affair far too seriously, so he abandoned her. She was pregnant by then and believed that Anson was the child's father. The baby, a boy, was born on February 15, 1828, and named Arthur Dudley Law. Ellenborough appears to have believed the child was his. A few months later, Jane attended a ball at the Austrian embassy and was introduced to the magnificently named Prince Felix Ludwig Johann von Nepomuk Friedrich zu Schwarzenberg. He was just a few years older than her twenty-one years, and he was entranced by her. Their affair didn't stay secret for long. They were soon the subject of gossip, below stairs and above. When friends told Ellenborough, he shrugged it off as a matter of no importance. Turning a blind eye to his wife's adultery left him free to behave in the same way.

Like Anson, Felix began to worry that Jane was making too much of their relationship. In the spring of 1829, she discovered that she was pregnant again. This posed a problem, as she hadn't shared a bed with her husband, Lord Ellenborough, for several months, so she couldn't pretend that he was the child's father. When the Austrian ambassador found out what had happened, he got Schwarzenberg out of the country as fast as possible to protect his reputation and career. Ellenborough left Jane and began divorce proceedings. A member of staff at Brighton's Norfolk Hotel, the same hotel where Jane and Ellenborough had honeymooned, stated that Jane and Schwarzenberg had stayed there and had spent a night together. He claimed to have listened at the door and to have heard the unmistakable sound of "cohabitation." A string of neighbors and servants gave evidence of Jane's meetings with Felix. Newspapers covered every juicy detail with lip-smacking disapproval. Ellenborough was granted his divorce. Shortly afterwards, Jane traveled to Basel to have her baby. Felix joined her a month later. On November 12, 1829, she gave birth to a little girl she named Mathilde after one of Felix's sisters. Just a month later, she learned that her first child, left in the care of her husband, had died.

When Mathilde was three months old, Jane moved to Paris. As a divorced woman with an illegitimate child, she was accorded the status of a demi-mondaine, a courtesan, and excluded from polite society. She became pregnant by Felix yet again—and once again, he refused to marry her. She gave birth to a boy and called him Felix after his father, but sadly the little boy died just a few days later. Jane and Felix had a particularly intense argument in May 1831, after which he left Paris.

A few months later, after a brief visit to England, Jane traveled to Munich in the vain hope of reaching a reconciliation with Felix. But a chance meeting with King Ludwig I changed everything. The forty-six-year-old king had an eye for attractive women, and he was captivated by this beautiful twenty-five-year-old Englishwoman. While her relationship with the king was developing, she had the misfortune to fall pregnant again by yet another admirer, Baron Karl Theodore Venningen. It was vital that news of the pregnancy be kept from the king and Felix, so she left for Italy to have the baby in secret. On January 27, 1833, she had a baby boy and called him Heribert. She left him behind in Italy when she returned to Bavaria.

A MARRIAGE OF CONVENIENCE

Jane finally accepted that she was not going to be able to win Felix back. Venningen wanted to marry her. And King Ludwig wanted the marriage to go ahead, because she would be more acceptable as his mistress if she were married. Her family wanted her married, too. So, on November 16, 1833, she entered a marriage of convenience with Venningen. In no time, she was pregnant yet again with her fifth child. The baby, a girl, was born on September 4, 1834, and named Bertha.

Jane didn't remain faithful to Venningen for very long. In 1835, bored with life at Schloss Venningen, she met a young, handsome Greek count, Spiridon Theotoky, and was instantly attracted to him. She reassured the king that her acquaintance with Theotoky was a harmless flirtation, but it was more than that. Inevitably, gossip about her clandestine meetings with Theotoky reached her husband. The two lovers eloped, with Venningen in hot pursuit. When he caught up with them, he challenged Theotoky to a duel—he'd had the foresight to take a pair of dueling pistols with him. Theotoky had no choice but to accept the challenge or be shown up as a coward. The two men faced each other. The less experienced Theotoky fired first, but he missed. Venningen took his time and aimed. Theotoky had to stand and await his fate. When Venningen fired, Theotoky felt the pistol ball slam into his chest and sank to the ground. He insisted that he was innocent of Venningen's accusations, probably to protect his lover.

The king wasn't happy that Jane was entangled in yet another scandal. Despite having suffered a serious chest wound, Theotoky survived and recovered. He agreed to leave Jane and return to Greece, while Jane agreed to stay with her husband. However, her relationship with her husband proved to be beyond repair. Then Theotoky returned. With an unhappy marriage and the king keeping his distance, she found Theotoky too hard to resist. They eloped for a second time. And once again, Jane's husband chased after them. He caught them, but this time he couldn't persuade her to come back with him. She set up house with Theotoky in Paris, and on March 21, 1840, she gave birth to Theotoky's son. She called him Leonidas. Although she had shown no interest in any of her previous children, having given up, neglected, or abandoned all of them, she finally discovered her maternal instinct and was a devoted mother to Leonidas. Soon afterwards, she converted to the Greek Orthodox Church, her marriage to Venningen was dissolved, and she married Theotoky. In 1841, they moved to the Greek island of Tinos, where Theotoky's father was the governor. The next year, they moved on to Corfu, where Theotoky managed the family estate. In 1842, Jane learned that her father and grandfather had both died.

She led a happy and contented life on Corfu until 1844. When Greece restored its monarchy in 1832, a descendant of previous Greek rulers was chosen as the new king. King Otto, the first king of modern Greece, was the second son of none other than King Ludwig I of Bavaria, Jane's ex-lover. Ludwig probably had something to do with Theotoky being offered a job as aide-de-camp to the new king. Theotoky took his family to Athens to take up his new appointment, but it wasn't long before they were ruffling feathers. Jane's income made her a wealthy woman in Athens. Courtiers and citizens were envious of the palatial mansion the Theotokys built for themselves. The queen was also irritated to find that Jane was an accomplished dancer, whom her husband enjoyed partnering with on the dance floor. The queen increasingly saw Jane as a rival for the king's affections. Then in 1846, Jane discovered that Theotoky had been unfaithful to her. While she was trying to come to terms with this, an even greater tragedy struck her. During a break in Italy, her six-year-old son, Leonidas, fell from the top of a staircase onto a marble floor below and died. With Leonidas dead, there was nothing to keep Jane and Theotoky together. They went their separate ways, and their marriage was terminated.

Jane then took up with a very unlikely suitor, Xristodoulos Hadji-Petros, the chief of a group of bandits from northern Greece. She was now persona non grata in London, Munich, and Athens. Her marriage to Hadji-Petros was imminent when she discovered that he had repeatedly tried to seduce her maid. In April 1853, she set out on a visit to Syria on the pretext of buying some Arab horses. In fact, she was leaving Hadji-Petros. She didn't return to Greece, but carried on traveling. Her escort, protector, and guide for part of the journey was a young bedouin man called Sheikh Medjuel el Mezrab.

CAPTIVATED BY SYRIA

Jane donned Arab dress and set out across the desert by camel, something very few Europeans had done in her time. It was a dangerous journey. At one point, Medjuel had to fight off raiders who attacked them. At the end of their journey, Medjuel stunned her by asking her to marry him. He was already married, but said he would leave his wife for her. By then she had decided to settle in Syria. After a brief visit to Athens to dispose of her property, she returned to the Middle East. Medjuel met her in Damascus and told her he was now free to marry her, despite his family's opposition. She finally accepted his proposal. The English admiral's daughter was going to marry a bedouin sheikh. The British consul in Damascus tried everything he could think of to talk her out of the marriage, but nothing would change her mind. Even being told that adultery by a bedouin wife was punished by decapitation didn't shake her resolve! On March 27, 1855, she married her sheikh. Their first home was in Homs. She threw herself into learning bedouin customs, and she impressed the tribesmen with her horse-riding skills. While Medjuel escorted visitors and tourists on their journeys across the desert, Jane stayed at home, but when Medjuel and his fellow bedouins went on their regular treks into the desert every year, she went, too.

She visited England for the last time at Christmas 1856. Friends and family, while thoroughly disapproving of the life she had chosen, were eager to see her and learn all about her adventures in Arabia. The saddest part of the visit was that she knew it would probably be the last time she would ever see her mother. Just after her fiftieth birthday, she set off for Syria, where she lived out the rest of her days with Medjuel. They moved to a large house in Damascus with stables for her horses, and she created a beautiful garden there. Her time in Syria was rarely boring. When she wasn't settling quarrels between staff, merchants, or neighbors, she had more serious issues to deal with, rarely those that any other English admiral's daughter encountered. In 1873, fighting broke out between two bedouin tribes over grazing land for their animals. Medjuel's tribe went to the support of its friends in one of the warring tribes. Jane, at the age of sixty-five, rode into battle with her husband. It was wrongly reported that she was one of those killed in the fighting. News of her death was telegraphed around the world. When she finally returned from the desert, she was more than a little surprised to find her own obituary in the newspapers.

In the spring of 1881, she bought a plot for herself in a Christian cemetery. In July, three months after her seventy-fourth birthday, she contracted dysentery, but she was too weak to fight it. She steadily declined until, on August 11, 1881, she died and was buried in the grave she had bought a few months earlier. She left nearly everything to her husband. Her son, Heribert, received a sum of one thousand pounds plus some jewelry. Her two brothers also received some jewelry. Medjuel never remarried.

THE DANCER WHO STARTED A
REVOLUTION—LOLA MONTEZ

Angering the volatile "Spanish" dancer Lola Montez, courtesan and mistress of King Ludwig I of Bavaria, was a risky endeavor. When an Australian newspaper criticized her, she attacked the unfortunate editor with a whip. She was also liable to pull out a knife or gun when she was riled.

The future courtesan and Spanish dancer wasn't Spanish at all. She was born in Ireland in about 1818 or 1820. She was the daughter of a British soldier and a local Irish girl. The baby girl was named Maria Dolores Eliza Rosanna Gilbert. She was known in the family as Dolores, but she found it too difficult to pronounce, so she called herself Lola. She later claimed to be descended from Spanish nobility, although there doesn't appear to be any hard evidence for this.

When Lola was about three years old, her father took the family to India, where he was to serve with his new regiment. It was an arduous six-month voyage. When they arrived, or shortly afterwards, he contracted cholera. Nothing could be done for him. Lola's mother found herself a widow in a strange, foreign country at the age of only nineteen. She quickly married another officer, the twenty-four-year-old Lieutenant Patrick Craigie of the 38th Native Infantry.

Little Lola grew into a pretty girl with hypnotic blue eyes. When she was eight years old, she was sent back from India to attend school in Montrose, Scotland, where Craigie's father and sisters lived. She quickly gained a reputation for mischief, which didn't go down well in the strict regime of her new home. She begged her parents to take her back, but instead they sent the eleven-year-old girl to Durham, across the border in England. She lived with Craigie's sister and husband, who had gone there to set up a boarding school. The teachers described Lola as rebellious and troublesome. About a year later, she was sent to a new school in the fashionable and grand spa city of Bath in South West England. Just before she left, Craigie's sister said to her, "Mark my words, miss, you will come to a bad ending." She spent nearly five happy years in Bath, which transformed her from a mischievous child into a beautiful, raven-haired young woman. When she was seventeen, her mother arrived to take her back to India to marry her off to a suitable husband—the richer, the better. The man selected for her was a sixty-four-year-old judge in Calcutta, Sir Abraham Lumley. As soon as the elderly judge saw Lola's picture, he was hot to trot. However, when Lola learned about the plans that had been made for her, she had no intention of becoming Lady Lumley.

Before they left Bath for India, they were visited by Lieutenant Thomas James, a twenty-nine-year-old soldier Lola's mother had met during her voyage from India to England. He quickly took a shine to Lola. She obviously thought the young soldier was a better prospect than an elderly judge, because she ran away with him to Ireland and married him. They settled in Lieutenant James's family home in County Wexford, but the restless Lola didn't take to life in rural Ireland. She was bored stiff. A brief spell in Dublin relieved the boredom for a while, but then it was time for Lieutenant James to return to military service in India. During the long voyage and overland journey to his regimental base at Karnaul, Lola and her husband argued. She felt trapped in an unhappy marriage.

While the pretty officer's wife was a great hit on the busy social round of parties, dinners, and dances, her husband showed little interest in her. Finally, they went their separate ways. According to one account, Lieutenant James left his wife for another woman. According to another, it was Lola who left. Lola was on her own now, as her mother didn't want her back. Instead, she paid for Lola to return to England. The passage was clearly eventful, because on her arrival in Portsmouth, England, on February 20, 1841, she moved in with a soldier, Captain Lennox (Lieutenant Lennox in some sources), whom she had met on the ship. However, her relationship with Lennox didn't last long. Reluctantly, she headed north to stay with her relatives in Scotland. When news of her affair with Lennox reached her husband in India, he divorced her, publicly accusing her of adultery. But the divorce was not absolute, so neither of them could marry while the other was still alive. This was a normal condition of divorce in Britain at this time. To obtain an absolute divorce with freedom to remarry required a private Act of Parliament, which was beyond the means of most people.

On her own again, in 1842, Lola embarked on a stage career. After taking acting lessons in London and dancing lessons in Spain, she reappeared in London in 1843 as Spanish dancer Lola Montez. Unfortunately, she was recognized as Mrs. James during her first performance at Her Majesty's Theatre. When challenged, she vehemently insisted that she was Lola Montez, born in Seville in 1823, but it was to no avail. The theater tore up her contract. Threatened with public exposure as a fraud, she decided to leave Britain and try her luck in another country.

She visited Prince Heinrich LXXII of Reuss-Lobenstein-Ebersdorf, whom she had met previously in London, but she quickly outstayed her welcome and was ordered out of his tiny German principality. She left for Dresden, where her performances enjoyed a mixed reception. Then she moved on to Berlin. Although critics continued to be unimpressed with her as a dancer, she was attracting a growing coterie of male admirers. The king, Friedrich Wilhelm IV, went to see her and introduced her to his son-in-law, who happened to be Tsar Nicholas I of Russia. Soon afterwards, she headed for Warsaw. Once again, her dance performances had a very mixed reception, and the theater director soon wanted rid of her. Yet again, she was ordered to leave. She continued her progress across Europe. The routine was the same in each city: Her reputation as a great Spanish dancer preceded her, thanks mainly to journalists whose friendship she made a point of cultivating. A theater charged premium prices for her performances, and then the audience went away disappointed. Her ultimate destination was Saint Petersburg, but she appears to have stayed there for only a short time before leaving again.

On her return journey, she read a newspaper story about the composer

Franz Liszt, the musical superstar of his day. On the spur of the moment, she set out to meet him. She attended his rehearsals and concerts until she managed to talk to him. Almost immediately, the two of them were being reported as a couple. Their stormy relationship didn't last long before he tired of her. The end was quick. He simply locked her in their hotel room and left. She spent twelve hours smashing everything she could get her hands on before anyone dared to release her.

By 1844, Lola was in Paris. The customary glowing press reports about her resulted in an engagement at the prestigious Paris Opera. As usual, the audience was unimpressed. This time she lost her temper with them. She tore off part of her costume and threw it at the unappreciative audience. Her contract was terminated after just two performances. Meanwhile, she met the leading lights of the literary and artistic community, including George Sand, Alexandre Dumas (father and son), Victor Hugo, and Balzac.

FLIRTING WITH *LA PRESSE*

Lola often gave interviews to journalists in the hope of a good review. One journalist made more of an impression on her than the others. He was Alexandre Dujarier, the co-owner and cultural editor of a newspaper called *La Presse*. They soon became lovers. A year after she was hissed and whistled off the stage at the opera, she appeared at the Théâtre de la Porte Saint-Martin. And for once, it wasn't a disaster. The critics were lukewarm, which ranked as a success for Lola. Things finally seemed to be going her way.

However, her relationship with Dujarier was suddenly cut short by his premature death in 1845. After a night of drinking at a party, he barely remembered an angry exchange he'd had with one of the guests, Jean-Baptiste Rosemond de Beaupin de Beauvallon. But the next day, two of Beauvallon's friends visited Dujarier and informed him that Beauvallon demanded satisfaction for the insults he'd suffered. According to the etiquette of the time, the two men would now have to fight a duel. If Dujarier declined the challenge or failed to turn up, he would be branded as a coward and he'd be a social outcast. He had no choice but to accept Beauvallon's challenge. It would be Dujarier's first duel, but his opponent was a veteran of several duels. Dujarier expected to be killed. He updated his will, wrote down his burial instructions, and penned a letter to his mother. In the morning, he wrote a letter to Lola and then went to meet his fate.

The two men were to fight with pistols—Dujarier's choice. On the bitterly cold morning of March 11, 1845, they stood facing each other in the Bois de Boulogne, thirty paces apart. Dujarier was so inexperienced with firearms that he had to be shown how to hold his pistol. When the signal was given, the two men took six paces toward each other and aimed their pistols. Dujarier fired first . . . but missed. Beauvallon took careful aim and fired. Dujarier was shot in the face. He fell backwards with blood pouring from his mouth and nose. A few moments later, he was dead. His body was delivered to Lola.

With Dujarier gone, Lola's fortunes changed. Her work dried up, and she had to rely on gifts of money from friends. Meanwhile, Beauvallon was arrested and put on trial for Dujarier's murder. The jury found him not guilty.

Lola left France after the trial and headed for Germany. She told a friend that she intended to hook a prince. As it turned out, she exceeded her own expectations. In Bavaria, she sought a meeting with the king, Ludwig I. It was 1846, and Lola was in her late twenties. The king was in his sixties. Luckily for Lola, he had a passion for all things Spanish, and he rather liked attractive women, too, so he granted her an audience. When he saw her, he was quite taken by her. One version of their meeting alleges that the king asked her if her impressive breasts were genuine. She is said to have produced a knife and sliced through the laces of her bodice to give him his answer. But the story is unlikely to be true. Another account is more likely—that he asked her to dance for him, after which he said he would issue orders to the director of the Hof Theatre to put her onstage. The king began spending more and more time with her, and spending more and more money on her. He ordered his architect to build a suitable home for her, and no expense was to be spared. Despite her good fortune, Lola's quick temper often erupted. She loudly and publicly insulted anyone who crossed her and often used a whip that she always carried with her.

The Bavarian people never accepted her or liked her, but the king was smitten. He even changed his will in her favor. Lola's temper continued to get her into trouble. She physically attacked a hotel owner and a delivery man, prompting a police investigation. The king let it be known that he wished Lola to have Bavarian nationality so that he could grant her a title. Her certificate of citizenship needed a cabinet minister's signature, but none could be found to do the job. The cabinet then sent a letter to the king saying that they would rather resign than grant Lola Bavarian citizenship. To their amazement, the king accepted their resignations. One of the appointees who replaced them showed his appreciation by signing Lola's citizenship certificate. The king quickly made her Countess of Landsfeld, a fictitious territory made up from two place-names, Landshut and Feldberg.

The aristocracy ostracized her. There were demonstrations on the streets, with protesters calling for Lola to be kicked out of the country. There was so much opposition to her among students that the king closed the university and ordered students who didn't live in Munich to leave the city. This outraged local traders, who were deprived of thousands of customers. When crowds surrounded Lola's home, she came out and faced them before servants dragged her back inside amid a hail of stones. Then a carriage burst out of the house's courtyard and raced away through the crowd, taking Lola to safety. In an attempt to win the king back again, she returned to Munich disguised as a boy. When the king was told that she was back, he rushed to see her, but with mobs searching for her, she had to leave again after a couple of hours. The opposition to Lola had grown into a revolutionary movement against the monarchy itself. The cabinet told the king that the only way to avoid revolution was to expel Lola from the country. He reluctantly issued one order revoking her Bavarian citizenship and another for her arrest. When she was found, she was deported to Switzerland. Ludwig felt humiliated and unable to continue as king. On March 20, 1848, he abdicated.

By late 1848, Lola was in London. Ex-king Ludwig, who was still sending her regular payments for her upkeep, discovered that she had taken at least two lovers while she was declaring her undying love for him. Knowing Ludwig's desire for her was on the wane, Lola met and quickly married a young cavalry officer, George Trafford Heald, who she learned had a substantial income. However, the marriage contravened the conditions attached to her divorce from Thomas James. When Heald's aunt discovered this, she had Lola arrested for bigamy. When the case went to court, it had to be adjourned partway through to give time for new evidence to be presented. When the case resumed, Lola's counsel announced to the court that his client had left the country. She had escaped to the Continent with her new husband. However, Heald quickly tired of her temper tantrums and abandoned her in Barcelona. She moved on to France and set up house in Paris. Now desperately in need of money, she prepared to return to the stage. Having heard that other European performers had been successful in the United States, she decided to try her luck there. First, she tried out several new dances with audiences in France and Belgium. This time she had the good sense to work with a choreographer, and for once her performances were generally well received.

Then, in 1851, she headed across the Atlantic to the United States. Critics who saw her performances were less than flattering, but even they accepted that her passion and enthusiasm could hold an audience. In 1852, she also starred in a play based on her life, *Lola Montez in Bavaria*. Her acting garnered better reviews than her dancing. New plays were written specially for her, and she toured all over the United States with them.

While she was on her way to California, she met Patrick Hull, a newspaper editor. They were married within two months and set up house in the small community of Grass Valley in California. Predictably, the marriage didn't last. Eventually, Lola threw Hull out. She stayed in Grass Valley and collected a menagerie of all sorts of animals, including a pet bear. She is remembered for encouraging investors to support the quartz gold industry there, enabling the mining industry in Grass Valley to prosper for another hundred years. Her house, the only one she ever owned, was demolished later because of its poor condition. A replica of the simple wooden cabin, now designated California Historical Landmark No. 292, was built on the same site at 248 Mill Street, where it houses a visitors' center.

In 1855, Lola was becoming restless, and she decided to return to the stage. This time, she prepared to tour Australia.

DANCING FOR THE DIGGERS

The 1850s was a good time to be an entertainer in Australia, because a gold rush in Victoria was attracting people from all over the world. Australia's population tripled. Lola traveled from place to place, acting and dancing for the gold diggers. When the *Ballarat Times* newspaper published a letter criticizing her in February 1856, she tracked down the paper's editor, Henry Seekamp, in a bar and attacked him with a whip. It wasn't the first time she had whipped someone. While she was riding a horse in Berlin, a police officer had taken hold of the reins to turn the horse round and lead it out of a VIP area. Lola reacted immediately and violently by striking him with her whip. She also had a reputation for carrying a knife, which she sometimes pulled out in moments of fury. But she didn't always come off better in her violent encounters. When she accused a theater manager of defrauding her out of money, his wife grabbed Lola's whip and lashed her with it so badly that she had to cancel an appearance onstage.

A few months later, she headed back to the United States. On the way there, her latest lover, an actor called Frank Folland, disappeared from their ship. No trace of him was found. One of the many rumors surrounding his death held that he had been driven to suicide by jumping overboard because of constant arguments with Lola.

Reviews of her performances reported that her acting had improved since she was last seen in California. After a successful tour, she decided to change tack and give a series of talks about her life. She gave her first talks in Hamilton, Ontario, and Buffalo. And they went down well. She gave repeat performances all over the United States. Then she cleverly capitalized on her success by publishing the text of her talks. She followed them up with a book called *The Arts of Beauty; or, Secrets of the Lady's Toilet* in 1858. This book did well, too. Another book, *Anecdotes of Love,* followed.

After successful lecture tours of Ireland, Britain, and America, she settled in New York, where she lived until her death. In her last few years, she turned to religion and helped women who had fallen on hard times. In June 1860, she suffered a stroke, which resulted in partial paralysis. She still managed to get out and about, albeit with a limp. However, during the cold winter of 1860, she developed pneumonia and was taken to the hospital. The woman who had captivated a king and caused a revolution died penniless on January 17, 1861, in her early forties. She was buried as Eliza Gilbert in the Green-Wood Cemetery in Brooklyn.

THE TEMPLE DANCER WHO WASN'T—
MATA HARI

Mata Hari is synonymous with sex and spying. She was an extraordinary woman who overcame all the difficulties and setbacks that life threw at her until she had the misfortune to come to the notice of the warring powers during World War I. Her pursuit of men, some of whom were military officers, and her readiness to accept money for espionage would ultimately cost her her life.

Mata Hari claimed to be a temple dancer from the Far East, but she actually hailed from the Netherlands. She was born in 1876 in the northern Dutch city of Leeuwarden. Her real name was Margaretha Geertruida Zelle. After Margaretha's happy childhood, her family suddenly fell apart when her father's business went bust and he left home. He divorced his wife, who died a year later. The children were split up and farmed out to relatives. Margaretha was sent to live with an uncle in a town called Sneek. Her uncle couldn't handle her, so he sent her away to school in Leiden, but she had to leave after rumors about a relationship with the head teacher. Another uncle in The Hague took her in. At that time, Holland was a colonial power, so military officers were a common sight on the city's streets. In 1894, when Margaretha was eighteen, she answered a newspaper advertisement from a soldier who was looking for a wife. The soldier turned out to be thirty-eight-year-old Rudolf MacLeod, home from the Dutch East Indies to recover from illness. Margaretha and MacLeod hit it off immediately. Within a week, they were engaged—and only three months later, they were married. The engagement was so short that there was gossip that Margaretha must be pregnant, but it wasn't true. They were married in June 1895, but their first child, a boy called Norman-John, wasn't born until January 1897.

When the boy was just a few months old, MacLeod was well enough to return to active service, so the family left for the Dutch East Indies. Their spacious home there came with a retinue of servants. Margaretha had a second child, a girl. She was called Jeanne-Louise, but nicknamed Non. However, the marriage was in trouble. Rudolf and Margaretha accused each other of adultery. Margaretha finally snapped and left her increasingly violent husband. After their return to Europe, he hit back at her by placing an advertisement in newspapers announcing that she was no longer his responsibility so that she couldn't obtain credit in his name. After failing to find work in the Netherlands, she tried her luck as a dancer in France. She invented her own dances, based loosely on dances she had seen in the Dutch East Indies. She started performing for private gatherings in people's homes. News of her performances spread by word of mouth, and she was soon being asked to dance in public.

Her transformation from Margaretha Zelle to Mata Hari occurred on

March 13, 1905. She had been invited to appear at the Musée Guimet by its proprietor, Émile Guimet. He encouraged her to choose an exotic stage name. She chose Mata Hari, meaning the "eye of the day," or "sunrise." And she invented a fictitious life as a Javan temple dancer to go with it. Mata Hari proved to be a huge success. She performed all over Europe, and now divorced from Rudolf, she had regular romances and affairs with military officers, businessmen, and diplomats. They were only too happy to pay for her company.

RECRUITED AS A SPY

At the outbreak of World War I, Mata Hari was in Berlin preparing for a season at the Metropol. She was anxious to return to France, but her train was stopped by German border guards. They sent her back to Berlin without her luggage. She managed to borrow enough money to get to Holland. There, a German diplomat called Karl Kroemer visited her and offered her a large sum of money to spy for Germany. She took the money, but later said she treated it only as compensation for the luggage that had been seized.

In 1915, a passenger ship called in at Folkestone, a port on the east coast of England. British secret service agents carried out routine checks on the passengers and became suspicious of Mata Hari as a possible German agent. When they discovered that she had met Karl Kroemer, a known recruiter of spies, it seemed to confirm their suspicions. They passed on their concerns about her to French officials. The next time she was in Paris, she realized that she was being followed. French police officers were tailing her. They saw her meeting a series of men. She used them to fund her extravagant lifestyle, but she was especially close to one, a twenty-one-year-old Russian soldier called Vladimir de Massloff. She was eighteen years older than he. Despite their age difference, they loved each other. She called him Vadim, and he called her Marina.

When Vadim was hurt in a gas attack, she wanted to visit him, but she needed permission to travel into the war zone. Her application for a travel permit came to the attention of counterespionage chief Georges Ladoux. Convinced that she was a German spy, he met her and tried to persuade her to turn double agent and spy for France. She saw it as an opportunity to earn enough money to give up her multiple relationships and settle down with Vadim, but to earn a big enough payment, she would have to deliver significant German secrets. She was now playing a very dangerous game.

She had the idea of seducing General Moritz von Bissing, governor-general of occupied Belgium, and prizing some military secrets out of him between the sheets. She would be risking her life. Bissing was the officer who signed Edith Cavell's execution warrant. Cavell was a British nurse working in Belgium. She had hidden British soldiers and helped them to get home. Eventually, she was betrayed and arrested. Found guilty of having "conducted Allied soldiers to the enemy of the German people," she was executed by firing squad on October 12, 1915.

However, Mata Hari didn't get to Bissing. She didn't get any further than Britain. British agents were on the lookout for a German spy called Clara Benedix. They suspected that Mata Hari and Benedix were the same person. They had instructions to arrest either of them on sight. When Mata Hari was discovered on board a ship docked at Falmouth, she was arrested and taken to London. Under questioning, she denied that she was Clara Benedix and claimed that she was working as a spy for the French secret service, which Ladoux confirmed. However, they wouldn't let her continue her journey and sent her to Spain instead. There, she went to see Major Arnold Kalle, a German officer stationed at the German embassy in Madrid. She learned from him that a submarine was due to land German and Turkish officers on the Moroccan coast. She rushed back to France and arranged a meeting with Ladoux, expecting a large payment for the information from Kalle. But she was disappointed. Ladoux refused to pay her anything. He said he already knew about the submarine landing, because the French were able to decode German military radio traffic.

ON TRIAL FOR HER LIFE

In January 1917, Vadim traveled to Paris on leave to see her. He was disobeying his commanding officer, who had warned him to steer clear of the notorious Mata Hari. Soon after he left, she was arrested. It was February 13, 1917. During four months of interrogations by Pierre Bouchardon, her health and mental state both deteriorated. Her lawyer's appeals for her to be moved to a hospital were refused. Her lawyer was seventy-four-year-old Édouard Clunet, a former lover. As a corporate lawyer, he was ill equipped to handle such a serious criminal case.

The trial began on July 24, 1917. The evidence against her included transcripts of German radio messages from Madrid to Berlin about an agent code-named H21. This agent's movements matched Mata Hari's. Curiously, the messages were sent using a code that the Germans knew the French had cracked. It appeared that the Germans wanted the French to read these messages. Perhaps they had decided that Mata Hari was no use to them and they wanted rid of her. Alternatively, they may have sacrificed her in order to distract the French from looking for other agents. She admitted receiving money from Karl Kroemer, but denied spying for Germany. Despite the absence of hard evidence against her, the prosecutor, André Mornet, described her as "perhaps the greatest woman spy of the century." The defense called several of Mata Hari's lovers, who confirmed that she had never shown any interest in military secrets. After a trial lasting only two days, the judges took forty-five minutes to come to their decision. Mata Hari was found guilty of all charges and sentenced to death. She was returned to prison to await her fate. All appeals and requests for clemency were rejected.

She was woken at 5 A.M. on the morning of October 15, 1917, and taken to the place of execution, where a firing squad was waiting for her. She declined an offer of a blindfold. When the command was given, the soldiers raised their rifles and took aim at her. She stared straight back at them. Moments later, they fired and Mata Hari sank to the ground. Then, in case any vestige of life remained, an officer walked up to her, drew his pistol, and shot her in the head. No one claimed her body. In a grisly aftermath to her execution, her head was removed from her body and sent to the Museum of Anatomy in Paris, where it joined the heads of about one hundred other execution victims. It later disappeared and has never been found.

THE END OF AN ERA

Courtesans and royal mistresses flourished in nineteenth-century Europe because the Continent had a multitude of aristocracies and royal families left over from the many Ruritania-like kingdoms and principalities that pre-dated today's nation-states. The ready availability of wealthy kings, princes, and dukes together with an extended period of peace and prosperity enabled Europe's aristocrats to squander their fortunes on gambling, entertaining, travel . . . and courtesans.

World War I reshaped Europe so dramatically that there was no longer any place for *les grandes horizontales*. Four empires vanished altogether (the German, Russian, Austrian, and Ottoman Turkish empires). The states that replaced them when the borders were redrawn had little use for kings, princes, and dukes. Many of Europe's aristocrats were displaced or fled dur-ing the war. They lost much of their property, wealth, and power. Postwar Europe was a different place, where power resided largely with men in suits. And they were *elected* men in suits. They could be removed by ordinary people, so their public behavior and private vices mattered. It wasn't so easy for mod-ern rulers to hide their indiscretions and disapproved-of behavior from the public gaze. They were subject to the same moral consensus as the rest of us. It didn't stop powerful men from taking mistresses, but they were no longer the showy, extravagant, and outrageous courtesans and *maîtresses-en-titre* of past centuries. The flamboyant demimondaines and their like receded into the shadows, lost their fortunes, and, like La Belle Otero, died in obscurity.

GLOSSARY

auletrides
Flute girls in Ancient Greece. They were female musicians and dancers who often performed naked and sometimes offered sexual services.

bon ton
High society in Britain during the Regency (1811–20) and the reign of King George IV (1820–30).

cocotte
A promiscuous woman or prostitute—from Old French, meaning a "small chicken."

cortigiana
The Italian word for courtesan.

cortigiani di lume ("courtesans of the light")
Courtesans who plied their trade in the inns and brothels of Venice in the sixteenth century, especially near the Rialto Bridge.

cortigiani onesti
Honest or honored courtesans, the highest class of prostitutes in sixteenth-century Venice.

courtesan
Originally a female courtier, but later a prostitute or kept woman with royal, noble, wealthy, or upper-class clients.

courtisane
The French word for courtesan.

demimondaine
Courtesan or prostitute of the demimonde.

demimonde
A twilight or shadow world, or parallel society, of people with hedonistic lifestyles, especially in Europe from the late eighteenth to early twentieth centuries.

demirep
A woman of ill repute, especially a prostitute in France; literally, a woman with only "half a reputation."

dolly-mop
Originally an English term for a mistress, but later a part-time prostitute.

Edo
The former name of Tokyo, Japan's capital city.

Edo period
A period of Japanese history from 1603 to 1868.

empress dowager
The mother of an emperor.

gay
An adjective that meant happy or joyful until the middle of the twentieth century, when it took on a new meaning—homosexual.

geisha
A Japanese hostess, skilled in conversation, music, and companionship, often wrongly taken to mean prostitute.

grisette
Originally a French workingwoman, from *gris* meaning "gray," describing the cheap gray dresses such women wore. During the nineteenth century, its meaning changed to a flirtatious workingwoman or a woman who was a part-time prostitute.

gynaekes
Wives in Ancient Greece.

hetaera
A female companion, one of a class of professional courtesans (hetaerae) in Ancient Greece.

kisaeng (also *gisaeng*)
Female entertainers in Korea, from the Goryeo dynasty (935–1394) to modern South Korea. Similar to geisha in Japan.

kotha
A house in India where *tawaifs* lived and entertained clients.

lorette
A woman in France supported by her lovers; a kept woman.

maîtresse-en-titre
The chief mistress of the king of France.

oiran
A Japanese courtesan.

pallakae
Concubines in Ancient Greece.

pilegesh
A biblical Hebrew word for a concubine.

pornai
In Ancient Greece, the lowest rank of prostitutes, who worked in the streets and brothels.

salon
A social gathering of friends in the home of a host. The salon was invented in Italy in the sixteenth century and flourished in Italy and France until the nineteenth century.

Shimabara
The pleasure quarter of Kyoto in Edo-period Japan.

Shinmachi
The pleasure quarter of Osaka in Edo-period Japan.

tawaif
A hostess or courtesan in India, especially during the Mughal empire from the sixteenth to nineteenth centuries.

tayu
The highest rank of Japanese *oiran* (courtesan).

yiji
A high-class entertainer in Ancient China, similar to a Japanese geisha. After the Ming dynasty, *yiji* started offering sexual services.

Yojo
A "woman of pleasure" in Edo-period Japan.

Yoshiwara
The pleasure quarter of Edo (Tokyo today), where prostitutes and courtesans were required to live until the early twentieth century.

yukaku
The pleasure quarter of a Japanese city during the Edo period.

APPENDIX:
COURTESANS, CONCUBINES,
AND ROYAL MISTRESSES

ANCIENT GREECE

Rhodopis (6th century B.C.)
Aspasia (ca. 470 B.C.–ca. 400 B.C.)
Thaïs (4th century B.C.)
Phryne (4th century B.C.)
Lais of Hyccara (4th century B.C.)

ANCIENT ROME

Clodia (born ca. 94 B.C.)

BYZANTIUM

Theodora (ca. 500–48)

INDIA

Amrapali (6th century B.C.)
Begum Samru (ca. 1753–1836)
Mah Laqa (1768–1824)
Moran Sarkar (19th century)

CHINA

Su Xiaoxiao (5th century)
Wu Zhao (624–705)
Li Shishi (11th/12th century)
Hwang Jin-I (ca. 1506–ca. 1560)
Dowager Empress Cixi (1835–1908)

VENICE

Tullia d'Aragona (ca. 1510–56)
Veronica Franco (1546–91)

PAPAL MISTRESSES

Pope Alexander VI	Giulia Farnese (1474–1524)
Pope Sergius III	Marozia (ca. 890–937)
Pope John X	Theodora (ca. 870–916)
Pope Gregory XIII	Maddalena Fulchini

FRANCE

King Charles VII	Agnes Sorel (ca. 1422–50)
	Antoinette de Maignelais
	(ca. 1430–ca. 1461)

King Louis XI	Phélisé Regnard (1424–74)
	Marguerite de Sassenage (ca. 1449–71)
King Francis I	Françoise de Foix (1495–1537)
	Anne de Pisseleu d'Heilly (1508–80)
King Henry II	Diane de Poitiers (1499–1566)
	Jane Fleming (ca. 1508–ca. 1553)
	Filippa Duci (born ca. 1520)
	Nicole de Savigny (1535–90)
King Charles IX	Marie Touchet (ca. 1553–1638)
King Henry III	Louise de La Béraudière du Rouhet (ca. 1530–ca. 1586)
	Renée de Rieux de Châteauneuf (1550–ca. 1586)
	Veronica Franco (1546–91)
	Marie van Kleef (1553–74)
King Henry IV	Diane d'Andoins (1554–1621)
	Françoise de Montmorency (1562–1614)
	Esther Imbert (1570–ca. 1593)
	Antoinette de Pons (1570–1632)
	Gabrielle d'Estrées (ca. 1571–99)
	Catherine Henriette de Balzac d'Entragues (1579–1633)
	Jacqueline de Bueil (1580–1651)
	Charlotte des Essarts (ca. 1580–1651)
	Charlotte-Marguerite de Montmorency (1594–1650)
	Charlotte de Sauve (ca. 1551–1617)
King Louis XIII	Marie de Hautefort (1616–91)
	Louise de La Fayette (ca. 1616–65)
King Louis XIV	Catherine Bellier (1614–89)
	Olympia Mancini (1638–1708)

Marie Mancini (1639–1715)
Henrietta Anne of England (1644–70)
Catherine Charlotte de Gramont (1639–78)
Bonne de Pons d'Heudicourt (1641–1709)
Louise de La Valliere (1644–1710)
Anne-Lucie de La Mothe-Houdancourt
  (1641–1709)
Isabelle de Loudres (1647–1722)
Françoise Athénaïs (1640–1707)
Gabrielle de Rochechouart (1640–1707)
Claude de Vin des Oeillets (ca. 1637–87)
Anne de Rohan-Chabot (1648–1709)
Françoise d'Aubigné (1635–1719)
Marie Angelique Scorailles (1661–81)
Charlotte-Éléonore Madeleine de La Motte
Houdancourt (1654–1744)

King Louis XV   Louise-Julie de Mailly (1710–51)
Pauline-Félicité de Mailly (1712–41)
Diane-Adélaïde de Mailly (1713–60)
Marie-Anne de Mailly (1717–44)
Madame de Pompadour (1721–64)
Marie Louise O'Murphy (1737–1815)
Madame du Barry (1743–93)
Françoise de Châlus (1734–1821)
Marguerite Catherine Haynault (1736–1823)
Lucie Madeleine d'Estaing (1743–1826)
Anne Couffier de Romans (1737–1808)
Louise Jeanne Tiercelin de La Colleterie
  (1746–79)
Irène du Buisson de Longpré (died 1767)
Catherine Éléonore Bénard (1740–69)
Marie Thérèse Françoise Boisselet
  (1731–1800)

King Louis XVI   Grace Dalrymple Elliott (1758–1823)

Napoléon Bonaparte   Marie Walewska (1786–1817)

LES DEMIMONDAINES

La Païva (1819–84)
Marie Duplessis (1824–47)
Cora Pearl (1835–86)
Virginia Oldoini (1837–99)
Blanche d'Antigny (1840–74)
Leonide Leblanc (1842–94)
Marguerite Bellanger (1838–86)
La Belle Otero (1868–1965)
Liane de Pougy (1869–1950)
Émilienne d'Alençon (1869–1946)
Marie Marguerite Alibert (1890–1971)

ENGLAND

King Edward IV

Jane Shore (ca. 1445–ca. 1527)
Elizabeth Lucy (ca. 1460s)

King Henry VIII

Anne Stafford, Countess of Huntingdon
    (ca. 1483–1544)
Jane Popincourt
Elizabeth "Bessie" Blount
    (ca. 1502–40)
Jane Stukley (ca. 1500–ca. 1559)
Joan Dingley (born ca. 1510)
Mary Perrot (ca. 1511–ca. 1586)
Mary Boleyn (ca. 1499–1543)
Anne Boleyn (ca. 1501–36)
Mary Shelton (1510/15–1570/71)
Jane Seymour (ca. 1508–37)

King Charles II

Lucy Walter (ca. 1630–58)
Barbara Palmer (1640–1709)
Louise de Kérouaille (1649–1734)
Nell Gwyn (ca. 1650–87)

Moll Davis (ca. 1648–1708)

Hortense Mancini (1646–99)

Winifred Wells (born ca. 1642)

Jane Roberts

Mary Bagot (1645–79)

Elizabeth, Countess of Kildare

Catherine Pegge (ca. 1635–ca. 1678)

King James II   Arabella Churchill (1648–1730)

Catherine Sedley (1657–1717)

King William III   Elizabeth Hamilton (ca. 1657–1733)

King George I   Ehrengard Melusine (1667–1743)

King George II   Henrietta Howard (1689–1767)

Mary Scott

Amelie von Wallmoden (1704–65)

King George III   Hannah Lightfoot (1730–59)

King George IV   Mary Robinson (1757–1800)

Maria Fitzherbert (1756–1837)

Grace Elliott (1758–1823)

Frances Villiers (1753–1821)

Marchioness of Hertford (1759–1834)

Elizabeth, Marchioness Conyngham
(1769–1861)

King William IV   Dorothy Jordan (1761–1816)

King Edward VII   Catherine "Skittles" Walters
(1839–1920)

Sarah Bernhardt (1844–1923)

Jennie Jerome (1854–1921)

Lillie Langtry (1853–1929)

Daisy Greville, Countess of Warwick
(1861–1938)

Alice Keppel (1868–1947)

Agnes Keyser (1852–1941)

King Edward VIII   Marie Marguerite Alibert (1890–1971)

Freda Dudley Ward (1894–1983)

Thelma, Viscountess Furness (1904–70)

Wallis Simpson (1896–1986)

Charles, Prince of Wales   Camilla Parker Bowles (born 1947)

SCOTLAND

King James IV   Marion Boyd (late 15th century)

Margaret Drummond (ca. 1475–1501)

Janet Kennedy (ca. 1480–ca. 1545)

Isabel Stewart of Buchan (1480–1555)

King James V   Margaret Erskine (died 1572)

Euphemia Elphinstone (1509–1542 or
after 1547)

Elizabeth Bethune/Beaton

BAVARIA

King Ludwig I of Bavaria   Jane Digby (1807–81)

Lola Montez (1821–61)

AUSTRIA

Emperor Franz Josef   Katharina Schratt (1853–1940)

SWEDEN

Charles VIII   Kristina Abrahamsdotter (1432–92)

Erik XIV	Agda Persdotter
	Karin Jacobsdotter
	Karin Månsdotter (1550–1612)
John III	Karin Hansdotter (1539–96)
Charles IX	Karin Nilsdotter (ca. 1551–1613)
Gustavus Adolphus	Ebba Brahe (1596–1674)
	Margareta Slots (died 1669)
Charles X Gustav	Märta Allertz (1628–ca. 1677)
Frederick I	Hedvig Taube (1714–44)
	Catharina Ebba Horn (1720–81)
Adolf Frederick	Marie Marguerite Morel (1737–1804)
Gustav IV Adolf	Maria Schlegel
Charles XIII	Augusta Fersen (1754–1846)
	Charlotte Eckerman (1759–90)
	Charlotte Slottsberg (1760–1800)
Charles XIV	Mariana Koskull (1785–1841)
Oscar I	Emilie Högquist (1812–46)
	Jaquette Löwenhielm (1797–1839)
Charles XV	Hanna Styrell (1842–1904)
	Wilhelmine Schröder
	Elise Hwasser (1831–94)
Oscar II	Marie Friberg (1852–1934)
	Emma Elisabeth Hammarström

THE AMERICAS

Clara Ward (1873–1916)
Klondike Kate Rockwell (1873–1957)

OTHERS

Mata Hari (1876–1917)
Eliza Lynch (1835–86)

FURTHER READING

Abbott, Elizabeth. *Mistresses: A History of the Other Woman*. New York: Overlook Press, 2010.

Algrant, Christine Pevitt. *Madame de Pompadour: Mistress of France*. New York: Grove Press, 2002.

Anand, Sushila. *Daisy: The Life and Loves of the Countess of Warwick*. London: Piatkus Books, 2008.

Aronson, Theo. *The King in Love: Edward VII's Mistresses*. New York: Harper & Row, 1988.

Beauclerk-Dewar, Peter, and Roger Powell. *Royal Bastards: Illegitimate Children of the British Royal Family*. Gloucestershire, England: History Press, 2008.

Bevan, Bryan. *The Duchess Hortense: Cardinal Mazarin's Wanton Niece*. London: Rubicon Press, 1987.

Borman, Tracy. *King's Mistress, Queen's Servant: The Life and Times of Henrietta Howard*. New York: Vintage Books, 2010.

Buckley, Veronica. *Madame de Maintenon: The Secret Wife of Louis XIV.* London: Bloomsbury Publishing, 2008.

Carlton, Charles. *Royal Mistresses.* London: Routledge, 1990.

Carroll, Leslie. *Notorious Royal Marriages: A Juicy Journey Through Nine Centuries of Dynasty, Destiny, and Desire.* New York: New American Library, 2010.

———. *Royal Affairs: A Lusty Romp Through the Extramarital Adventures That Rocked the British Monarchy.* New York: New American Library, 2008.

Castle, Charles. *La Belle Otero: The Last Great Courtesan.* London: Michael Joseph, 1981.

Cawthorne, Nigel. *The Empress of South America: The Irish Courtesan Who Destroyed Paraguay—and Became Its National Heroine.* London: William Heinemann, 2003.

Chang, Jung. *Empress Dowager Cixi: The Concubine Who Launched Modern China.* New York: Knopf, 2013.

Crosland, Margaret. *The Mysterious Mistress: The Life and Legend of Jane Shore.* Gloucestershire, England: Sutton Publishing, 2006.

Davenport, Hester. *The Prince's Mistress: A Life of Mary Robinson.* Gloucestershire, England: Sutton Publishing, 2004.

Davis, Irene Mary. *The Harlot and the Statesman: The Story of Elizabeth Armistead and Charles James Fox.* Abbotsbrook: Kensal Press, 1986.

Engel, Howard. *Lord High Executioner: An Unashamed Look at Hangmen, Headsmen, and Their Kind.* London: Robson Books, 1998.

Farquhar, Michael. *A Treasury of Royal Scandals: The Shocking True Stories of History's Wickedest, Weirdest, Most Wanton Kings, Queens, Tsars, Popes, and Emperors.* New York: Penguin Books, 2001.

Fraser, Antonia. *Love and Louis XIV: The Women in the Life of the Sun King.* Weidenfeld & Nicolson, 2006.

Friedman, Dennis. *Ladies of the Bedchamber: The Role of the Royal Mistress.* London: Peter Owen, 2003.

Gold, Claudia. *The King's Mistress: The True and Scandalous Story of the Woman Who Stole the Heart of George I.* London: Quercus, 2012.

Goldsmith, Elizabeth C. *The King's Mistresses: The Liberated Lives of Marie Mancini, Princess Colonna, and Her Sister Hortense, Duchess Mazarin.* New York: PublicAffairs, 2012.

Griffin, Susan. *The Book of the Courtesans: A Catalogue of Their Virtues.* London: Macmillan, 2002.

Hamel, Debra. *Trying Neaira: The True Story of a Courtesan's Scandalous Life in Ancient Greece.* New Haven: Yale University Press, 2003.

Hart, Kelly. *The Mistresses of Henry VIII.* Gloucestershire, England: History Press, 2009.

Haslip, Joan. *Madame du Barry: The Wages of Beauty.* London: Weidenfeld & Nicolson, 1991.

———. *The Emperor and the Actress: The Love Story of Emperor Franz Josef and Katharina Schratt.* London: Weidenfeld & Nicolson, 1982.

Her Royal Highness Princess Michael of Kent. *Cupid and the King: Five Royal Paramours.* London: HarperCollins, 1991.

Hickman, Kate. *Courtesans: Money, Sex, and Fame in the Nineteenth Century.* London: HarperCollins, 2003.

Lamont-Brown, Raymond. *Alice Keppel and Agnes Keyser.* Gloucestershire, England: Sutton Publishing, 2005.

Lever, Evelyne. *Madame de Pompadour: A Life*. Translated by Catherine Tremerson. New York: St. Martin's Griffin. 2003

Longstreet, Stephen, and Ethel Longstreet. *Yoshiwara: Geishas, Courtesans, and the Pleasure Quarters of Old Tokyo*. Rutland, VT: Tuttle Publishing, 2009.

Lovel, Mary S. *A Scandalous Life: The Biography of Jane Digby*. London: Richard Cohen Books, 1995.

Mancini, Hortense, and Marie Mancini. *Memoirs*. Edited and translated by Sarah Nelson. Chicago: University of Chicago Press, 2008.

Manning, Jo. *My Lady Scandalous: The Amazing Life and Outrageous Times of Grace Dalrymple Elliot, Royal Courtesan*. New York: Simon and Schuster, 2005.

Morgan, Lael. *Good Time Girls of the Alaska-Yukon Gold Rush*. Kenmore, WA: Epicenter Press, 1998.

Morton, Andrew. *Diana: Her True Story—In Her Own Words*. London: Michael O'Mara Books, 2003.

Munson, James. *Maria Fitzherbert: The Secret Wife of George IV*. London: Constable, 2001.

Pearl, Cora. *The Memoirs of Cora Pearl: The Erotic Reminiscences of a Flamboyant Nineteenth Century Courtesan*. Edited by William Blatchford. London: Granada Publishing, 1983.

Pougy, Liane de. *My Blue Notebooks: The Intimate Journal of Paris's Most Beautiful and Notorious Courtesan*. Translated by Diana Athill. New York: Jeremy P. Tarcher / Putnam, 2002.

Powell, Roger. *Royal Sex: The Scandalous Love Lives of the British Royal Family*. Stroud, England: Amberley, 2010.

Prioleau, Betsy. *Seductress: Women Who Ravished the World and Their Lost Art of Love*. New York: Viking Penguin 2003.

Rees, Siân. *The Shadows of Elisa Lynch: How a Nineteenth-Century Irish Courtesan Became the Most Powerful Woman in Paraguay.* London: Review, 2003.

Richardson, Joanna. *The Courtesans: The Demi-Monde in Nineteenth-Century France.* London: Phoenix Press, 2000.

Robinson, Mary. *Memoirs of Mary Robinson.* Edited by Joseph Fitzgerald Molloy. Philadelphia: J. B. Lippincott, 1895.

Rose, Andrew. *The Woman Before Wallis: Prince Edward, the Parisian Courtesan, and the Perfect Murder.* New York: Picador, 2013.

Rosenthal, Margaret F. *The Honest Courtesan: Veronica Franco, Citizen and Writer in Sixteenth-Century Venice.* Chicago: University of Chicago Press, 1992.

Rounding, Virginia. *Grandes Horizontales: The Lives and Legends of Four Nineteenth-Century Courtesans.* New York: Bloomsbury, 2003.

Schmidt, Margaret Fox. *Passion's Child: The Extraordinary Life of Jane Digby.* New York: Harper & Row, 1976.

Seymour, Bruce. *Lola Montez: A Life.* New Haven: Yale University Press, 1996.

Shipman, Pat. *Femme Fatale: Love, Lies, and the Unknown Life of Mata Hari.* London: Phoenix, 2008.

Sutherland, Christine. *Marie Walewska: Napoléon's Great Love.* London: Robin Clark Ltd., 1986.

Tomalin, Claire. *Mrs. Jordan's Profession: The Actress and the Princess.* New York: Viking, 1994.

Wilson, Christopher. *A Greater Love: Prince Charles's Twenty-Year Affair with Camilla Parker Bowles.* New York: William Morrow, 1994.

Wilson, Frances. *The Courtesan's Revenge: Harriette Wilson, the Woman Who Blackmailed the King.* London: Faber and Faber, 2004.

Wilson, Harriette. *Harriette Wilson's Memoirs: The Memoirs of the Reigning Courtesan of Regency London.* Edited by Lesley Blanch. London: Weidenfeld & Nicolson, 2003.

Wyndham, Horace. *The Magnificent Montez: From Courtesan to Convert.* New York: Hillman-Curl, n.d.

BIBLIOGRAPHY

Introduction

Coryat, Thomas. *Coryat's Crudities, 1611*. Republished by James MacLehose and Sons, 1905.

George III. http://www.britroyals.com/kings.asp?id=george3.

Harrison, Kathryn. "We're No Angels." *The New York Times,* September 30, 2007. http://www.nytimes.com/2007/09/30/books/review/harrison.html?pagewanted=all&_r=0.

"Portrait of Louise de Keroualle, Duchess of Portsmouth." The J. Paul Getty Museum. http://www.getty.edu/art/gettyguide/artObjectDetails?artobj=774.

Prioleau, Betsy. *Seductress: Women Who Ravished the World and Their Lost Art of Love.* New York: Viking Penguin, 2003.

Rosenthal, Margaret F. *The Honest Courtesan: Veronica Franco, Citizen and Writer in Sixteenth-Century Venice.* Chicago: University of Chicago Press, 1992.

"Sophie Friederike Auguste, Prinzessin von Anhalt-Zerbst." (2014). Biography.com. http://www.biography.com/people/catherine-ii-9241622.

Tannahill, Reay. *Sex in History.* London: Abacus / Sphere Books, 1981.

Tucker, Carol. "Portrait of a Poet-Prostitute." USC News. http://www.usc.edu/uscnews/stories/1083.html.

The Harlot's Progress

"Hogarth: Hogarth's Modern Moral Series: *A Harlot's Progress.*" Tate. http://www.tate.org.uk/whats-on/tate-britain/exhibition/hogarth/hogarth-hogarths-modern-moral-series/hogarth-hogarths.

1. LES DEMIMONDAINES

The Andalusian Volcano—La Belle Otero

1898: Mesguich Gets His Marching Orders. Movie Movie. http://www.moviemoviesite
.com/Years/19th%20Century/1898%20Articles/mesguich_gets_his_marching
_orders.htm.

Castle, Charles. *La Belle Otero: The Last Great Courtesan.* London: Michael Joseph, 1981.

"The Former Manager of the Eden Musee Kills Himself in Paris." *The New York, Sun* January 14, 1897. Chronicling America: Historic American Newspapers. Library of Congress. http://chroniclingamerica.loc.gov/lccn/sn83030272/1897-01-14/ed-1/seq-7/.

Griffin, Susan. *The Book of the Courtesans: A Catalogue of Their Virtues.* London: Pan Macmillan, 2002.

Hickman, Katie. *Courtesans: Money, Sex, and Fame in the Nineteenth Century.* London: HarperCollins, 2003.

Otero, Caroline. *My Story.* London: A. M. Philpott, 1927.

Prioleau, Betsy. *Seductress: Women Who Ravished the World and Their Lost Art of Love.* New York: Viking Penguin, 2003.

Richardson, Joanna. *The Courtesans: The Demi-Monde in Nineteenth-Century France.* London: Phoenix Press, 2000.

Rounding, Virginia. *Grandes Horizontales: The Lives and Legends of Four Nineteenth-Century Courtesans.* New York: Bloomsbury, 2004.

Le Grand Trois—Otero, Pougy, and d'Alençon

"Belle Epoque Postcards—Artists—Emilienne d'Alençon." Boudoir Cards. http://www
.helmut-schmidt-online.de/Boudoir-Cards/be-artists-alencon.html.

Castle, Charles. *La Belle Otero: The Last Great Courtesan.* London: Michael Joseph, 1981.

Griffin, Susan. *The Book of the Courtesans: A Catalogue of Their Virtues.* London: Pan Macmillan, 2002.

Pougy, Liane. *My Blue Notebooks: The Intimate Journal of Paris's Most Beautiful and Notorious Courtesan.* Translated by Diana Athill. New York: Jeremy P. Tarcher / Putnam, 2002.

The Queen of Kept Women—La Païva

Allen, Peter. "French 'Love Palace' Built by Famous Prostitute Restored." *The Telegraph,* March 28, 2010. http://www.telegraph.co.uk/news/worldnews/europe/france
/7533280/French-Love-palace-built-by-famous-prostitute-restored.html.

Prioleau, Betsy. *Seductress: Women Who Ravished the World and Their Lost Art of Love.* New York: Viking, 2003.

Rounding, Virginia. *Grandes Horizontales: The Lives and Legends of Four Nineteenth-Century Courtesans.* New York: Bloomsbury, 2003.

Schiller, Phyllis. "Crowning Jewels." *Rapaport*, December 2011. http://www.diamonds .net/Magazine/Article.aspx?ArticleID=38026&RDRIssueID=85.

Wright, Jennie. "Shelved Dolls: La Paiva—A Really Glamorous Monster." http://www .thegloss.com/2013/03/26/beauty/la-paiva-biography/.

The Lady of the Camellias—Marie Duplessis

Nockin, Maria. "The Real Traviata." (Originally printed in the Mexican magazine, *Pro Opera*). http://www.readliterature.com/R_camille.htm.

Richardson, Joanna. *The Courtesans: The Demi-Monde in Nineteenth-Century France.* London: Phoenix Press, 2000.

Ridley, Jane. "The Girl Who Loved Camellias, by Julie Kavanagh—Review." *The Spectator,* August 17, 2013. http://www.spectator.co.uk/books/8993011/the-girl -who-loved-camellias-by-julie-kavanagh-review/.

Rounding, Virginia. *Grandes Horizontales: The Lives and Legends of Four Nineteenth-Century Courtesans.* New York: Bloomsbury, 2003.

The Legendary Demimondaine—Cora Pearl

Hickman, Katie. "Cora Pearl: Bringing One of the World's Most Famous Courtesans Back to the Grosvenor Hotel." Huffington Post, February 22, 2012. http://www .huffingtonpost.co.uk/katie-hickman/cora-pearl-bringing-one-of-the-world_b _1293661.html.

Pearl, Cora. *The Memoirs of Cora Pearl: The Erotic Reminiscences of a Flamboyant Nineteenth Century Courtesan.* Edited by William Blatchford. London: Granada Publishing, 1983.

Prioleau, Betsy. *Seductress: Women Who Ravished the World and Their Lost Art of Love.* New York: Viking Penguin, 2003.

"Tart with a Heart Was the 'Pearl' of Plymouth." *Western Morning News,* July 22, 2009. http://www.westernmorningnews.co.uk/Tart-heart-pearl-Plymouth/story-11457 864-detail/story.html.

Zola's Nana—Blanche d'Antigny

"Antigny, Marie Ernestine Blanche d' (1840–1874)." Amis et Passionés du Père-Lachaise. http://www.appl-lachaise.net/appl/article.php3?id_article=107.

"Blanche d'Antigny." Les Amis du Vieux Martizay. http://amisduvieuxmartizay .pagesperso-orange.fr/en_ac_Blanche_d_Antigny.html.

Griffin, Susan. *The Book of the Courtesans: A Catalogue of Their Virtues.* London: Pan Macmillan, 2002.

"Music Events of 1874." Mark's Music Circus. http://www.marks-music-circus.co.uk /1815-1910=Romantic/1874/1874=Events.htm.

Richardson, Joanna. *The Courtesans: The Demi-Monde in Nineteenth-Century France.* London: Phoenix Press, 2000.

2. THE PETTICOAT BEHIND THE THRONE

Agnès the First

"Agnès Sorel." Encylopædia Britannica. http://www.britannica.com/EBchecked/topic /554867/Agnes-Sorel.

"Book Review: Agnes Sorel." *Examiner.com,* January 15, 2012. http://www.examiner .com/article/book-review-agnes-sorel.

ESRF—The European Synchrotron. "Press Release: Was Agnès Sorel, the First Official Royal Mistress of France, Poisoned?" April 2, 2005. http://www.esrf.eu/news /general-old/general-2005/sorel/index_html/.

"Françoise de Foix." Châteaubriant Histoire. http://chateaubriant.org/14-francoise-de -foix.

Prioleau, Betsy. *Seductress: Women Who Ravished the World and Their Lost Art of Love.* New York: Viking Penguin, 2003.

The Great Pox

Choi, Charles Q. "Case Closed? Columbus Introduced Syphilis to Europe." LiveScience, December 27, 2011. http://www.livescience.com/17643-columbus-introduced -syphilis-europe.html.

Harper, Zuckerman, Kingston Harper, and Armelagos. "The Origin and Antiquity of Syphilis Revisited: An Appraisal of Old World Pre-Columbian Evidence for Treponemal Infection." *American Journal of Physical Anthropology.* 146 no. S53 (2011): 99-133. http://onlinelibrary.wiley.com/doi/10.1002/ajpa.21613/abstract.

Hosein, Sean R. "Syphilis Beats Antibiotic—Caution Needed with Azithromycin." CATIE News, February 3, 2006. http://www.catie.ca/en/catienews/2006-02-03 /syphilis-beats-antibiotic-caution-needed-azithromycin.

Mitchell, S. J., J. Engelman, C. K. Kent, S. A. Lukehart, C. Godornes, J. D. Klausner. "Azithromycin-Resistant Syphilis Infection: San Francisco, California, 2000–2004." Clinical Infectious Diseases 42, no. 3 (2006): 337–45. http://cid.oxfordjournals.org /content/42/3/337.long.

"Syphilis, 1494–1923." Contagion: Historical Views of Diseases and Epidemics. Harvard University Library Open Collections Program. http://ocp.hul.harvard.edu /contagion/syphilis.html.

"Syphilis Outbreak in Europe." ColonialDiseaseDigitalTextbook. http://colonialdisease digitaltextbook.wikispaces.com/2.4+Syphilis+Outbreak+in+Europe.

Contraception

"A Brief History of Condoms." *BBC News Online,* October 16, 2005. http://news.bbc .co.uk/1/hi/programmes/panorama/4347796.stm.

"Contraceptive or Protective? The Slow Rise of the Condom." Science Museum,

London. http://www.sciencemuseum.org.uk/broughttolife/themes/birthanddeath/condom.aspx.

Rothstein, Edward. "Unrolled, Unbridled and Unabashed." *The New York Times,* February 4, 2010. http://www.nytimes.com/2010/02/05/arts/design/05sex.html?pagewanted=all&_r=0.

Queen in All but Name—Diane de Poitiers

Her Royal Highness Princess Michael of Kent. *Cupid and the King: Five Royal Paramours.* London: HarperCollins, 1991.

"History of the Château." http://www.chateaudanet.com/ahistorique.htm.

Bates, Claire. "Dying to Look Good: French King's Mistress Killed by Drinking Gold Elixir of Youth." Daily Mail Online, December 22, 2009. http://www.dailymail.co.uk/sciencetech/article-1236916/Dying-look-good-French-kings-mistress-killed-gold-elixir-youth.html.

Beck, Shari. "Diane de Poitiers." http://www.dianedepoitiers.sharibeck.com.

Prioleau, Betsy. *Seductress: Women Who Ravished the World and Their Lost Art of Love.* New York: Viking Penguin, 2003.

The Pursuit of Pleasure—Ninon de L'Enclos

"1911 Encyclopædia Britannica / Lenclos, Ninon de." Wikisource. http://en.wikisource.org/wiki/1911_Encyclop%C3%A6dia_Britannica/Lenclos,_Ninon_de.

Conley, John J. "Ninon de L'Enclos." Internet Encyclopedia of Philosophy. http://www.iep.utm.edu/lenclos/.

Hickman, Kate. *Courtesans: Money, Sex and Fame in the Nineteenth Century.* London: HarperCollins, 2003.

Ripley, George, and Charles A. Dana. "Ninon or Anne De Lenclos." *The American Cyclopaedia.* D. Appleton and Co, 1873. http://chestofbooks.com/reference/American-Cyclopaedia-9/Ninon-Or-Anne-De-Lenclos.html#.VBa19eeLZ20.

Rowsell, Mary C. *Ninon de L'Enclos and Her Century.* Hurst & Blackett, 1910. The Internet Archive. http://www.archive.org/stream/ninondelenclosan00rowsrich/ninondelenclosan00rowsrich_djvu.txt.

The Court of the Sun King

"1911 Encyclopædia Britannica / La Vallière, Louise Françoise de." Wikisource. https://en.wikisource.org/wiki/1911_Encyclop%C3%A6dia_Britannica/La_Valli%C3%A8re,_Louise_Fran%C3%A7oise_de

"1911 Encyclopædia Britannica / La Voisin." Wikisource. https://en.wikisource.org/wiki/1911_Encyclop%C3%A6dia_Britannica/La_Voisin

"Affair of the Poisons." Encyclopædia Britannica." http://www.britannica.com/event/Affair-of-the-Poisons.

Bevan, Bryan. *The Duchess Hortense: Cardinal Mazarin's Wanton Niece.* London: Rubicon Press, 1987.

"Catherine Deshayes." Murderpedia. http://murderpedia.org/female.D/d/deshayes -catherine.htm.

Fraser, Antonia. *Love and Louis XIV: The Women in the Life of The Sun King.* London: Weidenfeld & Nicolson, 2006.

Goldsmith, Elizabeth C. *The King's Mistresses: The Liberated Lives of Marie Mancini, Princess Colonna, and Her Sister Hortense, Duchess Mazarin.* New York: PublicAffairs, 2012.

Mancini, Hortense and Marie Mancini. *Memoirs.* Edited and translated by Sarah Nelson. Chicago: University of Chicago Press, 2008.

Mann, Natasha. "Beauty Secrets from the Past." Netdoctor. http://www.netdoctor .co.uk/healthy-living/beauty/beauty-secrets-from-the-past.htm.

Mapes, Diane. "Suffering for Beauty Has Ancient Roots." Health on NBCNews.com. http://www.nbcnews.com/id/22546056/ns/health/t/suffering-beauty-has-ancient -roots/#.VZg-G-dh60Y.

Powell, Roger. *Royal Sex: The Scandalous Love Lives of the British Royal Family.* Stroud, England: Amberley Publishing, 2013.

The Sun King's Wife?—Madame de Maintenon

Buckley, Veronica. *Madame de Maintenon: The Secret Wife of Louis XIV.* London: Bloomsbury, 2008.

Conley, John J. "Françoise d'Aubigné, Marquise de Maintenon (1635–1719)." Internet Encyclopedia of Philosophy. http://www.iep.utm.edu/mainteno/.

Dyson, C. C. *Madame de Maintenon: Her Life and Times.* John Lane the Bodley Head, 1922.

Fraser, Antonia. *Love and Louis XIV: The Women in the Life of The Sun King.* London: Weidenfeld & Nicolson, 2006.

Philbrick, Anne. "Françoise d'Aubigné." Find a Grave. http://www.findagrave.com/cgi -bin/fg.cgi?page=gr&GRid=84661263.

"The Story of M: Madame de Maintenon." *The Economist,* July 24, 2008. http://www .economist.com/node/11785001.

Louis XV's Mistresses

Lever, Evelyne. *Madame de Pompadour: A Life.* Translated by Catherine Temerson. New York: St. Martin's Griffin, 2003.

Louis XV. "Timeline of World History." Everyhistory.org. http://everyhistory.org /18thcentury/1710LouisXV_1.html.

"Marie-Anne de Mailly-Nesle, duchess de Châteauroux." Encyclopædia Britannica. http://www.britannica.com/biography/Marie-Anne-de-Mailly-Nesle-duchesse -de-Chateauroux.

Destined for Greatness?—Madame de Pompadour

"1757 Assassination Attempt of Damiens against Louis XV." Chateau de Versailles. http://en.chateauversailles.fr/history/the-significant-dates/most-important-dates /assassination-attempt-of-damiens-against-louis-xv.

Abbott, Elizabeth. *Mistresses: A History of the Other Woman.* New York: Overlook Press, 2010.

"Execution by Quartering." http://www.lordsandladies.org/execution-by-quartering.htm.

Her Royal Highness Princess Michael of Kent. *Cupid and the King: Five Royal Paramours.* London: HarperCollins, 1991.

Lever, Evelyne. *Madame de Pompadour: A Life.* Translated by Catherine Temerson. New York: St. Martins Griffin, 2003.

"Marie-Louise O'Murphy." Irish Paris. http://www.irishmeninparis.org/le-deuxieme -sexe/marie-louise-o-murphy.

Mitford, Nancy. "Jeanne-Antoinette Poisson, Marquise de Pompadour." Encyclopædia Britannica. http://www.britannica.com/EBchecked/topic/469399/Jeanne-Antoinette -Poisson-marquise-de-Pompadour.

Lawless, Erin. "Hidden Historical Heroines (#20: Marie-Louise O'Murphy)." January 7, 2013. http://erinlawless.wordpress.com/2013/01/07/hidden-historical-heroines-20 -marie-louise-o-murphy/.

Synon, Mary Ellen. "Casanova, Our Lady of the Potatoes and Cardinal Murphy-O'Connor's Racy Pedigree." *Daily Mail Online.* February 27, 2009. http://www .dailymail.co.uk/debate/article-1157183/MARY-ELLEN-SYNON-Casanova -Our-Lady-Potatoes-Cardinal-Murphy-OConnors-racy-pedigree.html.

A Peasant at Court—Madame du Barry

"1793: Madame du Barry, Who Hated to Go." http://www.executedtoday.com/2008 /12/08/1793-madame-comtesse-du-barry/.

Haslip, Joan. *Madame du Barry: The Wages of Beauty.* London: Weidenfeld & Nicolson, 1991.

Lamothe-Langon, Étienne-Léon. Memoirs of the Comtesse du Barry, with Intimate Details of Her Entire Career as Favourite of Louis XV. Walter Dunne, 1903. HathiTrust.

"Madame du Barry." *Find a Grave.* http://www.findagrave.com/cgi-bin/fg.cgi?page =gr&GRid=3236.

A Deadly Mistress—Madame La Guillotine

Bellis, Mary. "The History of the Guillotine: Doctor Joseph Ignace Guillotin, 1738–1814." http://inventors.about.com/od/gstartinventions/a/Guillotine.htm.

Croker, John Wilson. *History of the Guillotine, Revised from the Quarterly Review of December, 1844.* London: John Murray, 1853.

Engel, Howard. *Lord High Executioner: An Unashamed Look at Hangmen, Headsmen, and Their Kind.* London: Robson Books, 1998.

"The Guillotine." http://www.crimemuseum.org/crime-library/the-guillotine.

Wilde, Robert. "The Guillotine." http://europeanhistory.about.com/cs/frenchrevolution /a/Guillotine.htm.

Dr. Elliott's Wayward Wife—Grace Elliott

Alger, John Goldworth. "Elliot, Grace Dalrymple." *Dictionary of National Biography,* 1885–1900, volume 17. http://en.wikisource.org/wiki/Elliott,_Grace_Dalrymple _%28DNB00%29.

Manning, Jo. My *Lady Scandalous: The Amazing Life and Outrageous Times of Grace Dalrymple Elliot, Royal Courtesan.* Simon & Schuster, 2005.

Napoléon's "Little Polish Wife"—Marie Walewska

"Countess Walewska Relates How She Met the Emperor: From the Private Collection of Comte Alexandre Walewski, Paris." Napoleonic Society of America. http://www .napoleonicsociety.com/english/CountessWalewska.htm.

"Death Mask of Napoleon Makes £170,000 at Bonhams." Bonhams. http://www .bonhams.com/press_release/13967/.

Duell, Mark. "Cast of Napoleon's Death Mask Made After He Died in Exile on South American Island Almost 200 Years Ago Sells for £170,000." *Daily Mail Online.* http://www.dailymail.co.uk/news/article-2344801/Cast-Napoleon-Bonapartes -death-mask-death-St-Helena-1821-sells-170-000.html.

Her Royal Highness Princess Michael of Kent. *Cupid and the King: Five Royal Paramours.* London: HarperCollins, 1991.

Rounding, Virginia. *Grandes Horizontales: The Lives and Legends of Four Nineteenth-Century Courtesans.* New York: Bloomsbury, 2003.

Sutherland, Christine. *Marie Walewska: Napoléon's Great Love.* London: Robin Clark, Ltd. 1986.

UT Southwestern Medical Center. "Napoléon's Mysterious Death Unmasked." Science-Daily. January 16, 2007. http://www.sciencedaily.com/releases/2007/01 /070116131630.htm.

3. THE ANCIENT WORLD

Cinderella and Other Greek Tales

"Aspasia." Livius.org. http://www.livius.org/as-at/aspasia/aspasia.html.

"Aspasia." The Greeks: Crucible of Civilization. http://www.pbs.org/empires/thegreeks /htmlver/characters/f_aspasia.html.

"Aspasia of Miletus." http://penelope.uchicago.edu/~grout/encyclopaedia_romana/greece /hetairai/aspasia.html.

"Battle of Arginusae, 406 B.C." Military History Encyclopedia on the Web. http://historyofwar.org/articles/battles_arginusae.html.

Hamel, Debra. *Trying Neaira: The True Story of a Courtesan's Scandalous Life in Ancient Greece*. New Haven: Yale University Press, 2003.

Kapparis, K. "Women and Family in Athenian Law." The Stoa: A Consortium for Electronic Publication in the Humanities March 22, 2003. http://www.stoa.org/projects/demos/article_women_and_family?page=4.

Mark, Joshua J. "Alexander the Great and the Burning of Persepolis." Ancient History Encyclopedia. http://www.ancient.eu.com/article/214/.

McDevitt, April. "The Girl with the Rose Red Slippers." Ancient Egypt: The Mythology. http://www.egyptianmyths.net/mythslippers.htm.

"Phryne." Encyclopædia Britannica. http://www.britannica.com/EBchecked/topic/458409/Phryne.

Prioleau, Betsy. *Seductress: Women Who Ravished the World and Their Lost Art of Love*. New York: Viking Penguin, 2003.

Tannahill, Reay. *Sex in History*. London: Abacus / Sphere Books, 1981.

India's Dancing Girls

"Amrapali: Buddha's Gorgeous Disciple." The Tribune India—Spectrum, December 14, 2008. http://www.tribuneindia.com/2008/20081214/spectrum/main6.htm.

Bhise, Swati. "What Is Bharatanatyam?" Swati Bhíse. http://www.swatidance.org/whatis.html.

Dhiman, Kuldip. "Perfect Body Perfect Genes." The Tribune India—Spectrum, December 24, 2000. http://www.tribuneindia.com/2000/20001224/spectrum/main1.htm.

Mitra, Ipshita. "Amrapali Was More Than a Luscious Courtesan." The Times of India, January 31, 2013. http://timesofindia.indiatimes.com/life-style/books/Amrapali-was-more-than-a-luscious-courtesan/articleshow/12517919.cms?referral=PM.

Naidu, Jessica Sita. "Bharat Natyam: India's Classical Dance." Mahavidya.com. April 15, 2008. http://www.mahavidya.ca/?page_id=85.

China's Concubines

"Diaochan." *ChinaCulture.org*. http://www.chinaculture.org/gb/en_aboutchina/2003-09/24/content_22659.htm.

Emmott, Craig. "Princess Yang Kwei-fei (Yang Guiffei)." http://www.taleofgenji.org/yang_kwei-fei.html.

Empress Wu Zetian. "Women in World History Curriculum." http://www.womeninworldhistory.com/heroine6.html.

"Introduction to Four Ancient Beauties of Ancient China." *Cultureofchinese.com*. http://cultureofchinese.com/traditions/historical-figures-tales/introduction-to-four-ancient-beauties-of-ancient-china/.

Haiwang Yuan. "Diao Chan." http://people.wku.edu/haiwang.yuan/China/tales/diaochan_b.htm.

"Top Four Beauties of Ancient China." China International Travel Service. http://www.cits.net/china-guide/china-traditions/ancient-four-beauties.html.

"Wu Zetian." *ChinaCulture.org.* http://www.chinaculture.org/gb/en_aboutchina/2003-09/24/content_22879.htm.

"Xi Shi: Most Beautiful Woman in Chinese History Wall Scroll." *OrientalOutpost.com.* http://www.orientaloutpost.com/proddetail.php?prod=4bs-xishi2.

"Xishi—One of the Four Great Beauties in Ancient China." *Cultural China.* http://history.cultural-china.com/en/48History144.html.

Xi Yang. "Top 10 Most Glamorous Courtesans in Ancient China." *China.org.cn,* November 29, 2010. http://www.china.org.cn/top10/2010-11/29/content_21442642_10.htm.

"Yang Guifei." ChinaCulture.org. http://www.chinaculture.org/gb/en_aboutchina/2003-09/24/content_22669.htm.

"Yang Guifei." Encyclopædia Britannica. http://www.britannica.com/EBchecked/topic/651767/Yang-Guifei.

Ancient Rome

"Clodia." Encyclopædia Britannica. http://www.britannica.com/EBchecked/topic/122003/Clodia.

"Clodia." Universalium. http://universalium.academic.ru/263285/Clodia.

D'Ambra, Eve. *Roman Women.* Cambridge: Cambridge University Press, 2007.

Evans, James Allan. "Theodora (Wife of Justinian I)." University of British Columbia. http://www.luc.edu/roman-emperors/dora.htm.

Lewis, Jone Johnson. "Empress Theodora: Biography of Byzantine Empress Theodora." http://womenshistory.about.com/od/medbyzantempress/a/theodora.htm.

Prioleau, Betsy. *Seductress: Women Who Ravished the World and Their Lost Art of Love.* New York: Viking Penguin, 2003.

4. Honored Courtesans

The Courtesan Poet—Veronica Franco

"Franco, Veronica (1546–1591), Venetian Courtesan Poet." Italian Women Writers. University of Chicago Library. http://www.lib.uchicago.edu/efts/IWW/BIOS/A0017.html.

"Giambattista Tiepolo (Venice 1696–1770 Madrid): The Arrival of Henry III at the Villa Contarini." Lot Notes. Christie's. http://www.christies.com/lotfinder/paintings/giambattista-tiepolo-the-arrival-of-henry-iii-5529487-details.aspx.

Prioleau, Betsy. *Seductress: Women Who Ravished the World and Their Lost Art of Love.* New York: Viking Penguin, 2003.

"Prostitution in Renaissance Venice." *OpenLearn.* http://www.open.edu/openlearn /history-the-arts/history/prostitution-renaissance-venice.

Rosenthal, Margaret F. *The Honest Courtesan: Veronica Franco, Citizen and Writer in Sixteenth-Century Venice.* Chicago: University of Chicago Press, 1992.

Tucker, Carol. "Dressed (or Undressed) for Success: Researching the Life of an 'Honest Courtesan,' Margaret Rosenthal Unfolded a Closet Full of 16th Century Sartorial Secrets." USC News. March 27, 1995. http://www.usc.edu/uscnews/stories/1091 .html.

———. "Portrait of a Poet-Prostitute." *USC News.* http://www.usc.edu/uscnews /stories/1083.html.

"Venice History." *Lonely Planet.* http://www.lonelyplanet.com/italy/venice/history.

"Venice Quarantine Islands: Lazzaretto Nuovo." A Guide in Venice. http://aguideinvenice .com/en/venice-case-22-Venice-Quarantine-Islands-Lazzaretto-Nuovo.html.

"Veronica Franco: Biography." USC Dornsife. http://dornsife.usc.edu/veronica-franco /biography/.

Tantalizing Tullia—Tullia d'Aragona

Griffin, Susan. *The Book of the Courtesans: A Catalogue of Their Virtues.* London: Pan Macmillan, 2002.

Hairston, Julia. "Aragona, Tullia d'." Italian Women Writers. University of Chicago Library. http://www.lib.uchicago.edu/efts/IWW/BIOS/A0004.html.

Prioleau, Betsy. *Seductress: Women Who Ravished the World and Their Lost Art of Love.* New York: Viking Penguin, 2003.

Papal Mistresses

Lewis, Jone Johnson. "About Marozia." About.com Women's History. http://womens history.about.com/od/medievalchristianity/p/marozia.htm.

Kirsch, Johann Peter. "Pope John X." Catholic Encyclopedia (1913), volume 8. http://en .wikisource.org/wiki/Catholic_Encyclopedia_%281913%29/Pope_John_X .

"Pope Alexander VI." NNDB. http://www.nndb.com/people/159/000092880/.

Willey, David. "Fresco Fragment Revives Papal Scandal." BBC News Online, July 21, 2007. http://news.bbc.co.uk/1/hi/world/europe/6909589.stm.

5. MEANWHILE IN BRITAIN . . .

The Merriest Mistress—Jane Shore

Carroll, Leslie. *Royal Affairs: A Lusty Romp Through the Extramarital Adventures That Rocked the British Monarchy.* New York: New American Library, 2008.

Crosland, Margaret. *The Mysterious Mistress: The Life and Legend of Jane Shore.* Gloucestershire, England: Sutton Publishing, 2006.

"Jane Shore (1445?-1527)." Luminarium Encyclopedia Project. http://www.luminarium.org/encyclopedia/janeshore.htm.

"Jane Shore." Encyclopædia Britannica. http://www.britannica.com/EBchecked/topic/541589/Jane-Shore.

"Middle Ages Women: Jane Shore." Middle Ages. http://www.lordsandladies.org/jane-shore.htm.

More, Sir Thomas. *The History of King Richard the Third.* Written 1513–18.

The Ten Mistresses of Henry VIII

1533. The coronation of Anne Boleyn. http://englishhistory.net/tudor/prianne1.html.

"Anne Boleyn." Historic Royal Palaces: Tower of London. http://www.hrp.org.uk/TowerOfLondon/stories/palacepeople/anneboleyn.

Bilyeau, Nancy. "1541: Margaret Pole, Countess of Salisbury." ExecutedToday.com, May 27, 2103. http://www.executedtoday.com/2013/05/27/1541-margaret-pole-countess-of-salisbury/.

"Block and Ax." Royal Armouries. http://www.royalarmouries.org/tower-of-london/power-house/institutions-of-the-tower/prison/execution/block-and-axe.

Carroll, Leslie. *Royal Affairs: A Lusty Romp Through the Extramarital Adventures That Rocked the British Monarchy.* New York: New American Library, 2008.

Engel, Howard. *Lord High Executioner: An Unashamed Look at Hangmen, Headsmen, and Their Kind.* London: Robson Books, 1998.

"Execution by Decapitation." http://www.capitalpunishmentuk.org/behead.html.

Hart, Kelly. *The Mistresses of Henry VIII.* Gloucestershire, England: History Press, 2009.

Mantel, Hilary. "Anne Boleyn, Queen for a Day." *The New York Times,* January 22, 2010. http://www.nytimes.com/2010/01/24/books/review/Mantel-t.html?pagewanted=all&_r=0.

McCarthy, Michael. "The Jousting Accident That Turned Henry VIII into a Tyrant." *The Independent,* April 18, 2009. http://www.independent.co.uk/news/uk/this-britain/the-jousting-accident-that-turned-henry-viii-into-a-tyrant-1670421.html.

"Margaret Pole, Countess of Salisbury." TudorHistory.org. http://tudorhistory.org/people/mpole/.

"Mary, Queen of Scots." The Scotsman. http://www.scotsman.com/news/mary-queen-of-scots-1-465222.

"Tower Green and Scaffold Site." Historic Royal Palaces: Tower of London. http://www.hrp.org.uk/TowerOfLondon/stories/towergreen.

The Merry Monarch—Charles II

Ballard, Barbara. "The Face of Britannia." Britannia.com. http://www.britannia.com/history/articles/francesstuart.html.

"Barbara Villiers, Duchess of Cleveland." Encyclopædia Britannica. http://www.britannica.com/EBchecked/topic/121399/Barbara-Villiers-Duchess-of-Cleveland.

"Barbara Palmer, Duchess of Cleveland." English Monarchs. http://www.englishmonarchs.co.uk/stuart_20.html.

Carroll, Leslie. *Royal Affairs: A Lusty Romp Through the Extramarital Adventures that Rocked the British Monarchy.* New York: New American Library, 2008.

"Coranto." Encyclopædia Britannica. http://www.britannica.com/EBchecked/topic/137160/coranto.

Mahon, Elizabeth Kerri. *Scandalous Women: The Lives and Loves of History's Most Notorious Women.* New York: Perigree/Penguin, 2011.

"Wynne, S. M. Palmer (née Villiers, Barbara)." *Oxford Dictionary of National Biography.* http://www.oxforddnb.com/view/article/28285.

"History of Publishing." Early newspapers in Britain and America. Encyclopædia Britannica. http://www.britannica.com/EBchecked/topic/482597/history-of-publishing/28661/Commercial-newsletters-in-continental-Europe.

Patterson, Catherine. "No. 1983: Inventing the Newspaper." *Engines of Our Ingenuity.* http://www.uh.edu/engines/epi1983.htm.

The Mistress Who Married a King . . . Or Did She?—Lucy Walter

Carroll, Leslie. *Royal Affairs: A Lusty Romp Through the Extramarital Adventures that Rocked the British Monarchy.* New York: New American Library, 2008.

Clifton, Robin. "Walter, Lucy (1630?-1658)." *Oxford Dictionary of National Biography.* http://www.oxforddnb.com/templates/article.jsp?articleid=28639&back=,5144.

"Lucy Walter." Encyclopædia Britannica. http://www.britannica.com/EBchecked/topic/635108/Lucy-Walter.

Pepys, Samuel. "Lucy Walter." The Diary of Samuel Pepys. http://www.pepysdiary.com/encyclopedia/5743/.

Powell, Roger. *Royal Sex: The Scandalous Love Lives of the British Royal Family.* Stroud, England: Amberley Publishing, 2010.

Stephens, Sarah. "Lucy Walter." The Glorious Revolution of 1688. http://theglorious revolution.org/docs/lucywalter.htm.

The Orange-Seller, the Spy, and the Italian Temptress—Nell Gwyn, Louise de Kérouaille, and Hortense Mancini

Bevan, Bryan. *The Duchess Hortense: Cardinal Mazarin's Wanton Niece.* London: Rubicon Press, 1987.

Carlton, Charles. *Royal Mistresses.* London: Routledge, 1990.

Carroll, Leslie. *Royal Affairs: A Lusty Romp Through the Extramarital Adventures that Rocked the British Monarchy.* New York: New American Library, 2008.

Goldsmith, Elizabeth C. *The King's Mistresses: The Liberated Lives of Marie Mancini, Princess Colonna, and Her Sister Hortense, Duchess Mazarin.* New York: PublicAffairs, 2012.

Her Royal Highness Princess Michael of Kent. *Cupid and the King: Five Royal Paramours.* London: HarperCollins, 1991.

"The Lord Mayor's Orders." *HistoryLearningSite.* http://historylearningsite.co.uk/1665 _lord_mayor_orders.htm.

Mancini, Hortense, and Marie Mancini. *Memoirs.* Edited and translated by Sarah Nelson. Chicago: University of Chicago Press, 2008.

Powell, Roger. *Royal Sex: The Scandalous Love Lives of the British Royal Family.* Stroud, England: Amberley Publishing, 2013.

Prioleau, Betsy. *Seductress: Women Who Ravished the World and Their Lost Art of Love.* New York: Viking Penguin, 2003.

An Unpopular King—James II

Carlton, Charles. *Royal Mistresses.* London: Routledge, 1990.

Carroll, Leslie. *Royal Affairs: A Lusty Romp Through the Extramarital Adventures That Rocked the British Monarchy.* New York: New American Library, 2008.

"James II (1633–1701)." BBC History. http://www.bbc.co.uk/history/historic_figures /james_ii.shtml.

"James II (r.1685–88)." The Official Website of the British Monarchy. http://www .royal.gov.uk/HistoryoftheMonarchy/KingsandQueensoftheUnitedKingdom /TheStuarts/JamesII.aspx.

Kenyon, John P. "James II." Encyclopædia Britannica. http://www.britannica.com /EBchecked/topic/299989/James-II.

"King James II (1685–88)." Royal Family History. http://www.britroyals.com/kings .asp?id=james2.

Shuckburgh, Evelyn Shirley. "Churchill, Arabella." Dictionary of National Biography, 1885–1900, volume 10. http://en.wikisource.org/wiki/Churchill,_Arabella _%28DNB00%29.

The King and the Maypole—Ehrengard Melusine

"1911 Encyclopædia Britannica / Königsmarck, Philip Christoph, Count of." Wikisource. http://en.wikisource.org/wiki/1911_Encyclop%C3%A6dia_Britannica/K%C3%B6nigsmark,_Philipp_Christoph,_Count_of.

Carlton, Charles. *Royal Mistresses*. London: Routledge, 1990.

Carroll, Leslie. *Royal Affairs: A Lusty Romp Through the Extramarital Adventures That Rocked the British Monarchy*. New York: New American Library, 2008.

Day, Martyn. "The Monarch and the Maypole: Fun and Games At Kendal House." St Margarets Community Website. http://www.stmgrts.org.uk/archives/2010/07/the_monarch_and_the_maypole.html.

Gold, Claudia. *The King's Mistress: The True and Scandalous Story of the Woman Who Stole the Heart of George I*. London: Quercus, 2012.

Kilburn, Matthew. "Schulenburg, (Ehrengard) Melusine von der." Oxford Dictionary of National Biography. http://www.oxforddnb.com/view/printable/24834.

"Schrezenmaier, Christine. Melusine von der Schulenburg." Royal Genealogy. http://royal-genealogy.com/persons/nobility_germany/schulenburg/melusine_schulenburg_1667.html.

"South Sea Bubble." Encyclopædia Britannica. http://www.britannica.com/EBchecked/topic/556389/South-Sea-Bubble.

"South Sea Bubble Short History." Harvard Business School. http://www.library.hbs.edu/hc/ssb/history.html.

Waters, Florence. "The Georgians: How They Made Britain Great." The Telegraph. http://www.telegraph.co.uk/culture/tvandradio/10726622/The-Georgians-How-they-made-Britain-great.html.

White, Matthew. "Georgians." British Library: Learning Georgians. http://www.bl.uk/learning/histcitizen/georgians/georgianhome.html.

The Duelist's Daughter—Henrietta Howard

Borman, Tracy. *King's Mistress, Queen's Servant: The Life and Times of Henrietta Howard*. New York: Vintage Books, 2010.

Carroll, Leslie. *Royal Affairs: A Lusty Romp Through the Extramarital Adventures That Rocked the British Monarchy*. New York: New American Library, 2008.

"Henrietta Howard Countess of Suffolk: An Eventful But Uneven Life." http://www.twickenham-museum.org.uk/detail.asp?ContentID=61.

Kilburn, Matthew. "Henrietta Howard, Countess of Suffolk (ca. 1688–1767)." *Oxford Dictionary of National Biography*. http://www.oxforddnb.com/templates/article.jsp?articleid=13904&back=.

Kilburn, Matthew. "Wallmoden, Amalie Sophie Marianne von, suo jure Countess of Yarmouth (1704–1765)." *Oxford Dictionary of National Biography*. http://www.oxforddnb.com/templates/article.jsp?articleid=28579&back=&version=2004-09.

The Marble Hill Society. "History of the House." http://www.marblehillsociety.org
.uk/pages/2009/05/history-of-house.shtml.

Powell, Roger. *Royal Sex: The Scandalous Love Lives of the British Royal Family*. Stroud, England: Amberley Publishing, 2013.

Rigg, James McMullen. "Wallmoden, Amalie Sophie Marriane (DNBoo)." Dictionary of National Biography, 1885–1900, volume 59. http://en.wikisource.org/wiki /Wallmoden,_Amalie_Sophie_Marianne_%28DNB00%29.

"Worsley, Lucy. Henrietta Howard—The Mistress Who Saved a Royal Marriage." Daily Mail Online, May 4, 2010. http://www.dailymail.co.uk/home/you/article-1269820 /Henrietta-Howard–mistress-saved-royal-marriage.html.

The Dandy Prince

"George IV (1762–1830)." BBC History. http://www.bbc.co.uk/history/historic_figures /george_iv_king.shtml.

"George IV (ruled 1820–30)." The Official Website of the British Monarchy. http:// www.royal.gov.uk/HistoryoftheMonarchy/KingsandQueensoftheUnitedKingdom /TheHanoverians/GeorgeIV.aspx.

Parissien, Steven. "George IV: The Royal Joke?" BBC History. http://www.bbc.co.uk /history/british/empire_seapower/George_fourth_01.shtml.

The Mistress Who Blackmailed a King—Mary Robinson

Carroll, Leslie. *Royal Affairs: A Lusty Romp Through the Extramarital Adventures That Rocked the British Monarchy*. New York: New American Library, 2008.

Davenport, Hester. *The Prince's Mistress: A Life of Mary Robinson*. Gloucestershire, England: Sutton Publishing, 2004.

Ockerbloom, Mary Mark, editor. "Mary Darby Robinson (1758–1800)." A Celebration of Women Writers. http://digital.library.upenn.edu/women/robinson/biography.html.

Robinson, Mary. "Memoirs of Mary Robinson." Edited by Joseph Fitzgerald Molloy. Philadelphia: J. B. Lippincott, 1895. http://digital.library.upenn.edu/women/robinson /memoirs/memoirs.html.

An Illegal Royal Marriage—Maria Fitzherbert

"The Bathing Machine." The Mayor and Charter Trustees of Margate. http://margate .org.uk/index.php?page=the-bathing-machine.

Boyle, Laura. "Bucks, Beaus and Dandies." JameAusten.co.uk, April 14, 2014. http:// www.janeausten.co.uk/bucks-beaus-dandies/.

Boyle, Laura. "Was Beau Brummell a Dandy?" JaneAusten.co.uk, June 17, 2011. http:// www.janeausten.co.uk/beau-brummell-and-the-birth-of-regency-fashion/.

Carlton, Charles. *Royal Mistresses*. London: Routledge, 1990.

Carroll, Leslie. *Royal Affairs: A Lusty Romp Through the Extramarital Adventures That Rocked the British Monarchy*. New York: New American Library, 2008.

"Maria Fitzherbert." Encyclopædia Britannica. http://www.britannica.com/EBchecked /topic/208924/Maria-Fitzherbert.

"Maria Fitzherbert." The Twickenham Museum. http://www.twickenham-museum .org.uk/detail.asp?ContentID=78.

"Maria Fitzherbert: Maria Fitzherbert's House in the Old Steine." My Brighton and Hove. http://www.mybrightonandhove.org.uk/page_id__7540_path__0p224p1218p .aspx.

Munson, James. *Maria Fitzherbert: The Secret Wife of George IV.* London: Constable, 2001.

"Seaside Bathing Machines." Workshops for Schools Blog. http://www.workshops-for -schools.co.uk/blog/2012/11/02/seaside-holidays-in-the-past/bathing-machines -history-of-the-seaside/.

Spurned and Betrayed—Dora Jordan

Carroll, Leslie. *Royal Affairs: A Lusty Romp Through the Extramarital Adventures That Rocked the British Monarchy.* New York: New American Library, 2008.

"Dorothea Jordan: Actress and Royal Mistress." The Twickenham Museum. http:// www.twickenham-museum.org.uk/detail.asp?contentid=205.

"Dorothea Jordan." Encyclopædia Britannica. http://www.britannica.com/EBchecked /topic/306178/Dorothea-Jordan.

"Dorothea Jordan." NNDB. http://www.nndb.com/people/657/000101354/.

Tomalin, Claire. *Mrs. Jordan's Profession: The Actress and Prince.* New York: Viking, 1994.

"The Theatre." Discovering Leeds, Leeds City Council. http://www.leodis.net/discovery /discovery.asp?pageno=&page=2003218_251720608&topic=2003219_253704250 &subsection=2003625_449382961.

"Publish and Be Damned!"—Harriette Wilson

1911 Encyclopædia Britannica / Clarke, Mary Anne." http://en.wikisource.org/wiki/1911 _Encyclop%C3%A6dia_Britannica/Clarke,_Mary_Anne.

Brown, Susan, Patricia Clements, and Isobel Grundy, eds. Harriette Wilson Entry (Overview Screen). Orlando: Women's Writing in the British Isles from the Beginnings to the Present. Cambridge University Press Online, 2006. http://orlando .cambridge.org.

"Harriette Wilson: Courtesan and Blackmailer." Everything 2. http://everything2.com /title/Harriette+Wilson.

Wilson, Frances. *The Courtesan's Revenge: Harriette Wilson, the Woman Who Blackmailed the King.* London: Faber & Faber, 2004.

Wilson, Harriette. *The Memoirs of Harriette Wilson.* Volumes 1 and 2. Project Gutenberg, 2013. http://www.gutenberg.org/files/43617/43617-h/43617-h.htm.

6. PRINCES OF PLEASURE

Flirty Bertie—Prince Albert Edward

Aronson, Theo. *The King in Love: Edward VII's Mistresses.* New York: Harper & Row Publishers, 1988.

Bunbury, Turtle. "Nellie Clifden—The Irish Prostitute Who Nearly Brought the British Royal Family Crashing Down." http://www.turtlebunbury.com/history /history_heroes/hist_hero_nellie_clifden.html.

Carroll, Leslie. *Royal Affairs: A Lusty Romp Through the Extramarital Adventures That Rocked the British Monarchy.* New York: New American Library, 2008.

Costello, Eugene. March 22, 2010. *Daily Mail Online.* "A Love Seat Fit for a King: The Antique Chair That Gives an Eye-Popping Insight into Edward VII's Debauched Youth." Daily Mail.com, March 22, 2010. http://www.dailymail.co.uk/news/article -1259670.html.

"Edward VII (ruled 1901–10)." The Official Website of the British Monarchy. http:// www.royal.gov.uk/HistoryoftheMonarchy/KingsandQueensoftheUnitedKing dom/Saxe-Coburg-Gotha/EdwardVII.aspx.

Evans, Martin. "Duchess of Cambridge Treated at Hospital with a Long Royal Tradi- tion." *The Telegraph,* December 3, 2012. http://www.telegraph.co.uk/news/uknews /kate-middleton/9720259/Duchess-of-Cambridge-treated-at-hospital-with-a-long -Royal-tradition.html.

Holland, Evangeline. "The Amorous Life of Edward VII." Edwardian Promenade, August 10, 2010. http://www.edwardianpromenade.com/royalty/the-amorous-life -of-edward-vii/.

———. "The Many Scandals of the Marlborough House Set." Edwardian Promenade. August 27, 2007. http://edwardianpromenade.com/society/the-many-scandals-of -the-marlborough-house-set/.

"King Edward VII. (1901–10)." Royal Family History. http://www.britroyals.com /kings.asp?id=edward7.

Lamont-Brown, Raymond. *Alice Keppel and Agnes Keyser.* Gloucestershire, England: Sutton Publishing, 2001.

Porter, Bernard. "Bertie: A Life of Edward VII by Jane Ridley—Review." The Guardian, September 14, 2012. http://www.theguardian.com/books/2012/sep/14/bertie-life -edward-vii-jane-ridley-review.

"Queen Victoria: The Real Story of Her 'Domestic Bliss.'" BBC News Magazine, January 1, 2013. http://www.bbc.co.uk/news/magazine-20782442.

Sandbrook, Dominic. "One's Bit on the Side." *New Statesman,* July 9, 2009. http:// www.newstatesman.com/life-and-society/2009/07/royal-family-victoria-prince.

Thomas, Sean. "On the Trail of Edward VII's Sex Chair for Threesomes." *The Week,*

December 6, 2005. http://www.theweek.co.uk/28193/trail-edward-vii%E2%80%99s-sex-chair-threesomes.

Wilkes, Roger. "Sex Mad—and Off to the Asylum to Prove It." The Telegraph, January 16, 2002. http://www.telegraph.co.uk/property/3297489/Sex-mad-and-off-to-the-asylum-to-prove-it.html.

The Very Discreet "Skittles"—Catherine Walters

"Catherine Walters of Henderson Street Toxteth." Liverpool History Society. http://liverpoolhistorysocietyquestions.blogspot.co.uk/2012/03/catherine-walters-of-henderson-street.html.

"Catherine Waters ('Skittles')." The Library of Nineteenth-Century Photography. http://www.19thcenturyphotos.com/Catherine-Walters-%28%27Skittles%27%29-123604.htm.

Lawless, Erin. "Hidden Historical Heroines (13: "Skittles")." November 19, 2012. http://erinlawless.wordpress.com/2012/11/19/hidden-historical-heroines-13-skittles/.

McNeill, Maggie. "Skittles. The Honest Courtesan," April 18, 2013. http://maggiemcneill.wordpress.com/2013/04/18/skittles/.

Sherwood, James. "Miss Catherine Walters." Henry Poole & Co., November 28, 2012. https://henrypoole.com/hall_of_fame/catherine-skittles-walters/.

"Skittles—The Last Victorian Courtesan." Scandalous Women, March 22, 2012. http://scandalouswoman.blogspot.co.uk/2012/03/skittles-last-victorian-courtesan.html.

"Women of the Half-World." The Scotsman, September 16, 2014. http://www.scotsman.com/news/women-of-the-half-world-1-659333.

The Jersey Lily—Lillie Langtry

Aronson, Theo. The King in Love: Edward VII's Mistresses. New York: Harper & Row, 1988.

Carroll, Leslie. Royal Affairs: A Lusty Romp Through the Extramarital Adventures That Rocked the British Monarchy. New York: New American Library, 2008.

"Interviewed the Jersey Lily." Daily Telegraph, October 3, 1882, page 4. Papers Past. http://paperspast.natlib.govt.nz/cgi-bin/paperspast?a=d&d=DTN18821003.2.21.

"The Jersey Lily." The Genealogist. http://www.thegenealogist.co.uk/featuredarticles/2011/the-jersey-lily-67/.

"Lillie Langtry." Museum on the Internet. http://www.lillielangtry.com/.

"Lillie Langtry—Biography." The Royal Borough of Kensington and Chelsea. http://www.rbkc.gov.uk/subsites/visitkensingtonandchelsea/seedo/people/blueplaques/recordsh-l/lillielangtry.aspx.

"Lot 99 [Langtry, Lillie] Presentation Album of Photographs from Lillie (Lily) Langtry to Frederic Gebhard." Doyle New York. http://www.doylenewyork.com/content/more.asp?id=254.

Smyth, Sara. "Portrait of a Mistress: Album of King Edward VII's Lover Lillie Langtry Is Uncovered After 135 Years." *Daily Mail Online,* April 16, 2013. http://www .dailymail.co.uk/news/article-2309965/Edward-VIIs-mistress-pictures-woman -royal-affair-auction.html.

The Babbling Brooke—Daisy Greville, Countess of Warwick

"Alice Keppel." http://www.duchess-of-cornwall.co.uk/alice-keppel.htm.

Anand, Sushila. *Daisy: The Life and Loves of the Countess of Warwick.* London: Piatkus Books, 2008.

Aronson, Theo. *The King in Love: Edward VII's Mistresses.* New York: Harper & Row, 1988.

Carroll, Leslie. *Royal Affairs: A Lusty Romp Through the Extramarital Adventures That Rocked the British Monarchy.* New York: New American Library, 2008.

Dilley, Ryan. "Camilla's Inherited Role as Royal Mistress." BBC News Online, July 11, 2003. http://news.bbc.co.uk/1/hi/magazine/3055376.stm.

Fishburn, Victoria. "A Life of Contrast: Daisy, Countess of Warwick." Edwardian Prom- enade, March 27, 2009. http://www.edwardianpromenade.com/politics/a-life-of -contrast-daisy-countess-of-warwick/.

The Forgotten Gardens of Easton Lodge. The "Daisy" Years. http://www.eastonlodge .co.uk/content/%E2%80%98daisy%E2%80%99-years-1865-1938.

"Frances Evelyn Maynard." *The Peerage.* http://www.thepeerage.com/p1406.htm#i 14060.

"King Edward VII's Hospital: Sister Agnes." http://www.kingedwardvii.co.uk/military _history.cfm.

Lamont-Brown, Raymond. *Edward VII's Last Loves.* Gloucestershire, England: Sutton Publishing, 1998.

"Mariánské Lázně." Czech Republic: Land of Stories. http://stories.czechtourism .com/en/story/marianske-lazne/royal-care.aspx.

Meikle, James. "King Edward VII Hospital—The Royal Choice." *The Guardian,* De- cember 7, 2012. http://www.theguardian.com/uk/2012/dec/07/king-edward-vii -hospital.

Nicolson, Juliet. "Babbling Brook's Doomed Romance." *Daily Mail Online,* March 25, 2008. http://www.dailymail.co.uk/home/books/article-544634/Babbling-Brookes -doomed-romance.html.

Powell, Roger. *Royal Sex: The Scandalous Love Lives of the British Royal Family.* Stroud, England: Amberley Publishing, 2013.

"The Socialist Socialite." BBC Essex Local History. http://www.bbc.co.uk/essex/content /articles/2009/05/21/countess_of_warwick_feature.shtml.

The Queen of Pleasure House—Alice Keppel

Abbott, Elizabeth. *Mistresses: A History of the Other Woman.* New York: The Overlook Press, 2010.

Aronson, Theo. *The King in Love: Edward VII's Mistresses.* New York: Harper & Row, 1988.

Carlton, Charles. *Royal Mistresses.* London: Routledge, 1990.

Carroll, Leslie. *Royal Affairs: A Lusty Romp Through the Extramarital Adventures That Rocked the British Monarchy.* New York: New American Library, 2008.

Friedman, Dennis. *Ladies of the Bedchamber: The Role of the Royal Mistress.* London: Peter Owen, 2003.

Lamont-Brown, Raymond. *Alice Keppel and Agnes Keyser.* Gloucestershire, England: Sutton Publishing, 2005.

Powell, Roger. *Royal Sex: The Scandalous Love Lives of the British Royal Family.* Stroud, England: Amberley Publishing, 2013.

The Courtesan versus the Establishment—Marguerite Alibert

"Marie Marguerite FAHMY." *Murderpedia.* http://murderpedia.org/female.F/f/fahmy-marguerite.htm.

Rennell, Tony. "The Cover-Up That Saved the Prince of Wales' Murderess Lover from the Gallows." *Daily Mail Online,* March 15, 2013. http://www.dailymail.co.uk/news/article-2294153/The-cover-saved-Prince-Wales-murderess-lover-gallows.html.

Rose, Andrew. *The Woman Before Wallis: Prince Edward, the Parisian Courtesan, and the Perfect Murder.* New York: Picador, 2013.

A Crowded Marriage—Camilla Parker Bowles

"Announcement of the Marriage of HRH the Prince of Wales and Mrs. Camilla Parker Bowles." Clarence House press release, Feburary 10, 2005. http://www.princeofwales.gov.uk/media/press-releases/announcement-of-the-marriage-of-hrh-the-prince-of-wales-and-mrs-camilla-parker.

Cowell, Alan. "Prince Charles Postpones Wedding to Attend Funeral." *The New York Times,* April 4, 2005. http://www.nytimes.com/2005/04/04/international/europe/04cnd-wedding.html?_r=1&.

Friedman, Dennis. *Ladies of the Bedchamber: The Role of the Royal Mistress.* London: Peter Owen Publisher, 2003.

"Largest TV Audience—Wedding." Guinness World Records. http://www.guinnessworldrecords.com/world-records/largest-tv-audience-wedding/.

Olsen, Patrick, and Martin Gee. "Prince Charles, Camilla Change Wedding Plans." *Chicago Tribune,* February 18, 2005. http://articles.chicagotribune.com/2005-02-18/news/0502190039_1_charles-and-camilla-windsor-castle-charles-clarence-house.

"The Panorama Interview with Diana, Princess of Wales." BBC. http://www.bbc.co.uk/news/special/politics97/diana/panorama.html.

"Timeline: Charles and Camilla's Romance." BBC News Online. http://news.bbc.co.uk/1/hi/uk/4410551.stm.

"Timeline: Diana, Princess of Wales." BBC. http://news.bbc.co.uk/1/hi/uk/6214096.stm.

7. THE AMERICAS

The American Princess—Clara Ward

"Clara Ward Dies in Italy." *The New York Times*, December 19, 1916. http://query .nytimes.com/mem/archive-free/pdf?res=F50D15F9345B17738DDDA00994DA 415B868DF1D3.

"Clara Ward Left $1,124,935 Estate." *The New York Times*, December 23, 1916. http:// query.nytimes.com/mem/archive-free/pdf?res=F60C10F9345B17738DDDAA0A 94DA415B868DF1D3.

"Joseph, Prince de Caramas-Chimay." SR/Olympic Sports. http://www.sports-reference .com/olympics/athletes/de/joseph-prince-de-caramas-chimay-1.html.

Passante, Anna. *The Bayview Compass*. August 1, 2010. http://bayviewcompass.com /archives/4664.

"Princess Disinherited." *The New York Times*, May 29, 1915. http://query.nytimes .com/mem/archive-free/pdf?res=F10911F8385C13738DDDA00A94DD405B 858DF1D3.

The Queen of the Yukon—Klondike Kate

Houdek, Jennifer. "Klondike Kate: 'Queen of the Yukon,' 1876–1957." Lit Site Alaska, University of Alaska Anchorage. http://www.litsite.org/index.cfm?section=digital -archives&page=industry&cat=Mining&viewpost=2&contentid=2713.

John, J. D. Finn. Vaudeville's Famous "Klondike Kate" Became an Oregon Legend. Offbeat Oregon History, August 14, 2011. http://www.offbeatoregon.com/o1108b -vaudeville-legend-klondike-kate-bends-most-colorful-homesteader.html.

"Kathleen Eloise 'Klondike Kate' Rockwell." *Find a Grave*. http://www.findagrave.com /cgi-bin/fg.cgi?page=gr&GRid=1660.

"Klondike Kate 'Our Destitute Prostitue' or 'Aunt Kate.'" *The Source* Weekly. July 21, 2010. http://www.bendsource.com/bend/klondike-kate-our-destitute-prostitute -or-aunt-kate/Content?oid=2142156.

"Klondike Kate's Last Request to Be Granted." Eugene Register-Guard, July 16, 1958. http://news.google.com/newspapers?nid=1310&dat=19580716&id=9BVWA AAAIBAJ&sjid=reIDAAAAIBAJ&pg=4845,2365290.

Morgan, Lael. *Good Time Girls of the Alaska-Yukon Gold Rush*. Kenmore, WA: Epicenter Press, 1998.

Pedersen, Nathan. "Klondike Kate (1876–1957)." *The Oregon Encyclopedia*. http://www .oregonencyclopedia.org/articles/klondike_kate/#.U-jOuEiLZ20.

Taylor, F. Andrew. "Developers Named Casinos After Legendary Relative, Arizona Charlie Meadows." *Las Vegas Review-Journal,* October 4, 2011. http://www .reviewjournal.com/life/las-vegas-history/developers-named-casinos-after -legendary-relative-arizona-charlie-meadows.

New York Madam—Fanny White

Blankman, Edmon. "The Blankman Will Case." *The New York Times,* February 19, 1861. http://www.nytimes.com/1861/02/19/news/the-blankman-will-case.html.

"The Blankman Will Case; Surrogate's Court. Before Hon. Edward C. West, Surrogate." *The New York Times,* June 7, 1861. http://www.nytimes.com/1861/06/07/news/the-blankman-will-case-surrogate-s-court-before-hon-edward-c-west-surrogate.html.

"The Case of Mrs. Blankman; A Second Post-Mortem Examination Excitement Amount Medical Men Statement of Drs Finnell and Sands Other Interesting Particulars. Post-Mortem Examination. Statement of Drs Finnell and Sands." *The New York Times,* October 19, 1860. http://www.nytimes.com/1860/10/19/news/case-mrs-blankman-second-post-mortem-examination-excitement-among-medical-men.html.

"The Case of Mrs. Blankman; Coroner's Investigation—Testimony of the Husband of the Deceased and Other Witnesses—Verdict of Death from Apoplexy." *The New York Times,* October 22, 1860. http://www.nytimes.com/1860/10/22/news/case-mrs-blankman-coroner-s-investigation-testimony-husband-deceased-other.html.

Herts, Henry B. "Executor's Sale of Magnificent Household Furniture." *The New York Times.* Monday, October 28, 1861, page 7. http://fultonhistory.com/Newspapers%207/New%20York%20NY%20Times/New%20York%20NY%20Times%201861%20Oct-Nov%20Grayscale/New%20York%20NY%20Times%201861%20Oct-Nov%20Grayscale%20(224).pdf

"Law Reports; Court Calendar This Day. Surrogate's Court." *The New York Times,* March 4, 1861. http://www.nytimes.com/1861/03/04/news/law-reports-court-calendar-this-day-surrogate-s-court.html.

"Sudden Death of a Notorious Woman; Exhumation of Her Remains for the Purposes of a Coroner's Inquest." *The New York Times,* October 18, 1860. http://www.nytimes.com/1860/10/18/news/sudden-death-notorious-woman-exhumation-her-remains-for-purposes-coroner-s.html.

"Surrogate's Court; The Blankman Case Will Testimony of John H. Funk." *The New York Times,* March 5, 1861. http://www.nytimes.com/1861/03/05/news/surrogate-s-court-the-blankman-will-case-testimony-of-john-h-funk.html.

"Surrogate's Court; The Blankman Will Case Continuation of Contestants' Testimony. Matter of the Probate of the Will of Augusla J." *The New York Times,* February 28, 1861. http://www.nytimes.com/1861/02/28/news/surrogate-s-court-blankman-will-case-continuation-contestants-testimony-matter.html.

"Surrogate's Court; The Blankman Will Contest." *The New York Times,* February 22, 1861. http://www.nytimes.com/1861/02/22/news/surrogate-s-court-the-blankman-will-contest.html.

"Surrogate's Court; The Bankman Will Case Contestants Testimony Continued." *The New York Times,* March 2, 1861. http://www.nytimes.com/1861/03/02/news/surrogate-s-court-the-blankman-will-case-contestants-testimony-continued.html.

"Surrogate's Court; The Will of Fanny White." *The New York Times,* December 11,

1860. http://www.nytimes.com/1860/12/11/news/surrogate-s-court-the-will -of-fanny-white.html.

The Life and Death of Fanny White: Being a Complete and Interesting History of the Career of That Notorious Lady. New York, 1860. http://pds.lib.harvard.edu/pds/view /2968201.

The Empress of Paraguay—Eliza Lynch

Cawthorne, Nigel. *The Empress of South America: The Irish Courtesan Who Destroyed Paraguay—and Became Its National Heroine.* London: William Heinemann, 2003.

Lillis, Michael. "The True Origins of Eliza Lynch." http://www.irishtimes.com/culture /heritage/the-true-origins-of-eliza-lynch-1.1719349.

Murray, Edmundo. "Beauty and the Beast: A Beautiful Irish Courtesan and a Beastly Latin American Dictator." http://www.irlandeses.org/beautybeast.htm.

Podosyonov, Sergei. "War Turns Paraguay into Latin American Soybean." Pravda, March 23, 2012. http://english.pravda.ru/business/finance/23-03-2012/120879 -paraguay-0/.

Rees, Sian. "The Shadows of Elisa Lynch: How a nineteenth-century Irish courtesan became the most powerful woman in Paraguay." London: Review, an imprint of Headline Book Publishing, 2003.

Vila, Laura. "Elisa Lynch: Paraguay's Peron." http://theculturetrip.com/south-america /paraguay/articles/elisa-lynch-paraguay-s-peron/.

"War of the Triple Alliance [Lopez War] (1864–1870)." Global Security. http://www .globalsecurity.org/military/world/war/paraguayan.htm.

8. Asia

From Mughal Emperors to Bollywood

Gupta, Madhur. "The Rise and Fall of India's Courtesans." DesiBlitz. http://www .desiblitz.com/content/rise-fall-indias-courtesans.

"The Misconstrued Tawaif." Think Tome, March 15, 2010. http://thinktome.wordpress .com/2010/03/15/the-misconstrued-tawaif/.

Neville, Pran. "Nautch Girls: Sahibs Danced to Their Tune: Tribune India, July 25, 2004. http://www.tribuneindia.com/2004/20040725/spectrum/main1.htm.

The Courtesan Who Ruled a Principality—Begum Samru

"Fame and Infamy." The Hindu, August 14, 2009. http://www.thehindubusinessline .com/todays-paper/tp-life/article1086674.ece.

Kaur, Harpreet. "The Rebels." Dance with Shadows, March 26, 2006. http://www .dancewithshadows.com/society/courtesan.asp.

Vajpeyi, Yogesh. "Fall of a Culture." *Tribune,* India—Spectrum, September 20, 2009. http://www.tribuneindia.com/2009/20090920/spectrum/main2.htm.

Viage of the Moon—Mah Laqa

"Refurbished Garden Tomb of Mah Laqa Bai Inaugurated by Consul General." Consulate of the United States—Hyderabad, India, March 6, 2011. http://hyderabad.usconsulate.gov/pr030611.html.

"Tomb of Mah Laqa Bai Being Refurbished Through U.S. Ambassador's Fund for Cultural Preservation." Consulate General of the United States—Hyderabad, India, August 19, 2010. http://hyderabad.usconsulate.gov/pr081910.html.

"US Consulate Funds Renovation of Mah Laqa Bai's Tomb." DNA India, August 19, 2010. http://www.dnaindia.com/india/report-us-consulate-funds-renovation-of-mah-laqa-bais-tomb-1425862.

The Peacock Dancer—Moran Sarkar

Aujla, G. S. "Two Emperors in the Same Mould." *The Tribune of India,* February 10, 2002. http://www.tribuneindia.com/2002/20020210/spectrum/main4.htm.

Chopra, Rajni Shaleen. "Memories of a Dancing Peacock." *The Indian Express,* August 31, 2011. http://archive.indianexpress.com/news/memories-of-a-dancing-peacock/837545/1.

"The Court of Maharaja Ranjit Singh." Victoria and Albert Museum. http://www.vam.ac.uk/content/articles/t/the-court-of-maharaja-ranjit-singh/.

"Maharaja Ranjit Singh." History of the Sikhs. http://www.sikh-history.com/sikhhist/warriors/ranjit.html.

Nayar, Aruti. "Moran, the Mystery Woman." *The Tribune of India,* August 24, 2008. http://www.tribuneindia.com/2008/20080824/spectrum/main3.htm.

Singh, Amarinder. "The Man with 20 Wives." *The Telegraph of India,* March 7, 2010. http://www.telegraphindia.com/1100307/jsp/7days/story_12187144.jsp.

Walia, Varinder. "Maharaja-Moran Relationship in New Light." Tribune News Service, July 2, 2008. http://www.tribuneindia.com/2008/20080702/punjab1.htm.

A Rebellious Courtesan—Azizun Nisa

Ramesh, Randeep. "India's Secret History: 'A Holocaust, One Where Millions Disappeared. . . .'" *The Guardian,* August 24, 2007. http://www.theguardian.com/world/2007/aug/24/india.randeepramesh.

Sharma, Kabir. "Azizun: A Metamorphosis." *The Viewspaper.* http://theviewspaper.net/azizun_a_metamorphosis/.

Singh, Lata. "Making The 'Margin' Visible: Courtesans and the Rebellion of 1857." People's Democracy, vol. 31, no 38, September 23, 2007. http://archives.peoplesdemocracy.in/2007/0923/09232007_1857.htm.

Japan's Pleasure Quarters

Abbott, Elizabeth. *Mistresses: A History of the Other Woman*. New York: Overlook Press, 2010.

Graham (Diaz), Naomi. "Geisha FAQ." Immortal Geisha. http://immortalgeisha.com /faq_geisha.php.

Kakiuchi, Maria, and Akane Ogawa. "Oiran." The Kyoto Project. Kyoto University of Foreign Studies, February 17, 2014. http://thekyotoproject.org/english/oiran/.

Longstreet, Stephen, and Ethel Longstreet. *Yoshiwara: Geishas, Courtesans, and the Pleasure Quarters of Old Tokyo*. Rutland, VT: Tuttle, 2009.

"Oiran: Ladies of Pleasure." *Japan Slate,* December 19, 2009. http://www.japanslate.com /oiran-ladies-of-pleasure/.

Imperial China

Abbott, Elizabeth. *Mistresses: A History of the Other Woman*. New York: Overlook Press, 2010.

Cheng, Jennifer. "Liu Tienan: Hall Hath No Fury Like a Mistress Scorned." *Time,* August 2, 2013. http://world.time.com/2013/08/05/vice-doesnt-pay-10-scandalous -chinese-officials-who-landed-with-a-bump/slide/liu-tienan-hell-hath-no-fury/.

"Arsenic Killed Chinese Emperor, Reports Say." CNN.com/Asia, November 4, 2008. http://edition.cnn.com/2008/WORLD/asiapcf/11/04/china.emperor/index .html?_s=PM:WORLD.

Coonan, Clifford. "Welcome Back: Return of Capitalism to China Means a Major Comeback for the Concubine." *The Independent,* August 26, 2009. http://www .independent.co.uk/news/world/asia/welcome-back-return-of-capitalism-to-china -means-a-major-comeback-for-the-concubine-1777215.html.

Huang, Cary. "Ex-energy Chief Liu Tienan Expelled from Party over Graft." *South China Morning Post,* August 9, 2013. http://www.scmp.com/news/china/article /1295287/former-senior-official-liu-tienan-be-prosecuted-graft.

Li, Liu. "Wives Suing Mistresses over Gifted Properties." *China Daily,* January 2, 2006. http://www.chinadaily.com.cn/english/doc/2006-01/02/content_508674.htm.

"Revenge of the Evil Emperor: Mass Slaughter in Beijing's Forbidden City." *Daily Mail Online.* May 3, 2008. http://www.dailymail.co.uk/news/article-563688 /Revenge-evil-emperor-Mass-slaughter-Beijings-Forbidden-City.html.

Schwarck, Edward. "Xi Jinping's Anti-Corruption Campaign." Royal United Services Institute, October 28, 2013. https://www.rusi.org/analysis/commentary /ref:C526E43690AD78/#.U-O0F0hZAfc.

Yang, Jia Lynn. "Jilted Mistresses Expose Chinese Officials' Corruption." *The Washington Post,* July 25, 2013. http://www.washingtonpost.com/world/ji-yingnan-and -other-jilted-mistresses-expose-chinese-officials-corruption/2013/07/25/8d8d35f6 -eb02-11e2-aa9f-c03a72e2d342_story.html.

Yang, Jia Lynn. "Jilted Mistresses Step Forward to Expose Corruption in China." *The*

Independent, July 28, 2013. http://www.independent.co.uk/news/world/asia/jilted
-mistresses-step-forward-to-expose-corruption-in-china-8735583.html.

The Concubine Who Ruled China—Cixi

Bensen, Amanda. "Cixi: The Woman Behind the Throne." *Smithsonian Magazine.*
http://www.smithsonianmag.com/history/cixi-the-woman-behind-the-throne
-22312071/.

Chang, Jung. *Empress Dowager Cixi.* London: Vintage, 2014.

Schell, Orville. "Her Dynasty: Jung Chang's 'Empress Dowager Cixi.'" *The New York
Times Sunday Book Review.* http://www.nytimes.com/2013/10/27/books/review
/jung-changs-empress-dowager-cixi.html?pagewanted=all&_r=0.

Sit, Tony. "The Life of Empress Cixi." Society for Anglo-Chinese Understanding. http://
www.sacu.org/cixi.html.

9. AND THE REST . . .

The Admiral's Daughter and the Bedouin Sheikh—Jane Digby

Eleanor. "Royal Navy Bonus Culture in Action." Royal Museums Greenwich. http://
www.rmg.co.uk/researchers/collections/by-type/archive-and-library/item-of-the
-month/previous/royal-navy-bonus-culture-in-action.

Lovell, Mary S. "A Scandalous Life." Mary S. Lovell's Web site. http://lovellbiographies
.com/ascandalouslife.html.

Lovell, Mary S. *A Scandalous Life: The Biography of Jane Digby.* London: Richard Cohen
Books, 1995.

Prioleau, Betsy. *Seductress: Women Who Ravished the World and Their Lost Art of Love.*
New York: Viking Penguin, 2003.

Schmidt, Margaret Fox. *Passion's Child: The Extraordinary Life of Jane Digby.* New York:
Harper & Row, 1976.

The Dancer Who Started a Revolution—Lola Montez

Her Royal Highness Princess Michael of Kent. *Cupid and the King: Five Royal Paramours.*
London: HarperCollins, 1991.

"Lola Montez Home." Museums USA. http://www.museumsusa.org/museums/info
/1153769.

"People of Angus: Lola Montez—Uncrowned Queen of Bavaria." Angus Council.
http://www.angus.gov.uk/history/features/people/lolamontez.htm.

Prioleau, Betsy. *Seductress: Women Who Ravished the World and Their Lost Art of Love.*
New York: Viking Penguin, 2003.

Seymour, Bruce. *Lola Montez: A Life.* New Haven: Yale University Press, 1996.

Wilson, Bee. "Boudoir Politics." *London Review of Books.* http://www.lrb.co.uk/v29 /n11/bee-wilson/boudoir-politics.

Wyndham, Horace. *The Magnificent Montez: From Courtesan to Convert.* Hillman-Curl, n.d. Project Gutenberg.

The Temple Dancer Who Wasn't—Mata Hari

"The Execution of Mata Hari, 1917." *EyeWitnesstoHistory.com.* http://eyewitnessto history.com/matahari.htm.

"Mystery of How Mata Hari Lost Her Head (Disappeared from Macabre Museum)." Museum Security Network, July 13, 2000. www.museum-security.org/00/110 .html#2.

Noe, Denise. "Mata Hari." Crimelibrary, Criminal Minds & Methods. http://www .crimelibrary.com/terrorists_spies/spies/hari/1.html.

Rennell, Tony. "Mata Hari Was Only Interested in One Thing—and It Wasn't Espio-nage." *Daily Mail Online,* August 10, 2007. http://www.dailymail.co.uk/femail /article-474631/Mata-Hari-interested-thing–wasnt-espionage.html.

Shipman, Pat. *Femme Fatale: Love, Lies, and the Unknown Life of Mata Hari.* London: Phoenix, 2008.

INDEX